ALASKA NATIVE RESILIENCE

Indigenous
Confluences

CHARLOTTE COTÉ AND COLL THRUSH   *Series Editors*

Holly Miowak Guise

ALASKA NATIVE RESILIENCE VOICES FROM WORLD WAR II

University of Washington Press   *Seattle*

Alaska Native Resilience was supported by a grant from the Tulalip Tribes Charitable Fund, which provides the opportunity for a sustainable and healthy community for all.

A CAPELL FAMILY BOOK

This book was also made possible in part by the Capell Family Endowed Book Fund, which supports the publication of books that deepen the understanding of social justice through historical, cultural, and environmental studies.

Additional support was provided by a generous gift from Jill and Joseph McKinstry.

Design by Mindy Basinger Hill / Composed in Minion Pro

28   27   26   25   24   5   4   3   2   1

Printed and bound in the United States of America

UNIVERSITY OF WASHINGTON PRESS *uwapress.uw.edu*

LIBRARY OF CONGRESS CATALOGING-IN-PUBLICATION DATA

Names: Guise, Holly Miowak, author.

Title: Alaska Native resilience : voices from World War II / Holly Miowak Guise.

Description: Seattle : University of Washington Press, [2024] | Series: Indigenous confluences | Includes bibliographical references and index.

Identifiers: LCCN 2023051412 | ISBN 9780295752518 (hardback) | ISBN 9780295752525 (paperback) | ISBN 9780295752532 (ebook)

Subjects: LCSH: World War, 1939–1945—Alaska—Aleutian Islands. | Aleuts—Forced removal and internment, 1942–1945. | Aleuts—Relocation. | Aleuts—Alaska—Social conditions—20th century. | World War, 1939–1945—Evacuation of civilians—Alaska. | Attu, Battle of, Alaska, 1943. | Attu Island (Alaska)—History—Japanese occupation, 1942–1943. | World War, 1939–1945—Campaigns—Alaska—Aleutian Islands. | World War, 1939–1945—Alaska. | World War, 1939–1945—Personal narratives, American. | Aleutian Islands (Alaska)

Classification: LCC D810.A53 G85 2024 | DDC 940.54/28—dc23/eng/20240227

LC record available at https://lccn.loc.gov/2023051412

For all the elders who shared
their stories with me—*quyaanaqpaq*

CONTENTS

ACKNOWLEDGMENTS

SEVERAL ELDERS, community members, intellectuals, and family members made this project possible. The appendix includes my effort to name every person who helped me along the way with oral history research. It truly took community effort to compile this Alaska history.

With funding from the University of New Mexico (UNM) Feminist Research Institute (FRI), three scholars significantly influenced this book before submission to the press: Cynthia Enloe, Frederick Hoxie, and Jeffrey Ostler. I am incredibly grateful to all three for shaping my work in conversation in the fields of gender and women's studies, Native history, and history of the US West. I am also grateful to Shanon Fitzpatrick (Style & Spine) for going through a draft with me before I sent it to my FRI readers. With coordination by Brett Rushforth and Ryan Jones, we workshopped chapter 2 with the history department and Native studies at the University of Oregon. A panel at the Organization of American Historians with Maurice Crandall, Julian Lim, Rosina Lozano, and Evan Taparata influenced and strengthened chapter 1. I am deeply appreciative of my editor Larin McLaughlin, Charlotte Coté, Coll Thrush, Alja Kooistra, Joeth Zucco, Ishita Shahi, the anonymous reviewers, Joshua Reid, and Judi Gibbs for creating the index. The American Council of Learned Societies Fellowship and the Ford Foundation Postdoctoral Fellowship gave me time to thoughtfully integrate revisions while working on my related World War II Alaska website, ww2alaska.com. While I have tried to be as precise as possible in citing oral histories and in writing history, any mistakes in this text are my own.

My work as an oral historian began as an undergraduate majoring in Native American studies at Stanford University. When my initial advisor from an unnamed department declined to support my research on segregation history, I found an incredibly encouraging honors thesis advisor in C. Matthew Snipp, who mentored me while helping me to secure research funding. In 2008, I received the Community Service Research Internship through the Center for Comparative Studies in Race and Ethnicity to interview elders. From Stanford, I am grateful to my generous teachers and mentors who informed my early and continued development as a scholar: JoEllen Anderson, Albert Camarillo, Gordon Chang, Michele Elam, Estelle Freedman, Maud Gleason, Tamar Herzog, Allyson Hobbs, Benjamin Hoy, Teresa LaFromboise, Beth Lew-Williams, Christina Mesa, Sharon Nelson-Barber, Rand Quinn, Ian Robertson, Kelly Summers, Richard White, Michael Wilcox, and Sylvia Yanagisako. Alongside an opportunity to connect with conservation biologists, I found campus employment with Jai Ranganathan, Berry Brosi, and Sevan Suni.

During graduate school at Yale University, I found engaging scholarship and community activities organized by my advisor Ned Blackhawk with the Yale Group for the Study of Native America. I will cherish my time as a teaching fellow for Ned's Writing Tribal Histories class when he secured funding to bring the class to First Nations sites in Montreal and Kahnawà:ke. My dream team committee members—Birgit Brander Rasmussen, Jonathan Holloway, and Matthew Jacobson—taught me to think critically about empires and to advocate for human rights. I am deeply appreciative of friends and colleagues from New Haven: Wendell Adjetey, Genevieve Carpio, Jenny L. Davis, Sarah Derbew, Marilyn Flores, Tiffany Hale, Emily Hauser, Katherine Hindley, Craig Holloway, Khalil Anthony Johnson, W. Chris Johnson, Tess Lanzarotta, Juliet Nebolon, Andrew Offenburger, Melissa Pa-Redwood, Sebastian Perez, Alec Reichardt, Tyler Rogers, Miranda Sachs, Brian Tennyson, and Jacqueline Yen. I am also thankful for faculty, including Jessica Cattelino, George Chauncey, Kathleen Cleaver, Alejandra Dubcovsky, Jay Gitlin, Joanne Meyerowitz, Michelle Nearon, Steven Pincus, and Stephen Pitti; for my Iñupiaq language instructor through Yale's Directed Independent Language Study, Maggie Pollack- quyaanaqpaq!; and for funding from the Yale Oral History Travel Fellowship, the Office for Diversity and Equal Opportunity Fellowship, and the A. Bartlett Giamatti Fellowship. The Ford Foundation Predoctoral Fellowship freed me from campus duties so I could write my dissertation in San Francisco.

Thank you to my Ford conference roommate, Arianne Eason, who hosted me in Seattle while I visited the University of Washington's archives. While in Seattle, I connected with Stephanie Fryberg and Sven Haakanson.

Although the pandemic shortened my time on campus with the University of California President's Postdoctoral Fellowship (UCPPF), I found a vibrant community within the University of California, Irvine (UCI) Humanities including my cherished postdoc advisor Sharon Block, who helped me navigate submitting my first article, "Who Is Doctor Bauer?," and continued professional development. I am grateful to several other scholars at UCI, including John Marquez; Sarah Orem; Stephanie Narrow, who created a master interview spreadsheet for my elder oral histories using Sharon Block's digital history funds; Dwayne Pack, UCI's computing director who helped me launch my YouTube channel "World War II Alaska" and plan my website ww2alaska.com; Noah Dolim; David Fedman; Andrew Highsmith; Adria Imada; Makanani Sala; Heidi Tinsman; Jeffrey Wasserstrom; and Judy Tzu-Chun Wu. Special thanks to my National Center for Faculty Development and Diversity (NCFDD) team for helping me navigate academia and life: Deisy Del Real, Roya Ebtehaj, and Tina Post. With funds from UCPPF, Nathan Ellstrand created a searchable Excel spreadsheet of the Felix Cohen collections at the Beinecke Library that I had previously photographed.

At UNM, I am grateful for the following grants and funding: the FRI Faculty Research Grant, the UNM Faculty Support Program ADVANCE, the UNM Investing in Faculty Success Faculty Scholarship Time, and WeR1 Faculty Success Summer Funding. Other fellowships and grants supported my research in Alaska, including the American Philosophical Society's Digital Knowledge Sharing Fellowship and Phillips Fund for Native American Research, the Walter Rundell Award, and the Cook Inlet Historical Society.

My time at UNM has been engaging with inspiring colleagues from the Institute for American Indian Research: Jennifer Denetdale, Nick Estes, Alyosha Goldstein, Sarah Hernandez, Lloyd Lee, and Melanie Yazzie. Several scholars from history and Native studies have been supportive: Durwood Ball, Judy Bieber, Melissa Bokovoy, Sarah Davis-Secord, Tiffany Florvil, Kimberly Gauderman, Fred Gibbs, Wendy Greyeyes, Elizabeth Hutchison, Luis Herrán Ávila, Robert Jefferson, Sarah Kostelecky, Karen Leong, Katherine Massoth, Virginia Scharff, Samuel Truett, and Shannon Withycombe. Special thanks to my oral history transcript editor and teaching assistant Sean Lausin and my graduate teaching assistant Emily Heimerman. Brian Carpenter of the Center for Native American and Indigenous Research at the American Philosophical Society has been essential for archiving my oral histories, alongside support from American Philosophical Society director Patrick Spero. #Twitterstorians is a lively group, and I appreciate Jason Herbert's #HATM community. Co-convening with the German Historical Institute (GHI) on the Indigenous Migrations workshop with Sören Urbansky and Nino Vallen has broadened my perspective on transnational Indigenous migration history. In addition to connecting with global scholars through GHI, I spent a week learning public history in Sitka with Alaskan historians Colton Brandau and Ian Halter.

Maria Shaa Tláa Williams encourages collaborations and activism, and with her I found an ideal mentor when visiting Alaska. At the University of Alaska Anchorage (UAA), I found support from Jeane Ta'aXi'waa Breinig, Ian Hartman, Shirley Kendall, and Paul Dunscomb, who connected me with the Japan Studies Association. I also thank Alaska Native studies scholars Pearl Kiyawn Nageak Brower, Beth Gigondidoy Leonard, Heidi Aklaseaq Senungetuk, Olga Skinner, Thomas Swensen, and Sean Asikłuk Topkok. In Juneau, inspiring scholar Rosita Worl advised me on research at the Sealaska Heritage Institute. While living in the Bay Area, I attended Native studies events at UC Berkeley, connecting with Shari Huhndorf, Caitlin Keliiaa, and Beth Piatote, who graciously organized a writing group with Jen Rose Smith.

Many archivists and librarians assisted my research. Those who shared specific collections guiding my research include Rita Anderson, Jon Bolsa, Christie Burke, Richie Cahoon, Veronica Denison, Abby Focht, Leah Geibel, Denise Henderson, Gwen Higgins, Charles Hilton, Ken House, Zachary Jones, Roxana Kashatok, Lisa Krynicki, Marguerie La Riviere, Marina La Salle, Mike Livingston, Rachel Mason, Millie McKeown, Patty McNamee,

George Miles, Bruce Parham, Emily Pastore, Sara Piasecki, Jason Russell, Robyn Russell, Angela Schmidt, Arlene Schmuland, Crystal Shurley, Chuck Smythe, Rose Speranza, Gary Stein, Sally Swetzof, Valerie Szwaya, Zane Treesh, Robert Vanderpool, Teressa Williams, and Timothy Young. Special thanks to Mike Livingston at the Aleutian Pribilof Islands Association (APIA) for helping me obtain the correct spelling of names of several Unangax̂ from oral histories and archival references. Colton Brandau checked my glossary for *Alutiit* and *Sugpiat*. Lauren Peters and Haliehana Stepetin helped me with the glossary definition for *Unangax̂*.

In addition to the libraries and archival collections consulted, public museums have been a great resource. I feel that public history is so important and that more scholars should be using public history sources for their research—especially when trying to understand a memory of war or a social history for which Indigenous voices are less prevalent in Western archives. I visited the following museums in my research: Alaska Aviation Museum, Anchorage; Alaska Native Heritage Center, Anchorage; Alaska Veterans Museum, Anchorage; Aleutian World War II Visitor Center, Unalaska; Alutiiq Museum, Kodiak; Anchorage Museum and Atwood Resource Center, Anchorage; Duncan Cottage Museum, Metlakatla; Iñupiat Heritage Center, Utqiaġvik; Juneau-Douglas City Museum, Juneau; Museum of the Aleutians, Unalaska; University of Alaska Museum of the North, Fairbanks; and Wing Luke Museum, Seattle, Washington.

More personally, I am most thankful to the matriarchs in my family, including my mother, criminal defense attorney Ella Anagick (Annikan); sisters Alaska Native Medical Center physician Christina Darby (Siuvaq/Qaquaqtuaq) and business researcher for Diné Development Corporation Jennine Jordan (Camuqin); my rock-solid matriarch Grandma Betty Anagick; and my aunts. Thanks also to my Uncle Edgar, rest in peace. When I was a graduate student, my dad, David Stebing, a former history teacher and attorney, gave me an MP3 recorder for oral histories. My brilliant mapmaker is my cousin, earth scientist Sarah Aarons, PhD, whom I consider my best friend since we were babies. My cousin Elizabeth Aarons, an Alaska Native Tribal Health Consortium nurse, generously accompanied me to Bethel, where Andy Angstman's family hosted me.

Friends who have supported me throughout various writing stages of my life include, but are not limited to, Tanya Aylward, Jamie Cornejo, Zjok Durst, Samantha Englishoe, Monique Eniero, Jennette Heidrich, Emma Huntington, Yuki Kondo-Shah, Erika Kuempel, Yinshi Lerman-Tan, Alyssa London, Julia McCord, Freddie Olin IV, Michael Pascual, Ramine Ross, Carmen Sebro, Jayme Selanoff, Peter Shannon, Noelle Trujillo, Sabrina Walker, Gwen Watson, and Crystal Worl.

My spouse, Max Guise, an engineer, inspires me to integrate technology in various capacities within my scholarship—I believe that my humanist tendencies have influenced him as well. I will never forget visiting historic World War II ruins at the seventy-fifth anniversary of the bombing of Dutch Harbor, with the shoreline overlooking the ocean and coastline, and Max held baby Jada in possibly one of the most scenic locations on earth. Max watched baby Jada in Utqiaġvik while she played with the kids at Tuzzy Consortium Library and with Wesley Ugiaqtaq Aiken's great-grandkids at his house. My children, Nash (Nashoalook) and "Jada bug" (Benisak), accompanied me on several research travels in Alaska, including meetings with Marie Matsuno, Al Wright, and Jorgy Jorgensen. And finally, I am grateful to my ancestors who challenged colonialism in whatever capacity possible. While the US government damaged our language fluency for the current moment through mission and boarding schools, in my family we have retained our Native names and continue to claim our history.

FORMS OF SEPARATION, EXCLUSION, AND SEGREGATION IN THE ALASKA TERRITORY DURING WORLD WAR II

February 19, 1942	The US government issues Executive Order 9066, relocating approximately 240 Japanese Americans in Alaska to incarceration camps in the US mainland.
June 1942	The US Navy and government relocate over 880 Unangax̂ from their home islands to camps in Southeast Alaska until 1944 and 1945.
1942–1943	Segregated Black American platoons arrive in Alaska, representing about 3,700 out of 10,000 troops building the 1,390-mile Alaska-Canada (ALCAN) Highway. Lieutenant General Simon Bolivar Buckner of the Alaska Defense Command reluctantly accepts segregated Black American platoons in Alaska.
1942–1944	The military forbade association between Native women and servicemen in Southeast Alaska. Native women and Native men protest until the order is rescinded. However, the military continued to restrict intermarriage between Native women and servicemen through 1948.

February 16, 1945   The Alaska Equal Rights Act is signed into law
to address the racial segregation at businesses
and public venues directed at Native people and
minorities in Alaska towns that had existed without
consequence. The act failed to pass in 1943. While
schools in certain Alaskan towns integrated after
unrelenting Native activism, school segregation
through boarding schools and mission schools
widely continued.

ALASKA
NATIVE
RESILIENCE

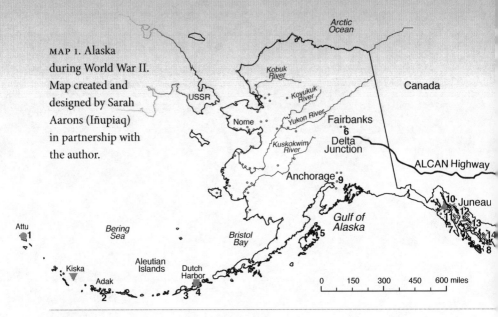

MAP 1. Alaska during World War II. Map created and designed by Sarah Aarons (Iñupiaq) in partnership with the author.

Battlefields and Select Military Bases

▼ Invasion of Kiska, June 6, 1942
● Invasion of Attu, June 7, 1942
● Battle of Attu, May 11–30, 1943
■ Dutch Harbor bombing, June 3–4, 1942
▲ Prisoners of War Camp for German prisoners, June 1945 to November 1945

1 Attu Battlefield and US Army and Navy Airfields
2 Adak Army and Naval Operations Base
3 Cape Field at Fort Glenn
4 Dutch Harbor Naval Operating Base and Fort Mears
5 Kodiak Naval Operating Base and Fort Greely
6 Ladd Field/Fort Wainwright
7 Sitka Naval Operating Base and Fort Rousseau

8 Annette Island Air Field
9 Fort Richardson/Elmendorf Field
○ Alaska Territorial Guard locations

Unangax̂ Relocation Camps

10 Funter Bay
11 Killisnoo
12 Wrangell Institute
13 Burnett Inlet
14 Ward Lake

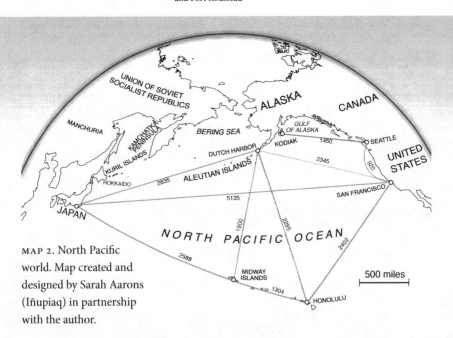

MAP 2. North Pacific world. Map created and designed by Sarah Aarons (Iñupiaq) in partnership with the author.

AN ALASKAN INTRODUCTION
REGAINING INDIGENOUS EQUILIBRIUM AS WARTIME RESISTANCE

"WE ALMOST LOST HER. She had pneumonia. We didn't even have aspirin to relieve the pains of the people. And we didn't know. . . ."[1] Alice Petrivelli, an Unangax̂ elder (also known by the Russian colonial term *Aleut*) who survived the measles epidemic in a wartime government camp, paused before she collected her words: "The only thing, plant, we recognized was dandelion. In Atka, we could use the plants to help the people. And we didn't have that in Killisnoo. My sister almost died." During an interview in November 2014, Alice described her memories about the epidemics that hit her community at a wartime relocation camp from 1942 to 1945. Over seventy years had passed since the US Navy *evacuated*—this was the navy's benign term—Alice's community from Atka in the Aleutian Islands to a camp in Killisnoo in Southeast Alaska. Wartime relocation of Unangax̂, an era also known by scholars of the twentieth century and the Commission on Wartime Relocation and Internment of Civilians as "Aleut internment," brought dire circumstances causing the deaths of 10 percent of the Unangax̂ population.[2] Over the past eight decades, Unangax̂ survivors have shared stories about being targeted during World War II by the US government's war-waging policies, about the hurt they and their relatives experienced, about treatment of neglect, and about the resultant epidemics that caused rampant deaths.

These stories of wartime loss and suffering, however, are matched, I have discovered, by ones of Indigenous resiliency and defiance. While wartime relocation camps are scarcely seen as spaces of Indigenous defiance, it is within these sites of colonial control and oppression that a powerful force of Indigenous resistance emerged, one mighty enough to upend the colonial government's intended outcome of Indigenous erasure by relocation.

One story in particular, as told by Alice, exhibits what I see as a moment of "equilibrium restoration." Throughout this study, I use this concept of equilibrium restoration to refer to actions taken consciously by Indigenous Alaskan women and men during World War II to restore an Indigenous order that disrupts colonial actors, thereby thwarting colonial efforts of complete control. Thus, when Atkans banished a US government doctor from a government-controlled internment space, as Alice describes, that, I have come to understand, was a defiant action designed by Atkans to restore equilibrium. Such actions were intentionally made to generate order during a time of disorder and chaos brought by colonial forces.

Alice recalled this time of change during wartime when her Uncle William "Bill" Dirks expelled a Bureau of Indian Affairs (BIA) physician from the camp at Killisnoo.[3] She relayed, "[Doctor] Bauer tried to control our lives. Uncle kicked him out." Doctor H. O. K. Bauer had committed a long list of offenses. Native women and government officials in northern Alaska had written letters of complaint to the BIA describing that Bauer had sexually assaulted Iñupiat women and teenage girls.[4] During the BIA's investigation, Bauer transferred from northern to Southeast Alaska where he administered medical services to Unangax̂ at relocation camps. According to Alice, while serving as a government physician, Bauer sexually assaulted and impregnated an Atkan woman and then defied her bodily integrity by forcing an abortion on her. Alongside this medical abuse, Alice recalled that Bauer experimented on her and other Atkans with spinal taps. Among these grievances, Bauer violated the Hippocratic oath by refusing to treat Alice's cousin who died from a ruptured appendix. Furthermore, as a federal authority figure wielding power over Native bodies, he tried imposing a curfew on the entire camp.

Atkans defied Bauer's authority by responding actively against his medical neglect, unethical experimentation, and attempts at control. For example, Alice told of how when Bauer tried to enforce a curfew at the camp, she coordinated with the other children to "play games at 7 o'clock curfew to have him [Bauer] chase us around." In a similar manner, when Bauer refused to treat Alice's cousin who died of a ruptured appendix, Alice's Uncle Bill asserted personal autonomy by banishing the doctor. The agency—positive, intentional action—asserted by Alice's uncle and the Atkan children, along with Alice's own testimony about this history, provide evidence of larger patterns of Indigenous resistance that limited and subverted US colonial projects carried out by colonial officials, like Bauer, in Alaska.

Continued Reevaluation of the "Good War"

Making visible, as Alice was doing, those Indigenous actions serves to upend simplistic, incomplete, often nationalist US portrayals of World War II as the alleged "good war," as critically identified by historian John Bodnar.[5] Likewise, literary scholar Elizabeth D. Samet offers an overview of military history uncovering postwar US cultural memory as it relates to a burgeoning US national identity.[6] Stories of Alaska Indigenous wartime resistance fit in the growing field of scholarly studies that aims to shine a critical light on the ways that US military officials and the US government chose to wage war. Scholars in the field of political science and military studies such as renowned scholar Cynthia Enloe have centered a feminist approach to understanding war, global studies, and how gender informs militarization of a wartime landscape and cultural history.[7] These understandings show not only that gender was central to imperialism and soldier/civilian relations but also that an Indigenous feminist understanding of war is essential to interpretations of Alaska.

This good war involved labeling Japanese Americans, including elders, women, and children, as potential wartime enemies and incarcerating civilians in heavily guarded concentration camps in the US heartland. Asian American studies scholar Gary Okihiro identifies these wartime incarceration stories as not just "internment" but "concentration camps."[8] Here, Okihiro explains that what has been historically identified as "concentration camps" in Nazi Germany were indeed coordinated death camps of Jews, homosexuals, and political enemies. In the United States, where the military and federal government forced Japanese Americans into concentration camps, the federal government deemed all bodies of Japanese ancestry as culpable enemies of the state after Japan's attack on Pearl Harbor on December 7, 1941. Indeed, as writers such as Jeanne Wakatsuki Houston and James Houston show, Japanese American incarceration unraveled families, leaving lasting legacies.[9]

The similarity between the wartime incarceration of Japanese Americans and Unangax̂ resides within the concept of white supremacy embedded in the US governmental system, in which bodies of color did not possess equal citizenship rights as exercised by white Americans; one-third of Japanese immigrants incarcerated in the United States during World War II were not citizens and therefore lacked human rights to freedom.[10] This good war involved wartime incarcerations on the territorial periphery of Alaska in addition to the US heartland, including Japanese Latin Americans from South America incarcerated at Crystal City, Texas.[11] Such an extensive geography of camps with incarcerated bodies of color indicates a widespread exhibition of anti-Indigeneity, anti-Asian xenophobia, and US global reach of Latin America. The federal and military treatment of Japanese Americans differed from that of Unangax̂, whom the government treated not as wartime enemies but rather as Indigenous wards of the state.[12]

On citizenship rights, it bears significant mention that anti-Black segregation was prevalent practice in the armed forces in addition to segregated schools on the home front. At this time, structural inequalities designed to maintain a racial hierarchy through institutional segregation existed at businesses that regularly exercised separation and exclusion, housing discrimination, and job discrimination that predated the 1964 Equal Employment Opportunity Commission.[13] As historians such as Robert Jefferson have illuminated, African American servicemen fought a double victory campaign for each of their own unique reasons in addition to fighting discrimination on the home front and fascism abroad.[14]

Across the Pacific, the good war involved killing over 200,000 Japanese civilians, mostly women, children, and the elderly, with the US dropping of atomic bombs on Hiroshima and Nagasaki, from the initial impact to the subsequent radiation poisoning.[15] The bilingual website JapanAirRaids. org, co-managed by historian David Fedman and a team of scholars, details

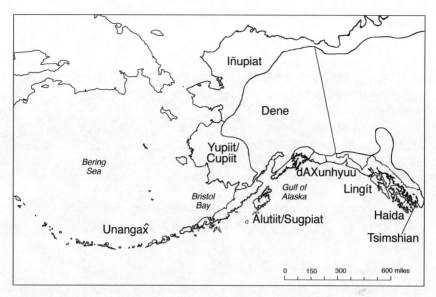

MAP 3. Alaska Native tribal geographies of Indigenous Alaskan nations.
Map created and designed by Sarah Aarons (Iñupiaq) in partnership
with the author.

how US air raids and incendiary bombings of Japan's cities rendered "nine
million people homeless, killed an estimated 187,000 civilians, and injured
214,000 more."[16] And yet, for the most part, the teaching of the atomic bomb
in US schools presents a story of a calculated measurement of human lives;
in this case, soldiers propelling the US war effort versus Japanese civilians.
Historian Ronald Takaki has argued that the calculation that the bomb
would save 500,000 US soldiers is inflated from 40,000. Takaki locates these
numbers from a report dated June 15, 1945, which speculates on US casualties if Truman had sent troops to invade Japan's island of Kyushu followed
by a land invasion of Tokyo.[17] In teaching about the Pacific War, I found
that many of my students had not seen photographs of the survivors of the
atomic bombs and the charred earth in their aftermath. The photographs of
the people and land reveal a dehumanization of Japanese civilians and the
land devastated into oblivion. Historian Dmitri Brown (Tewa) illuminates
the imperial nature of the Manhattan Project from a Tewa perspective; his
scholarship shows that although the locations and peoples of the atomic age

seem distant, ranging from testing sites on Tewa lands in the US Southwest to Japan, they are indeed entangled by empire.[18]

Empires and Indigenous Nations in Alaska

When Japan invaded the Aleutian Islands of Attu and Kiska in June of 1942, just six months after the attack on Pearl Harbor, Alaska Natives from all tribal geographies responded by asserting their sovereignty. Spanning diverse ecologies including the Arctic, subarctic, taiga, rainforests, and vast mountain ranges, the Alaska territory contains more than 660,000 square miles. Texas, the next largest US state, is just over 268,000 square miles. The name *Alaska* itself derives from the Unangax̂ word *Alaxsxix̂*, translating to "mainland" (from the eastern dialect recorded in 1761), where "mainland" refers only to what is known today as the Alaska Peninsula.[19] Russian fur traders applied this name to define the entire territory. Alaska's tribal nations are equally diverse to the entire region. For over ten thousand years, Native peoples have inhabited their homelands in Alaska. Recent archaeological studies show that Alaska Natives and Asians created extensive trade networks bringing European goods to northern Alaska, predating the Columbian exchange and European migration to the Americas.[20]

To date, Alaska has 228 federally recognized tribes that are linguistically diverse and geographically distant. Alaska Natives are generally grouped into three broad categories that correspond to various geographies and linguistic groups, including Iñuit, Aleut (Unangax̂ and Sugpiat), and Alaskan Indians. Spanning a vast Arctic geography occupied by various colonial empires, Alaskan Iñuit have the same language family as Iñuit from land colonially occupied by Russia, Canada, and Greenland. Along the western coast of Alaska, Cupiit and Yupiit are Alaska's southern Iñuit, while Iñupiat live along Alaska's northern coast. The Aleutian Islands and the Pribilof Islands are Unangax̂ homelands. The Aleutian archipelago extends from western Alaska through the Bering Sea, bordering the international dateline reaching toward the Russian-occupied Kamchatka Peninsula. Sugpiat span lands from the Prince William Sound, Kenai Peninsula, Alaska Peninsula, and Kodiak Island. Pivoting inland and to the southern coast, Alaskan Indians have ancestral lands in central, South Central, and Southeast Alaska. Dene (Athabascans) of Interior Alaska share the same language family as the Diné in the American Southwest. In South Central Alaska, dAXunhyuu speak a distinct language closely related to the Athabaskan language, and they live and protect the land and waters along the Gulf of Alaska. Among the topography of the rainforests of Southeast Alaska, Tlingit, Haida, and Tsimshian hold ancestral lands along Alaska's southern coast and the waters of the Inside Passage. All these Native nations chose to ally with the US military in defeating and further preventing Japan's invasion of Alaska, a key location of war in the North Pacific.

Shifting Demographics of an Alaskan Settler Colony

War brought hundreds of thousands of servicemen and a mostly male contingent of civilian workers to Alaska to advance imperial and settler colonial projects. While individually these incomers may not have thought of themselves in 1942 as colonizers but simply as war-deployed US personnel, nonetheless their arrival from the south in such large numbers had the effect of intensifying Alaska Native women's and men's experiences of white-dominated US imperial and settler colonial projects. According to the 1939 prewar census data, Alaska had a total population of 72,000, of which white people were 54 percent of the population; "Native stock" including "Aleut, Esk*mo, and Indian" represented about 45 percent of the population; and Asian, Black, and all other races represented about 1 percent of the population.[21]

Comparing prewar and wartime census data reveals how the presence of the US military—both uniformed and civilian military—fundamentally changed Alaskan demographics. In 1943, 150,000 troops resided in three hundred separate military installations across Alaska, and 300,000 personnel served.[22] After American forces defeated Japanese forces in the Battle of Attu in May 1943, the federal government redeployed forces in Alaska to fight in other regions. As a result, the number of US Armed Forces stationed in Alaska markedly declined to 60,000.[23] With the wartime construction of new roads and runways, including the 1,390-mile Alaska-Canada (ALCAN) Highway for which one-third of the laborers were segregated Black platoons, the federal government's wartime operations brought significant military infrastructure to the so-called Great North. While designed for the waging of war, these extensive wartime infrastructure projects would have a notable impact on postwar Alaskan politics, economics, and culture, each of which can be best understood by taking seriously Indigenous Alaskan experiences of white expansionism.

Regardless of the Washington imperial intent, Alaskan territorial governor Ernest Gruening, appointed by President Franklin D. Roosevelt in 1939, had his own vision of what wartime influxes of people from the south and, with them, massive infrastructure building could bring to postwar Alaska. Prior to his position as governor, while serving as the head of the Department of the Interior's Division of Territories and Island Possessions, Gruening opposed a resettlement plan in Alaska for Jewish Holocaust refugees, as did Alaska delegate Anthony Dimond.[24] And yet, in January 1945, Gruening appealed to the legislature to retain veterans with veteran benefits so they would be more likely to remain in Alaska.[25] A year earlier, in 1944, he voiced opposition to establishing Indian reservations in Alaska, claiming it would "incit[e] racial animosity" with Native people putting up signs like "no tres-passing-by-whites" and would "preclude the development of Alaska as a home for the thousands of veterans who have already expressed their interest in coming to Alaska when their war services come to an end."[26] Refashioning military personnel into civilian pioneers propelled US settler colonialism. Such an expansionist postwar call to demobilized mostly male soldiers to colonize what the governor imagined to be the Alaskan "frontier" left out the crucial detail: the original peoples and their sovereign right to their land.

Native nations navigated territorialization of Alaska, which signified a key part of US westward imperial expansion to non-contiguous territories reaching the Pacific and north to the Arctic. For the US audience, Alaska characterized this epic "frontier" of Western resource extraction that in-tended to erase the presence of Native nations who, contrary to colonial propaganda, continue to hold sovereignty to these lands.

"Go North, Young Man!" This recruitment slogan is familiar because it mirrors the popular "Go West, Young Man!" of the nineteenth century. In 1944, this phrase rang through Congress and called white men to colonize the Great North, the Arctic, and the ever-expanding Pacific territories.[27] The call for westward expansion cannot be divorced from the concept of manifest destiny, a nineteenth-century concept that encouraged not only theft of property by Western settlers, squatters, and colonial authority figures who willingly broke treaty rights and opted to ignore the formality of the treaty-making process, but also the extraction of Native lands and resources compounded by genocide of American Indians. According to historian Jeffrey Ostler, this genocide through removal extended from the Eastern Seaboard to the Pacific Rim.[28] Such an understanding foregrounds that Alaska became a primary place to continue the extension of the American West and to connect the United States to Asia, which was comprehended by both the US settler state and alliances to Indigenous nations in Alaska. Alaska and Hawai'i are just two examples of non-contiguous US territories in the Pacific that illuminate the power of US empire to continue reaching for frontiers into the twentieth century.[29] Indeed, examining Asian transpacific histories, scholar Moon-Ho Jung underscores the emergence of the US state by expanding empire and "the entangled history of colonial conquest, white supremacy, and anticolonial struggle."[30]

Previous scholars have oriented Alaska as a major component of the US West and projects of settler colonial expansion. Historian Stephen Haycox identifies the colonial nature of Alaska history beginning with eighteenth-century Russian occupation and dating to US arrival.[31] Relatedly, historian Robert Campbell highlights how during the Gilded Age, Alaska represented more than a popular tourist destination as the United States expanded in the Pacific Northwest for capitalist extraction.[32] On racial segregation in the US West reaching Alaska, historian Terrence Cole highlights Alaska Native activism.[33] Similarly, historians Ian Hartman and David Reamer have continued the study of African American history in Alaska as a history of the US West.[34]

The Pacific War Overlapping World War II

The Pacific War shows that the US West indeed extended to Asia, where Alaska represents one territory of imperial pursuit colliding with US wartime efforts of the Pacific War. As wars can overlap involving various geographies and empires, the Pacific War, from the perspective of the United States, is generally regarded as resistance against Japan's imperialism dating from December 1941 to 1945. Situating Alaska in the Pacific War reveals this northern geography as a puzzle piece in a greater effort to control the Pacific. The territories of Alaska, Hawai'i, Guam, the Philippines, and numerous islands in the South Pacific were never assisted in their sovereignty but rather calculated as places where US empire could maintain a stronghold in the Pacific.[35] During World War II, the United States framed its imperialism as protecting other countries from Japan.[36] As noted by historian John Dower, this form of Pacific imperialism quickly extended to military control of Japan.[37] Following acts of civilian genocide with the Japan air raids and the dropping of two atomic bombs on cities, the United States extended imperialism to Japan, thereby disrupting Japan's colonial control in Eastern Asia and the Pacific.[38] As historian Daniel Immerwahr has highlighted, global imperialism occurred as an obvious sign to countries afflicted by US empire, and yet US citizens on the continental mainland remained largely unaware of the darker legacies of colonialism by their empire that ruthlessly took hold of global geographies.[39]

An analysis of Alaska during World War II shows that the United States was never as powerful as it purported to be, because there was never any certainty that the United States could hold the Pacific territories from the reach of Japan's empire or subsequently from the Soviet Union's empire during the Cold War. While the United States assessed Japan's empire for risk in the early years of war, the country largely ignored Japan until the attack on Pearl Harbor in December 1941 followed by the Aleutian campaign from 1942 to 1943. Japan presented a substantial and historically proven threat in Asia and the Pacific, even while advocating for a united Asia independent from Westernization. Invasion of Alaska could have extended to Siberia or the contiguous states. Prior to Pearl Harbor, the United States ignored Japan's imperialism of the Pacific world, aside from a trade embargo, because the government racialized the Japanese Empire as nonthreatening. This was contrary to evidence dating to Japan's invasion of Manchuria in 1931 that proved otherwise, which unfolded into the events of the Pacific War involving Japan's invasion of several Pacific geographies.[40] Manchuria, a region in China seized by the Russian Empire in the aftermath of the First Sino-Japanese War (1894–1895) and then by the Japanese Empire, reveals how quickly borderlands collapsed between various empires of the Pacific world and Asia spanning several decades.[41] Alaska, strategically located in the North Pacific, could have been part of the shift of borderlands between the forces of empires.

Alaska the Borderland

Far from a frontier of an empty wilderness, Alaska represented a borderland of the North Pacific and the Arctic. Alaska is first a Native land that happens to be a borderland where various empires attempt to claim it and its resources. Turning to other Pacific Northwest tribal geographies and the concept of Native borderlands, maritime historian Joshua Reid (Snohomish) identifies specifically the Makah as holding a unique Indigenous "ča·di· borderland" defined as an Indigenous-held land and sea.[42] Other historians have highlighted Alaska as a borderland along the Pacific. Historian Andrea Geiger describes Alaska as "shifting borderlands of the North Pacific coast" linking North America, Asia, and various empires, including Russian America, British and Spanish exploration, the United States, Japan, and Canada.[43] A majority of Alaska's borders touch the Pacific Ocean, and Alaska resides between the major empires of the Pacific world, including the Soviet Union (Russia pre-1922 and post-1991), Japan, Canada, and the United States.

In this book, I have tried to be as specific as possible distinguishing between Soviet and Russian colonial history in Alaska. However, given the centuries of Russian colonial influence in Alaska, a slippage occurs particularly in oral histories with elders who describe Siberian pilots through the Alaska-Siberia Lend-Lease program (1941–1945) as "Russian." Even territorial officials such as Gruening described the Soviets as "Russians" during this World War II era.[44] Evidencing borderlands that change at the whims of empires, sharing planes from Alaska to Siberia and the alliance between the United States and Soviet Union with the Lend-Lease Act of 1941 quickly shifted to animosity in July 1945 after US military planners drew a military boundary in Korea separating Soviet control.

This book is not just about World War II Alaska; it is about the expansion of US empire and the ways that Alaska Native nations refused erasure by multiple competing settler colonial empires. The US Congress's purchase of Alaska from Russia in 1867 remains a folly because the empires never consulted with the Native nations. Native consultation would change when Alaska Native nations adapted to destabilizing conditions, choosing to ally with the US over the Soviet Union and Japan during World War II. Fighting alongside the United States to maintain their homelands, this alliance between Alaska Natives and the US government did not exist without consequence.

Alaska therefore shows how the West orients north and to the Pacific. After Pacific battles including ones on Alaskan islands, the United States reached Eastern Asia by imperial force and established military bases in Japan. For Alaska Native nations, protecting their land and allyship meant imperial expansion of US empire into their Indigenous homelands from World War II well into the Cold War that followed. Notably, the shift from the nineteenth century to the twentieth century involved seeing colonial bodies as relative allies compared to the enemies of other empires.

Equilibrium Restoration

Alongside and in defiance of colonial powers and (dis)order, Indigenous peoples have exerted their own subversive structure and powers. Indeed, they disrupt colonial projects daily, as exhibited by Alice's uncle who banished a government doctor. As critical Indigenous studies scholar Jodi Byrd (Chickasaw) shows, US empire depends upon Indigenous peoples. A decolonial future relies upon Indigenous agency.[45] How then can we capture the phenomena of continued patterns of sustained Indigenous resistance against what Byrd has labeled "a cacophony" of colonial violence in American history? I borrow language from the fields of sociology and economics to illustrate an Indigenous movement that must be characterized as more than just "agency." I call to recognize and name the subversive structure and powers that Indigenous peoples exercise through a focus on Alaska at war because this region encapsulates Native assertions of sovereignty with diplomacy and the establishment of nation to national alliances.

I put forth the term *equilibrium restoration* to highlight how Indigenous peoples balance their lives during continuous waves of colonial violence.[46] The root words of both *equilibrium* and *restoration* relay anti-colonial assertions of Indigenous agency. For example, the word *equilibrium* references a stable and balanced condition, whereas *restoration* emphasizes positive rebuild. Colonialism attempts to tear down both with imbalance, destruction, and the replacement of Indigenous bodies with settler colonial bodies. Approaches to Native American studies and history often emphasize persistent and resilient survival of Native peoples amid settler colonialism. I expand on these important concepts of agency, resistance, resilience, and refusal to assist in identifying the numerous ways that Alaska Natives obtained equilibrium restoration. An analysis of Alaska Native history during World War II shows that Indigenous peoples indeed shaped colonial structures, finding ways to maintain Indigenous spaces while retaining Indigenous sovereignty.

Pivoting back to Alice's story illuminates a social and Indigenous history made possible only through oral history. In banishing Bauer, Alice's Uncle Bill not only restored equilibrium but also asserted Unangax̂ sovereignty. Rather than tolerate a government physician who caused trauma and harm, Atkans chose to fend for themselves by declining US medical aid. The action of banishment in addition to the children's taunting of Bauer illustrates how on the wartime Alaskan landscape, even within the confines of government relocation camps, Indigenous resistance flourished at multiple interlocking levels.

The term *agency* has been widely debated among various academic fields specifically when removal or unfreedom emerge. Critics of the term have shown that an individual's level of agency is limited by the structures of power imposed upon that individual. The field of African American studies maintains a rich analysis on the concept of agency. Literary scholar Saidiya V. Hartman identifies agency as limited by the slaveholders' exercise of power, yet Hartman explored "instances of insurgency" and possibilities of resistance.[47] Historian Robin D. G. Kelley called for a reframing of history to recognize that the oppressed, even if inhibited by structures of power, need to dismantle the very structures that prevent observations of agency.[48]

Concepts of resistance and refusal prove particularly useful in understanding Indigenous agency.

For every form of oppression exerted by a colonizing power, Indigenous peoples resisted in tailored ways producing a proliferation of Indigeneity. Of note, my intent is not to homogenize Native nations, or diverse Native experiences, but rather to situate Alaska Native studies in the broader field of Native studies. By documenting various forms of Kanaka Maoli resistance against US colonization in Hawai'i, political scientist Noenoe K. Silva (Kanaka Maoli) "refute[d] the myth of passivity."[49] American studies scholar Nick Estes (Lower Brule Sioux Tribe) has also underscored the power of Indigenous resistance linked to sovereignty.[50] Relatedly, anthropologist Audra Simpson (Mohawk) theorized "nested sovereignty" of Mohawks of Kahnawà:ke asserting sovereignty that refuses "settler logics of elimination."[51] Equilibrium restoration builds upon these concepts of resistance and refusal from Native studies to show times when Alaska Natives have restructured their lives, propelling Indigeneity forward against colonial forces, such as removal.

Equilibrium restoration provides a term for the anti-colonial structure that pushes against settler colonialism to maintain an Indigenous order. Indigenous Kenyan literary scholar Ngũgĩ wa Thiong'o (Gĩkũyũ) assists with understanding this framework in which Indigenous peoples push against colonizers at an equal rate.[52] Equilibrium restoration shows how Indigenous peoples survive, reject, overthrow, and even appropriate colonial structures to maintain an Indigenous livelihood while their land and governments remain intact and protected. An analysis of equilibrium restoration debunks the Western assumption that colonialism is an all-powerful entity with zero counterbalances by Indigenous actions.

Adoption and adaptation are key components to understanding Indigenous agency as well. When Indigenous peoples exhibit elements of colonial projects, it is not because they are colonized but rather because they have chosen to appropriate elements of colonialism and to Indigenize these colonial projects to serve their own purposes, thus restoring equilibrium. Such an analysis fits historian Matthew Sakiestewa Gilbert (Hopi), who argues that when confronted by colonial projects in education or politics, Indigenous peoples use them.[53] Thus, when Alaska Natives chose US military service, they seized the opportunity to ally with the United States to protect their homeland from further invasion by Japan. False assumptions that downplay Indigenous persistence and resistance serve the purpose to silence Indigenous agency and to aggrandize the power of settler colonialism.

Indigenous sovereignty exists and persists, and nothing—other than complete genocide—can remove that. Even in the face of blatant colonial powers, such as the conditions of a government-led wartime relocation camp, Indigenous sovereignty is retained, and sometimes it is only practiced in discursive settings. I am going to borrow from political scientist James C. Scott and apply his concept of a "hidden transcript" to illustrate that Indigenous peoples adhere to their sovereignty; at times this meant the adoption of Western bureaucracies until such structures could be expelled and rejected in favor of Indigenous control.[54] Sometimes Indigenous sovereignty took the form of accepting certain components of colonization while dispelling others. Historian Frederick Hoxie shows that assertions of Indigenous agency include Indigenous activists who maintain Indigenous nationhood while "coexist[ing]" alongside "the expanding continental empire that became the United States."[55] Here, we see how American Indians truly are dual citizens.

Policies and actions by settler institutions such as the government continue to compromise according to Indigenous actions, reactions, and resistance. Equilibrium restoration acknowledges that Indigenous peoples and their nations balance chaotic actions of colonialism with calculated and organized Indigenous resistance both on an individual and coordinated group level. This system, considering Alaska as a case study, is theorized and enacted by layered, what I call, "survivance alliances" forged between sovereign Alaska Native nations. Acclaimed literary scholar Gerald Vizenor (Minnesota Chippewa Tribe, White Earth Reservation) termed *survivance* as "an active sense of presence, the continuation of Native stories, not a mere reaction of survivable name."[56] Building from Vizenor, I see these survivance alliances as revealing solidarities: when Native people ally with one another, they accelerate not only their own survivance but also a collective anti-colonial body. These alliances make it harder for colonialism to chip away at multiple Native sovereignties.

Alaska Native Oral History Methods

Only by taking both Indigenous men's and Indigenous women's ideas and experiences seriously—that is, explicitly investigating each through oral history—can one create a reliable history of any colonial project, of any war, or of any collective resistance. On methodologies in constructing this Alaskan Indigenous history, I would be remiss to leave out the fundamental role that tribal archives, Native newspapers, and, in particular, oral histories play in elucidating this Indigenous social history. Testimonies provide not only a means to understand the past but also a way to illuminate a history otherwise shaded by colonial narratives of declension and the myths of Indigenous nations as non-existent, non-purposeful, and incapable of shaping empire. Truly, the concept of equilibrium restoration itself was not immediately evident to me until after I met Alice, listened to her stories, and thought broadly on what her stories meant in the larger schema of Alaskan colonization projects.

While diverse Alaska Natives did not have the same experience with the US military and government, they have a common experience of coping and navigating US imperial projects and wartime strategies. Over ninety oral histories that I have conducted from 2008 to 2022 for this study relay Native memories and such strategies. Each chapter in this book reveals that Native people unrelentingly negotiated events and situations. Unless cited otherwise in the text, I conducted all oral histories with elders, sometimes alongside their family members. In addition to official oral histories conducted for this study, I frequently visited with elders and their families; those stories shared in a personal context are not included, although the relationships that I developed with elders did inform my understanding of Alaska history and community solidarities. Haliehana Stepetin (Unangax̂) has written about the central role of "visiting" as "intentional" and an Indigenous feminist practice, where "visiting is not only a way to connect, but it is also how our histories, family stories, values, lessons, and ways of life are transferred."[57]

Oral history is, or should be, a reciprocity, a mutual exchange between members of the community and an oral historian. I have interviewed elders from tribes across Alaska in Anchorage, Bethel, Dutch Harbor, Fairbanks,

FIG. 1. Gifts from elders in Juneau and Metlakatla, 2014. Signed book from Carol Brady (Tlingit), Southeast Traditional Values magnet from Marilyn Doyle (Tlingit), tea from Rosa Miller (Tlingit), copper earrings from Donald Gregory (Tlingit), kippered salmon from Dorothy Own (Tlingit/Filipina), and doll fashioned by Roxee Booth (Tsimshian). Photo by the author.

Juneau, Kodiak, Metlakatla, Nome, Unalakleet, Utqiaġvik, and Wasilla. Elders had the option to participate anonymously, to be audio or video recorded, and to include a photograph.[58] At the conclusion of each interview, the elder received a small gift to thank them for their time. These gifts ranged from bakery loaves to fresh fruit, tea, hard candies, small tote bags, and—after I had received grant funding from the American Philosophical Society Library—Visa gift cards. Some elders and their families reciprocated with gifts of personalized fish camp key chains, jars of homemade jam or kippered salmon, Native dolls, books, and handpicked Labrador tea (fig. 1).

I developed the practice of transcribing each interview and mailing it to the respective elder, providing elders an opportunity to offer feedback with edits, revisions, and omissions. On multiple occasions, elders called me or wrote to correct the spellings of names and places that do not exist from a basic online search. On one occasion, one elder asked to be removed; I redacted their interview(s) from this study. While I primarily sought to interview Native elders, non-Native elders and veterans provided valuable perspective as well. Since I met with many elders on multiple occasions, I decided to refer to each elder by their first name. If an elder identified their Native name, I prioritized this in my writing.

Crucial support from community members made interviews possible. While it helped to circulate recruitment flyers on bulletin boards, at senior centers, and on various listservs, the best way to find elders was referrals from within the Native community. Friends and community members gave me names of their grandparents and elders (the bibliography includes a list of all interviews and dates). I visited senior lunch programs and senior activities centers where I introduced myself by bringing photobooks from research travels. All photographs from the photobooks included consent. Over time, I developed the practice of showing elders a research photobook before their interview. Many elders enjoyed viewing these since they recognized friends from boarding school, and they enjoyed seeing pictures of my Alaska adventures. After I met with an elder, I asked if they knew other elders whom I should connect with; this snowball method proved most effective.

I believe that my background as a young Iñupiaq woman with family from Unalakleet helped in soliciting participation in this oral history project. I also believe that my age, familial background, and gender contributed to oral history outreach. I perceived that many elders saw me as relatively close in age to their grandchildren or grandnieces and grandnephews. I also believe that some of the best interviews I conducted occurred when I was visibly pregnant in 2016 and 2018. I am not sure why; perhaps elders saw me as a link between generations.

Outside of tribal archives, such as those of the Sealaska Heritage Institute, the Tuzzy Consortium Library, and the Aleutian Pribilof Islands Association (APIA) Heritage Library, scant archives from specifically Native perspectives make oral histories all the more powerful as a source. These oral histories prioritize traditional knowledge passed down from elders in the community and fit what Linda Tuhiwai Smith (Ngāti Awa and Ngāti Porou, Māori) called "decolonizing methodologies," in which research methods fit an "Indigenous research agenda."[59] During a guest lecture for JoEllen Anderson's class at Stanford University, Diné student Nataanii Hatathlie thoughtfully asked why I had not conducted or translated oral histories from Alaska Native languages.[60] The truth is I am only a historian and not a linguist. To interview and translate oral histories in each Native language would have been an amazing undertaking, and it was ultimately beyond the scope of this project. Relatedly, I chose not to Indigenize the phrase *equilibrium restoration* as this would involve applying a Western concept to Native languages and privileging one Alaska Native language over another.[61] Overall, elder interviews reveal that Alaska Natives pushed against colonialism to counteract, subdue, and manipulate colonial projects.

Alaska Natives at War

Reverberations of war swept the wartime landscape from the Aleutian Islands to every Alaskan region, and Alaska Natives responded to restore Indigenous lands. As the military and Indigenous peoples navigated each other, equilibrium restoration emerged from the relationship between Alaska Natives and the US military. Each chapter of this book shows how Alaska Native people, working with, through, and sometimes against the arrival of the US military, shaped the wartime Alaskan landscape.

Situated within scholarship from the field of Alaska history, wartime Alaska offers a compelling case study about colonization. In recent years, there have been significant contributions to Alaska Native history. This includes literary scholar Juliana Hu Pegues's work on entanglements between the Alaskan Indigenous and Asian peoples with "space-time colonialism."[62] Other works include art historian Emily Moore's study on Tlingit totem pole carving during the New Deal era.[63] Centering environmental history, Bathsheba Demuth has linked Siberia to Alaska, underscoring the trans-Arctic nature of colonial resource extraction.[64] Highlighting Gwich'in activism in protesting oil development, Finis Dunaway underscores Indigenous-led grassroot movements that partnered with environmentalists to bring about change.[65] These works pair with major contributions in Alaska Native studies, such as Maria Shaa Tláa Williams's (Tlingit) foundational anthology *The Alaska Native Reader*.[66] In addition, scholarship by Native studies scholar Dian Million (Tanana Athabascan) illuminates the need for healing since colonialism brings endemic violence impacting Indigenous women.[67] Firmly placed in expansive oral history scholarship, Nora Marks Dauenhauer (Tlingit) and Richard Dauenhauer remain foundational to studies on Alaska.[68]

Equilibrium restoration emerges in each chapter, showing that Alaska Natives fought to retain their lands and restore an Indigenous agenda amid colonial projects. In negotiating with colonial forces, Native people mastered their futures by exerting their sovereignty.[69] While this book opens with Unangax̂ history in the first two chapters, they are not the main focus of this book. Chapters 3 and 4 detail experiences of Native men in the service and Native men and women in guerrilla platoons, showing how given the option to ally with Japan, the Soviet Union, or the United States, Alaska Natives overwhelmingly chose to ally with the United States to preserve their lands. Chapter 5 highlights the challenge that Alaska Natives confronted with structures of segregation and assimilation imposed by Western schools and settlers alike. Chapter 6 articulates stories of diverse Alaska Native women's experiences with the military, gendered segregation, and sexual violence.

Uncovering Alaska Native equilibrium restoration shows that US colonialism failed to colonize Alaska and its Native people and that the US government negotiated with unrelenting Indigenous nations. Identifying equilibrium restoration meant different things in each diverse colonization projects. For example, as chapter 1 shows, equilibrium restoration at relocation camps meant Unangax̂ men exerting labor rights and Unangax̂ women writing protest letters to the government as an organized Indigenous government while creating homes for children amid deplorable conditions, all while Unangax̂ advocated to restore their nation's bodies to their Pribilof and Aleutian home islands in 1944 and 1945. Chapter 2 reveals that equilibrium restoration relied on survivance alliances generated between Unangax̂ and Tlingit who collaborated through giving and accepting tribal mutual aid.

Zooming out, as chapters 3 and 4 show, equilibrium restoration meant using the resources of empire, such as the US military, to fight a war on— and for—your homeland. All these actions/reactions/refusals amalgamate to produce a larger web of not just Indigenous resistance; they collectively illustrate an exercise of Native sovereignty that is inherent, involving not only political choice but also selective allyship during war. Even the youngest members of society, Native children, found ways to restore equilibrium, as shown in chapter 5, by Indigenizing school settings through whispering Native words to one another at recess. Native children rejected the colonizer's tongue, retaining their Native languages with friends in whatever limited formats possible. Equilibrium restoration derives from elders who survived the boarding school era and chose to teach their Native language to Native youth today, literally teaching banned Indigenous languages and restoring Native tongues in the future generation. Other times, as chapter 6 shows, equilibrium restoration derived from Native organizing efforts to end the Alaska Defense Command ban on interracial relations between servicemen and civilian Native women in Southeast Alaska. Centering Native women's voices, this chapter brings to light gendered racial violence directed at Native women that was augmented by the conditions of war and the arriving military personnel.

The actions of Native people obtaining equilibrium restoration during wartime Alaska reveal a landscape overwhelmed by manifestations of Native sovereignty. Perhaps we have not identified this as sovereignty because we have victimized Indigenous peoples to the point of not recognizing their agency and skills to manipulate empire. When Native people deny this sovereignty, it is because we have been indoctrinated by reeducation programs from Western assimilationist schools to deny the visibility and presence of our own sovereign rights.

ONE
UNANGAX̂ RELOCATION
FORCED REMOVAL
AND FORCED LABOR

LAWRENCE "LARRY" CHERCASEN (Unangax̂), who was born in 1935 in Nikolski on the Aleutian Islands, described the Unangax̂ relocation camp: "It took our past and our future. It took our elders, which was our past; and it took our children, which were the future. And we had a gap there. And there's a gap that's gonna be there forever because there's no way to replace it."[1] During the Second World War, 10 percent of Unangax̂ died at the relocation camps due to poor housing conditions, rampant illnesses, impotable water, and a lack of medical care. Larry himself survived the measles epidemic. He explained, "TB, pneumonia, flu, measles, mumps, you name it. It killed us because we weren't used to the diseases."

The voices of Unangax̂ elders like Larry and their stories of death, survival, and resiliency regarding wartime removal offer a counter-history to a broader understanding of the United States during war. Truly, the causalities of this war occurred not only overseas but also within US territorial boundaries and most importantly within the lands of Indigenous nations. In line with the doctrine of manifest destiny, US officials deemed Indigenous bodies dispensable to expand US empire. Historian Jeffrey Ostler reveals dispossession of numerous Native nations to be an act of genocide.[2] Many are familiar with Cherokee Removal in the 1830s and the Indian Wars in the nineteenth century, but fewer people outside Alaska are knowledgeable on Unangax̂ relocation and internment of the mid-twentieth century that occurred after Japan's invasion of the Aleutian Islands. This removal followed other patterns of US removals of Native nations into the twentieth century, including the Warner's Ranch removal of Cupeño Indians in California in 1903 and attempted removals such as the failed Rampart Dam project of Interior Alaska proposed in 1954.[3]

Unangax̂ relocation is a story of the US government exploiting Indigenous bodies, labor, and land, under the guise of protecting Indigenous wards. This concept of wardship itself denotes an infantilization of Indigenous peoples and nations, thereby generating the federal government as paternal and benevolent.[4] With this in mind, following Japan's invasion of the Aleutians in 1942, the US Navy evacuated over 880 Unangax̂ to six relocation camps fifteen hundred miles away from their home islands. These camps in Southeast Alaska existed at the Funter Bay cannery, the Funter Bay mine, the Killisnoo herring reduction plant, the Wrangell Institute boarding school, the Burnett Inlet cannery, and, in Larry's experience, the Ward Lake Civilian Conservation Corps (CCC) camp.[5] The camp locations read like random sites because they were. These makeshift camps existed at whatever dormant and non-coincidentally dilapidated buildings and campsites could host hundreds of people. The government chose these camp locations in Southeast Alaska to consolidate Unangax̂ laborers.[6]

Unangax̂ relocation is a story that has parallels to histories of American Indians and other marginalized groups, yet it is unlike any other history that Alaska Native nations encountered. The story of Alaska at war reveals that different branches of the US government exercised not only bureaucracy but also varied forms of colonial control when government organizations treated certain Indigenous groups differently than others. Not only did Unangax̂ encounter a different fate than any other Alaska Native group, but within the Unangax̂ nation, individual islanders faced diverse experiences. Put simply, Unangax̂ internment can be divided into two categories. In one category, Pribolobians, also known as Unangax̂ from the Pribilof Islands of St. Paul and St. George, were placed into camps, and the government forced men to work harvesting seal pelts to profit the US government. In the second category, Unangax̂ from the Aleutian Islands were relocated and forced into camps, but they did not all serve as laboring bodies that profited the US government. Although all Unangax̂ endured internment, evacuation, and relocation, their experiences varied depending on whether or not the government forced them to labor.

This story of Unangax̂ relocation reframes our understanding of, among other subjects, the Fish and Wildlife Service (FWS) as a profit-seeking entity that had partnered with the Missouri-based Fouke Fur Company to exploit Indigenous labor. During the 1940s, the FWS and this private corporation conscripted Unangax̂ men from camps to a warzone to prepare seal pelts for the US market. As this history shows, there are indeed a wide range of institutional actors like the FWS who propelled US colonizing projects. The Unangax̂ experience is valuable in understanding US colonial practices of forced labor; government war-waging policies; Indigenous politics; and the ongoing, not-finished-yet Alaskan history. Although this chapter documents hardships and suffering, writing this history only through the language of internment, evacuation, and prisoners of war (POWs) would fail to capture the story that shows Native sovereignty where Native people defied colonial projects and asserted an Indigenous agenda in whatever capacity possible.

Camps, detention centers, and mass civilian deaths characterize many World War II histories and geographies across the Pacific and globally. The experiences of Unangax̂ during World War II in Alaska follow a long history of placing ethnic bodies in encampments. And while this chapter does not illuminate the stories of German POWs brought from Seattle to Excursion Inlet, roughly forty miles from Juneau, after Germany's surrender from July 1945 until November 1945, their stories contrast that of Unangax̂ relocation since all seven hundred German POWs survived.[7] This chapter will, in addition to addressing Japan's POW camp on Hokkaido, outline some experiences of mixed Japanese/Alaska Native men incarcerated by US empire in the US heartland.

Despite the deprivation of human rights illuminated by survivor testimonies, Unangax̂ remained resilient, resisting forms of US colonialism while advocating to return home. In this instance, equilibrium restoration meant agency exerted by Unangax̂ to push against colonial violence by organizing and asserting their voices. In the context of removal, this specifically involved Unangax̂ adaptability in their (im)mobility and unrelenting advocacy to return to their home islands, revealing that community activism occurred on the groundwork to upend colonial plans for permanent relocation.[8] Alongside this primary example, there are other examples of equilibrium restoration. Unangax̂ confounded imposed colonial racial categories, as in the case of mixed Japanese American/Native individuals. At the camps, they exerted activism through labor negotiation, with Native women organizing and reporting government abuse through correspondence to government officials; in taking control of daily life by creating positive structures in the community, such as providing clothing for children and facilitating religious services; and in the decades after the war by pursuing lawsuits coordinated alongside Japanese Americans, thereby establishing bonds in Indigenous-immigrant relations.

Land Invasion

On June 3 and 4, 1942, Japan bombed Dutch Harbor, invading Kiska Island on June 6, followed by Attu Island on June 7.[9] Japan initiated these projects in the Aleutians to prevent US military expansion in the North Pacific and to divert attention from the Battle of Midway. And yet Unangax̂ from Attu anticipated Japan's attack. Chief Mike Hodikoff of Attu warned US war correspondent Corey Ford that Japan's military had previously landed on Attu Island, taken measurements, and raped the women.[10] No record has been found detailing the perspective of the Attuan women. Much like the way that sexual violence against Native women has been systematic and also dismissed by government officials, the war correspondent showed ambivalence toward Chief Hodikoff and his speculation of Japan's invasion. According to Chief Hodikoff, thirty years prior to the war, Japanese marauders raided fox skins from hunters on the far side of the island and killed some Attu men, including Hodikoff's father.[11] Chief Hodikoff knew that Unangax̂ occupied an archipelago at the center of conflict between Japan, the Soviet Union, and the United States, including settlers, fishermen, trappers, and military alike. From his perspective, in relaying previous encounters with the Japanese to a US war correspondent, he sought to both bring awareness to this history and build an alliance with the US military to defend his homeland.

On the day of Japan's arrival between June 3 and 7, 1942, Charles Jones, an elderly man born in 1879, who worked for the BIA and operated the radio as a weather reporter, sent out a radio message: "J*ps are here." Invasion included airplanes and one large naval vessel with smaller boats as landing barges. Japanese soldiers shot an Attuan woman in her leg. According to Etta Jones, a BIA teacher and spouse to Charles, members of the Japanese military instructed her to read a statement to the Attuans that Japan liberated them from exploitation and tyranny of the US government.[12] Such a statement aligned with others read to imperial-occupied Asian and Pacific geographies. The military looted Attuan homes, rounding everyone up including women, children, and the two white BIA teachers. Charles died in the first few days of Japan's occupation. In interviewing Etta Jones, the Japanese tried to see if an alliance existed between the Americans and the Soviets in Kamchatka. Tensions between the Japanese and the Soviets remained high following the aftermath of the Russo-Japanese War from 1904 to 1905. This ended with the Treaty of Portsmouth in New Hampshire coordinated by US president Theodore Roosevelt, enabling Japan to extend their empire to Korea and railroad lines in southern Manchuria.[13] In 1931, Japan invaded Manchuria and the nearby Kuril Islands where these regions exchanged hands between Japan and the Soviet Union.[14]

After Japan's imperial invasion of Attu, the military took forty Attuans to a POW camp in Otaru on Hokkaido. Japanese military officials threatened Attuans, telling them not to help the white BIA employees. Before being taken as captives to Japan, Attuans buried Charles Jones on their island. Here, the Attuans recognized the integrity of Charles's humanity, and in honoring his humanity they honored their own humanity. In burying this BIA official on their land, Attuans recognized an affinity or pre-established allyship with a US government employee that preceded a new imperial power. Sequential colonialisms can indeed be complex as civilians are forced to navigate which empire is a lesser evil and at times choose to ally with more familiar colonizers over newly arrived colonizers. Another poignant testimony, that of Alex Prossoff, details Japan's removal of Attuans into a coal carrier: "Some of the children do not want to leave Attu. They cry but J*p soldiers pick them up and throw them down the holds, too."[15] Japanese soldiers instructed Attuans to bring barrels of fish with them to Otaru.

At the POW camp in Otaru, where the Japanese military forced Attuans to work in factories, 40 percent of Attuans died. In January 1945, Chief Hodikoff himself passed away in captivity. Food was scarce across Japan toward war's end, and both Chief Hodikoff and his son George died from food poisoning after foraging food from waste bins. Other accounts by Attuans at POW camps inform that the Japanese treated Attuans slightly better than other POWs with better rations when food was not scarce. Alongside these deaths, some unlikely friendships emerged between Attuans and members of the Japanese military. Scholar Henry Stewart's report for APIA in 1978 mentions two names of Japanese individuals from Shimizu-cho on Hokkaido who "played with the Aleut children when the Aleuts were at Shimizu-cho."[16] Masami Sugiyama describes that while a foreign affairs section of the Otaru Police Department surveilled Attuans, one local housewife never got caught giving vegetables to Attuan women from her window, who in turn gave her baked bread.[17] Also, according to Sugiyama, Japanese and Attuan children played together "in a playground behind the house." Nick Golodoff (Attuan), for example, described his childhood friendship with a Japanese soldier named Mr. Kamani in his biography *Attu Boy*.[18] Illustrating the power of interpersonal connection, the lives of Golodoff and Kamani intersected across geographies and time—more than fifty years after war ended, they reunited. While extra food and friendships undoubtedly went a long way to aid survival, it cannot be discounted that Attuans barely survived war as prisoners on foreign territory.

Japanese American Concentration Camps

Japanese American incarceration illuminates another dimension to removals from Alaska, as camps in the US heartland provide evidence of nationalism that incarcerated innocent civilians. Following Executive Order 9066 dated February 19, 1942, the US Department of War relocated 120,000 Japanese Americans, a majority being citizens, to concentration camps; 240 Japanese Alaskans, including men of mixed Japanese and Indigenous ancestry, were sent to these camps in the US mainland.[19] A letter to Governor Gruening from former Ketchikan resident Michael Hagiwara at the Minidoka camp explained that the government incarcerated more than 120 Alaskans at Minidoka and that roughly fifty were children under the age of eighteen and many Japanese men had Native wives.[20]

Evacuation of Japanese Alaskans relied on gender and race. The Alaska Defense Command sent "all persons of Japanese percentage of greater degree than half blood and all males over sixteen years old or half Japanese blood, whether American citizens or otherwise."[21] Children could voluntarily accompany a parent to the concentration camp, but Native women married to Japanese men could not join their spouse. With their Japanese husbands, sons, and brothers removed to camps outside the territory, Native wives remained at their homes and were dependent on meager allowances from the BIA.[22] However, there was some fluidity here. According to oral histories of Marie Matsuno (Japanese/Aleut), who was born at the Minidoka camp in 1943, her Native mother wrote to the US government requesting to join her Japanese American husband at the Minidoka camp.[23] Similarly, the government exempted Japanese women married to Native men, thereby linking Native identities to a national white identity. The notion that Japanese Alaskan women conformed their identity to that of their husbands, either Native, white, or Japanese ancestry, exuded the concept of patriarchy. The federal government first relocated Japanese Alaskans to Puyallap, Washington, at "Camp Harmony." The name itself is a euphemism. After separating Japanese Alaskan men from their families, the government transported them to Texas and New Mexico, and six months later they rejoined their families at the Minidoka War Relocation Center in Idaho.[24]

Individuals of mixed Alaska Native/Japanese ancestry confounded racial categories ascribed by the US government, revealing entangled relationships between Indigeneity and Asian immigration. Estimating the demographics of these Alaskans is difficult, yet oral histories including Marie's and Melva Wither's (Aleut/Japanese ancestry), whose mixed Native/Japanese father passed as Alaska Native during removal thereby remaining in their hometown of Seward, and publications including the *Magazine Alaska* from 1941 account for these multiracial individuals.[25] In northern Alaska, for example, in the Iñupiaq town of Ipnatchiaq (English name Deering), the federal government detained and deported some Iñupiat to Idaho because of their mixed Japanese ancestry.[26]

Seeking to return to Alaska, individuals of mixed Alaska Native and Japanese ancestry wrote to Governor Gruening requesting reunification with their families in Alaska. These protest letters from Japanese Alaska Native men reveal persistent attempts to forge familial reunifications and a call for the government to examine their cases for freedom. Personal requests may be interpreted as efforts of equilibrium restoration to physically return home and rejoin their families. In November 1943, Charles Foode began his letter from the concentration camp in Idaho to Governor Gruening with "I am an evacuee from Cordova Alaska, and would like to know whether my three brothers and I can be sent back home. We are half Japanese and half Alaska Indian, our sisters and brothers are still in Cordova with our mother."[27] Similarly, Fairbanks resident Alice Stuart wrote to Governor Gruening in April 1942, begging him not to ship Henry Hope, a seventh-grade boy from Wiseman, to a camp. She described Hope as an adopted "half-breed Esk*mo . . . Henry has never seen his father, who was Japanese. His mother was Esk*mo."[28] With no regard for splitting families, in Southeast Alaska, the US Army separated Harvey Sharai "one half Tsimshian half Japanese" from his "full Tlingit" wife and their several children.[29] Their letters indicate not only the prevalence of mixed Japanese Alaska Natives across tribal geographies but also the degree to which gendered ordinances impacted these multiracial men whom the government took from their families. In this case, being Indigenous did not prevent someone from being presumed an enemy of the state. And like the history of boarding school separations, camps separated Japanese Alaskan families.

Other letters reveal tragic fates of families of Japanese ancestry separated by the US government. Specific names include the Kito family, Sakamato family, and Okegawa family of Petersburg, the Hama family of Seward, the Kawata family and Miyasato family of Wrangell, and the Mayeda family of Hoonah. In Petersburg, before government relocation, Japanese Alaskan children tried to sell their bicycles and wagons.[30] With their possessions seized, many relocated Japanese Americans would never return to Alaska. Sometimes, as Melva Withers (Aleut/Japanese ancestry) identified, a white family overtook a Japanese-owned business such as the laundromat in Seward.[31]

Other times, Japanese Alaskans wrote to the government asking to return to Alaska in the postwar years, as was the case of Marie Matsuno's father, Fred Matsuno. Her father had a compelling case to return to Alaska as a decorated war veteran who received medals including the Purple Heart from serving in the segregated 442nd Infantry Regiment made up of Japanese Americans who fought in the European theater. Nonetheless, when their family returned to Ugashik, their house and all their belongings had been stolen, most likely seized by other villagers or fishermen who might have assumed the family would never return from incarceration. The Matsuno family stayed in a relative's tiny house until Marie's father built a new house next to it. Equilibrium restoration meant returning to Alaska from Minidoka and rebuilding an entirely new home.

While the two stories of wartime camps seem separate, the story of Japanese American incarceration and Unangax̂ relocation are indeed strongly linked. Unangax̂ possessed US citizenship rights, and a majority of Japanese Americans in concentration camps were citizens too.[32] Both groups also encountered forced labor during incarceration, as historian Stephanie Hinnershitz illuminates.[33] Yet the government placed these Indigenous peoples and immigrants into camps for divergent reasons. In forcing over 120,000 Japanese Americans into camps, under the guise of protecting the home front, the US government villainized Japanese Americans as "outside" white America.[34] In contrast, the United States placed Unangax̂ in camps to purportedly protect them from invasion by Japan, which thereby rendered Unangax̂ wards "inside" white America. There are distinctions between the way that relocation projected Japanese Americans as "outsider foreign enemies" and Unangax̂ as "protected insiders." Both colonial projections dichotomize ethnic others while reinforcing xenophobia and settler colonialism that seizes Native lands.

Unangax̂ Relocation and Internment Camps

Unangax̂ on the remaining Aleutian and Pribilof Islands not invaded by Japan encountered an entirely different fate. They remained captive to another empire, the more familiar one of the United States, which used wartime powers to impose not only relocation but to fill capitalist labor demands. Into the twentieth century, the US federal government partnered with a private corporation, the Fouke Fur Company based in Missouri, extracting

Unangax̂ labor for profit. Predating this era of forced labor, in addition to bringing diseases, Russians enslaved Unangax̂ during the fur trade, forcing them to harvest seal pelts from the Pribilof Islands during the eighteenth and nineteenth centuries.[35] In 1743, *promyshlenniki*, Russian fur trappers, began sealing operations in the Aleutians, where a majority of the pelts went to China's market.[36] As Unangax̂ internment shows, labor demands imposed on Indigenous bodies by empire continued into the twentieth century with US occupation, in which a paternal wardship relationship masked the darker motive of colonial labor extraction.

Soviet influence on Unangax̂ relocation is only speculative as federal archives and findings by the US Federal Commission investigation including the attorney hired by APIA show no indication that this had any bearing on removal.[37] The links between Unangax̂ and the Soviets did not exist; however, Russian colonialism extended east to Alaska predating the Soviet Union. Unangax̂ spoke Unangam Tunuu as their primary language, Russian as their second language, and English as their third. To this day, Unangax̂ have Russian surnames and sometimes first names. Yet Unangax̂ having Russian names is no different from Native people in other regions; Great Plains Indians carry French surnames yet never assimilated to French colonialism during the fur trade. Indeed, the history of Unangax̂ with Russian colonial influence is complicated. In fact, Americans and Soviets allied during the war. Through the Lend-Lease program from 1941 to 1945, the United States shared airplanes with Soviet pilots, who retrieved planes from Alaska, learned to fly at Ladd Field in Fairbanks, and brought these wartime weapons of assistance to the Soviet Union to fight the Nazis on their western border.

In never asking Unangax̂ for consent to be removed, to occupy their land with imperial powers, or to work alongside them to develop an evacuation plan, the United States denied Indigenous sovereignty while assuming the role of a paternal colonial authority determining the fate of an Indigenous nation during war. When asked about government consultation regarding relocation, Korean War veteran General Jake Lestenkof (Unangax̂), born on St. George Island in 1932, replied, "No. No, we only had one day notice."[38] Relatedly, Alfred Stepetin (Unangax̂) longed to understand why the US government evacuated Unangax̂ yet allowed white men to remain on the

Aleutian Islands. He detailed, "There was always one thing on my mind the whole time, was why us Aleuts had to be evacuated when the Caucasians could remain in the village. This has been on my mind since I was fourteen years old. And this question I feel, should be answered by somebody."[39]

Following the attack on Pearl Harbor in December 1941, and prior to Unangax̂ relocation, Lieutenant General Simon Bolivar Buckner, head of the Alaska Defense Command, ordered an evacuation of all white women and children from Unalaska and Japonski Island near Sitka.[40] The name "Japonski" itself reveals early Japanese influences in Alaska of stranded Japanese fishermen in 1805 who Russians returned to Hokkaido in 1806. This story itself represents yet another example of the entangled histories between multiple empires and peoples in the North Pacific. Contrasting the ways that the government evacuated Unangax̂, Lieutenant General Buckner allowed white evacuees ample luggage, including 1,000 pounds baggage per family.[41] Making clear the links between white settler colonialism, patriarchy, and military occupation, civilian white men who remained on the Aleutians were treated as autonomous individuals alongside the military. Within six months of Unangax̂ removal, in December 1942, the secretary of war, Henry Stimson, wrote to the secretary of the interior about evacuation as a "military necessity" since it vacated Native houses for troops and eased shipment facilities within the Aleutians.[42] Expanding a settler colonial project of replacement, US servicemen resided in the vacant Unangax̂ homes. Of note, some white women, such as Mrs. Fry of Kodiak, who married a soldier and gave birth to twins, sought to remain in Alaska against Buckner's command by using the courts.[43]

In parallel to Japanese American removal, racial blood quantum, a colonial measurement imposing the notion of fractions onto one's Native identity, informed Unangax̂ removal. Indeed, government employees from the BIA, including the director John Collier himself, oversaw the execution of Executive Order 9066, supervising incarcerated Japanese Americans on Indian reservations in the US mainland.[44] Other historians, including Hana Maruyama, have explicitly linked Japanese American incarceration as a product of US settler colonialism.[45] On the race-based measure, Captain Hobart W. Copeland wrote to the commanding general in Seattle: "About

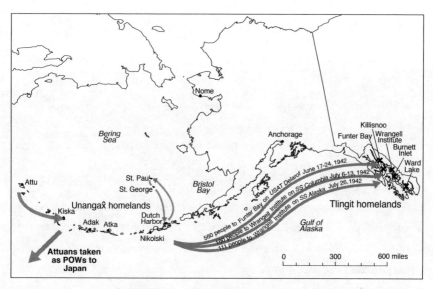

MAP 4. Alaska Unangax̂ Relocation, 1942. Map created and designed
by Sarah Aarons (Iñupiaq) in partnership with the author.

19 July 1942, the S.S. Alaska docked at Unalaska and [N]atives were placed
aboard subject to the following regulations prescribed by Commander Up-
degraf: All [N]atives, or persons as much as one eighth (1/8) [N]ative blood
were compelled to go."[46] Here, blood quantum accelerated Indigenous land
dispossession.[47] The number denotes a fraction of non-whiteness that could
supposedly be erased from Native people over generations by assimilation
into white mainstream society. Conversely, the "one-drop rule," dating to
early colonial American history and which asserted that any African ancestry
meant total non-whiteness, projected Black Americans as unassimilable.

Foreshadowing the challenging conditions at camps in Southeast Alaska,
ships relocating over 880 Unangax̂ from the Aleutians lacked basic infra-
structure such as water, food, privacy, bathrooms, and medical care. The
Delarof, a US Army transport ship, arrived on June 15, 1942, loading Pribolo-
bians from St. Paul and St. George Islands without knowing its destination.[48]
Already overcrowded, the *Delarof* retrieved residents from Atka and Nikolski
Island. The ss *Columbia*, a passenger ship, evacuated remaining Aleutian
Unangax̂ from Dutch Harbor. The doctor from St. George Island refused

to enter the *Delarof*'s bowels where an infection circulated among Unangax̂ passengers. The first fatality occurred on the transport ship when Haretina Kochutin (Unangax̂) gave birth—unassisted by the doctor who refused to provide care—to baby Susan "Dela" Kochutin, who died three days later from bronchial pneumonia.[49] Unangax̂ elders recalled saying a prayer as they dropped deceased baby Dela into the Gulf of Alaska. More deaths of children and elders would follow when Unangax̂ arrived at the camps.

When they disembarked on June 24, 1942, at Funter Bay in Southeast Alaska, Unangax̂ children ran through the trees chasing frogs while exploring new plants and an environment that contrasted with their treeless Aleutian homelands. Having to adapt to the new ecology, with children unknowingly touching stinging nettles, paled in comparison to other pressing uncertainties. They did not know how to differentiate plants as poisonous, medicinal, or supplemental food.

Underscoring a deprivation of bodily autonomy at the camps, a government doctor conducted invasive medical procedures on Unangax̂ women. Harriet Hope (Unangax̂) described that upon entry to the camp, the government doctor subjected her older sister to immodest medical exams. She explained, "I remember . . . the urgency of once we got there they had to give us all medical treatment of some kind. And my sister, again being of a certain age group she was subjected to physical examinations that were so degrading to her. And we felt really bad about that. But we had no say in the matter."[50] These medical procedures monitored Unangax̂ women's bodies and fit familiar patterns of government control over women's bodies.[51] As highlighted in the introduction, a BIA government doctor, H. O. K. Bauer, engaged in unethical sexual relations with an Atkan woman at the Killisnoo camp, showing that he preyed on one of the most vulnerable populations.[52]

Medical neglect, malpractice, and death at the camps indicate that the United States abandoned Unangax̂ with no resources to survive, and this included neglect by local colonial officials. Father Ishmael Gromoff described such mistreatment in his testimony to the Commission on Wartime Relocation: "When I was there a lot of older people died. . . they got sick with the flu and died. But I remember some of them were already sick when they left the Pribilofs so they got sick and died. I don't remember seeing a doctor there the first year, I don't think we had any."[53] Linking this refugee population to reports in nearby towns, local newspapers such as the *Alaska Weekly* reported on the frequency of Unangax̂ deaths, including one newsreel that read, "Friday, November 19, 1943. Several deaths occurred among little children of the [N]atives of southeastern Alaska during the last month from measles and other causes."[54] As an example of how colonial leaders in predominantly white towns navigated the influx of sick Unangax̂, J. A. Talbot, the mayor of Ketchikan, wanted Unangax̂ to receive their medical services in the Native village of Saxman rather than the majority white town of Ketchikan.[55]

Ella Kashevarof (Unangax̂), born in 1926, from St. George Island, became sick while attending the Wrangell Institute boarding school in Southeast Alaska. She explained, "I get skinny; I catch tuberculosis. In September, they send me to Wrangell Institute with the kids that go to school there. I like it there. Then by February they do x-ray, and they find out I have tuberculosis with one of my girlfriends."[56] Ella and her friend went to the Ketchikan hospital, the very place Mayor Talbot tried to exclude Natives from: "They take us to Ketchikan hospital; I stay there for six months. . . rest in bed for six months. You just get up to use bathroom. But they gave me, nuns are in there, they give me stuff to do, embroidery and stuff like that." Ella recovered while her future spouse, Andronik Kashevarof (Unangax̂), recovered from the measles.

Territorial officials such as Governor Gruening did relatively nothing when confronted with the camp conditions, whereas other federal employees tried to sound the alarm within the federal government. In August 1943, Governor Gruening landed at Funter Bay, saw the conditions firsthand, and met with internees for an hour, after which he did not issue aid nor, that can be ascertained from his autobiography or archival collections including the National Archives and Records Administration, implore the feds for assistance.[57] In September 1943, Gruening wrote to the FWS about the living conditions, stating "the hope that these [N]atives can be sent back to the Pribilofs at the earliest possible moment."[58] In contrast to Gruening, N. Berneta Block, a medical doctor of the Territorial Department of Health, wrote an impassioned report about her trip to Funter Bay on October 14, 1943: "As we entered the first bunkhouse the odor of human excreta and waste was so pungent that I could hardly make the grade. . . . The overcrowded housing condition is really beyond description. . . . Children were found naked and actually covered in excreta."[59] These descriptions of squalor matched the shocking number of sick evacuees: "Many of the 118 or so patients had shown a little improvement during the past twenty-four hours" and many had complications including otitis media (middle ear infection) and pneumonia. Her description of the camp reveals a lack of manpower to wash, clean, and cook for an entire village that was relegated to an abandoned cannery amid various epidemics.

Medical neglect paradoxically paired with other forms of government control over Pribolobians, including government surveillance. As an example, the FWS prevented an Unangax̂ couple from divorcing in 1941, thereby dictating Native domestic life.[60] A surveillance system, known as the "official log," by the FWS accounted for each Unangax̂ body that moved between the camps. Dating back to US occupation of Alaska in the mid-nineteenth century, the so-called official log recorded the daily production of Pribolobian sealing operations. During relocation, the FWS recorded data on Pribolobian labor, migration, and the number of sick and deceased Unangax̂ to maximize sealing profits for the government.[61] It is unclear if Unangax̂ knew of the log.

Forced Sealing Labor

"A dead Aleut can't slaughter seals."[62] These chilling words of Ruth Gruber, field representative from the Department of the Interior, underscored that since the government only valued Unangax̂ labor and not their bodies, it was of financial interest to ensure Unangax̂ survival at the relocation camps. Her advocacy as a lone federal employee on behalf of Unangax̂ challenging the larger federal government to intervene parallels Dr. Block's impassioned report on the camp conditions in October 1943. Gruber's question "Are the Aleuts Animals or People?" implored the government to recognize Unangax̂ humanity rather than continue to reduce them to laboring bodies for sealing profit (fig. 2). Flore Lekanof's memories from an Unangax̂ perspective

FIG. 2. "Aleut skinners at work," August 10, 1945. Courtesy of the Alaska State Library, Evan Hill Photo Collection, P343-612.

mirrored these feelings of dehumanization: "We were treated a little better than animals for service to the government."[63]

The history of forced Unangax̂ labor and fur sealing dates to Russian colonization and the Russian fur trade of the eighteenth century.[64] In partnership with Tanadgusix (TDX) Corporation, based in St. Paul, journalist Susan Hackley Johnson has illuminated a history of St. Paul Island and sealing operations dating from the Russian-American Company that managed Russian interests in Alaska since 1800.[65] Johnson reveals that during US occupation, various corporations followed by the federal government oversaw Unangax̂ labors for sealing, from the Alaska Commercial Company, to the North American Commercial Company, to the Bureau of Fisheries (later part of the FWS) that eventually took over in 1910 to regulate the decreased seal herd. Alaskan scholar Barbara Boyle Torrey accounts for the long colonial histories of forced sealing in the Pribilof Islands followed by activism after the 1971 Alaska Native Claims Settlement Act (ANCSA) era.[66] According to Torrey, in 1977, TDX Corporation brought labor independence by negotiating on behalf of St. Paul Unangax̂ with the federal government to take over sealing operations through the 1980s.[67]

Gruber's informative letter to her employer, the secretary of the interior, reveals her role in attempting to hold the government accountable for their actions in neglecting Unangax̂ health, housing, and labor. The United States indeed deployed intimidation tactics forcing Unangax̂ to harvest seal pelts. Gruber observed this practice: "While I was at the camp last spring, I was told by everyone, whites and non-whites, that the Aleuts were being intimidated into going back to the Pribilofs for the six weeks sealing season. Government employees had told them that if they didn't go, they would never be allowed to return home." These threats of permanent displacement from their ancestral islands pressured Unangax̂ men to leave their wives and children at the camps and return to an active warzone to harvest seal pelts in the summer of 1943.

Underscoring that empire relied on capital gains from Indigenous lands, resources, and even labor, bodies that could have contributed to the war effort instead contributed to US profit. The FWS had Unangax̂ men suspended from military service and granted furloughs during the summer of 1943 to harvest seal pelts to profit the US government.[68] The FWS pulled Pribolobian students, like Flore Lekanof, out of the Wrangell Institute boarding school for sealing.[69] The military excused sixteen Pribolobian men for sealing on the Pribilof Islands.[70] Paul E. Thompson, acting chief of the Division of Alaskan Fisheries, described Nicolai Stepetin, Gregory Nozekof, Daniel Malavansky, and Stefan Lekanof as more valuable in sealing than as soldiers in the war against fascism: "They are experts in their work; they will be employed in an active theater of war; they will be producing substantial revenue for the government. It is believed that they will be of greater service to the country in the capacity of sealing men than in the armed forces during the period for which deferment is requested."[71] Other names listed by Thompson of men deferred for forced labor include Ferman Galanin, Laurence Galanin, Moses Galanin, Ermogen Lekanof, Nicholai S. Merculief, Alexay Merculief,

Andrine Merculief, Isiah Merculief, Alexay Prokopiof, Michael Prokopiof, Ferapont Swetzof, and Simeon Swetzof. As the government pried 116 Pribolobian men away from their families at the camps in preparation for forced sealing, the entire community mourned, saying goodbyes and singing in Unangam Tunuu at the waterfront.

Father Gromoff, from St. Paul, revealed his own story of forced labor by the government with unpaid wages. Accordingly, in the summer of 1943, the military excused Father Gromoff to harvest seal pelts for the FWS. Father Gromoff detailed that he never received payment, recalling, "I just got paid Army pay; I didn't get any extra money or bonuses from that catch. I remember they used to pay the Aleut twenty cents a pelt and when they sold it, it was one hundred dollars a skin so we really lost [sic] out. And they told us, when we asked about it, we'd be paid after we got out of the Army, I never saw the money after that."[72] According to Father Gromoff, Superintendent Edward Johnston of the FWS told him that the Pribolobians would be paid more later, but Johnston died before Father Gromoff ever saw his wages. It is unclear if Johnston purposefully misled Pribolobian men like Gromoff with false promises of payment.

In their attempt to negotiate with federal agents, Pribolobian men pushed against unfair labor expectations. In March 1943, L. C. McMillin identified Native resistance toward government sealing operations: "The [N]ative gang here at Funter wish for me to notify you that they do not want to make the trip to the Islands until the war is over."[73] He reiterated, "Some here and one I know in Juneau says they will not return while the war lasts. Others say they will go only if ordered to do so." Pribolobian men believed that sealing operations would delay their return to their home islands with their families so they tried to leverage that.

Despite efforts by Pribolobian men to resist labor control and to negotiate wages, the government intimidated Pribolobians into compliance. Government workers threatened banishment from their home islands if Pribolobians refused to comply. In March 1943, Edward C. Johnston articulated sanctions to Pribolobians and their descendants for anyone who rebelled: "If any St. George workman refuses to return to the island at the time of rehabilitation, I would recommend that he forfeit all rights to return to the island at any future time as a resident. This would apply to his dependents as well."[74] Even locals who lived in towns near the camps knew of government coercion with Unangax̂ sealing operations. Juneau resident Mary Jane Gaither wrote protest letters to Alaskan territorial delegate Anthony Dimond describing Pribolobians as "in virtual slavery."[75] Gaither understood this mistreatment while she likely observed the abundant propaganda circulated by the United States about saving other marginalized groups from oppression by other countries.

To resist labor demanded by the FWS during internment, Pribolobian men exercised as much labor autonomy as they could by voicing protest to government agents at town hall meetings. They also wrote letters, such as one dated April 10, 1943, in which twelve Pribolobians from St. George and twenty Pribolobians from St. Paul sought equal pay to Juneau sealers plus a sealing bonus. Pribolobian men organized, communicated with Juneau sealers, learned of their wages and freedom to contract their labor, and in turn tried to coordinate fair payment from the federal government. Pribolobian men also requested a meeting with Johnston to negotiate their labor and to ask for housing for their families in Juneau until they returned to their home islands.

Demonstrating varied attempts at protest, in addition to organizing as a collective, some men organized in smaller groups. For example, three Pribolobian men declared in a protest letter dated April 26, 1943, "We communities of St. Paul and St. George undersigned the [sic] we not infavor [sic] of going up for sealing this year unless we get a dollar a skin. St. George are not infavor [sic] of taking women and children until after the war."[76] The normal rate was sixty cents per pelt. Unbeknownst to Pribolobians, they qualified for war zone pay at a higher rate, but government officials never informed Pribolobians about this.[77]

To stall government operations, Unangax̂ protested sealing and coerced labor through mundane inconveniences. As an act of defiance, Sergie Shaishnikoff used the main control to shut lights off in a government building.[78] Shaishnikoff's action is akin to the mischievous ones of Unangax̂ children, as told by Alice Petrivelli, who forced a BIA physician to chase them after an imposed curfew. These actions of stalling federal efforts of profit or

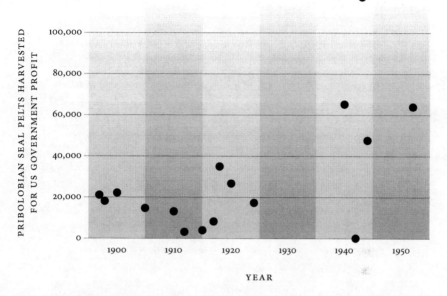

FIG. 3. Pribolobian seal pelt harvests for US government profit. Graph created by Sarah Aarons (Iñupiaq).

control, the protest letters demanding fair wages, and the men's organizing and demanding fair wages for their labor cumulatively reveal equilibrium restoration. That is, they create an Indigenous structure that continuously thwarts the expectation of colonial structures to completely control Native bodies, their labor, and sealing resources from their home islands.

And yet the threat of permanent displacement by the federal government led Pribolobian men to harvest a record number of seal pelts in 1943.[79] A comparison of sealing numbers reveals that wartime harvest proved staggering (fig. 3). For example, in 1897, the number of fur seals killed on St. Paul Island totaled 18,600, with 2,362 on St. George Island, for a total of 20,962.[80] From 1898 to 1911, harvested seal pelts numbered 11,726 to 23,301, and in 1912 they dipped to 3,191. From 1913 to 1917, harvested pelts numbered between 2,406 and 8,170. These lower numbers reveal how the FWS tried to stabilize sealing numbers after their control in 1910. Prior to the war years, these numbers hit between 15,000 to 35,000 seal pelts. In June 1942, before relocation, Pribolobians harvested 96 pelts on St. Paul Island and 31 pelts on

St. George Island, totaling only 127 seal pelts.[81] This minimal number reveals the impact of relocation on the seal harvest in 1942. Taken away from their families at the camps in the summer of 1943, Pribolobian men harvested 95,342 seals on St. Paul Island and 21,822 seals on St. George Island, totaling a record 117,164 pelts.[82] In 1944, Pribolobians harvested substantially fewer seal pelts, numbering 39,775 on St. Paul Island and 7,806 pelts on St. George Island, for a total of 47,581.[83]

Sealing numbers represent significant unpaid labor by Pribolobian men in 1943. Accordingly, Fouke Fur Company owed the US Treasury $465,598.30 at the end of 1943 ($8.28 million adjusted to inflation for the year 2023).[84] If the men had received $1 per pelt in 1943, they would have divided $117,164 ($2.08 million adjusted to inflation for the year 2023), which is still only a fraction (about one-fourth) of the US Treasury's revenue from Pribolobian sealing operations that year. However, the government never made payment, and some Pribolobians saw only a mere fraction of their earnings. Unstated regulations by the War Department prevented Fouke Fur Company from fully compensating St. George Island Natives.[85] In this instance, colonial entities colluded, and the government and a private corporation reaped financial benefit during an imperial project of war, yet Pribolobians faced labor exploitation and death of their family members at relocation camps.

Equilibrium Restoration in the Camps

Equilibrium restoration sometimes meant taking control in daily life to create positive structures in the community to support children and Native domestic livelihood. Specifically, Unangax̂ women, a tight-knit collective of matriarchs, banded together demanding the government provide reliable living conditions and stability. Figure 4 shows community laundry drying and children socializing.

In protesting deplorable conditions at the camps on behalf of their children and families, Native women asserted a governing identity. In a letter addressed to the FWS dated October 10, 1942, forty-nine Unangax̂ women from St. Paul signed a protest letter demanding basic infrastructure. They spoke primarily Unangam Tunuu, Russian, and English, with English as

FIG. 4. "Funter Bay Relocation Camp, St. Paul villagers." Fredericka Martin Collection, 91.223.272. Courtesy of the Archives at University of Alaska Fairbanks.

their third language; in broken English, the letter began with, "We the people of this place wants a better place than this to live." [86] Modeled on the US Declaration of Independence, the letter represented an Unangax̂ declaration of rights against tyrannical government in which the women asserted a governing Unangax̂ identity. Unangax̂ women identified rampant illnesses from poor water quality that hurt their children: "This place is no place for a living creature. We drink impure water and then get sick the children's get skin disease even the grownups are sick from cold." Identifying not only the lack of privacy but also biohazards, the women continued: "We ate from the mess house and it is near the toilet only a few yard away. We eat the filth that is flying around." The women lamented the lack of bathhouses and access to clean water: "We got no place to wash our clothes or dry them when it rains. We women are always lugging water up stairs and take turns warming up and the stove is small."

The second half of the Unangax̂ women's protest letter expressed concern over poverty and the need for sustainable jobs to support their families in Southeast Alaska. The women described their needs: "We need clothes and shoes for our children how are we going to clothe them with just a few dollars[?]" They advocated for local jobs to support their families outside the realm of government-mandated jobs with meager salaries. The women implored, "Why they not take us to a better place to live and work for our selve's and live in a better house. Men and women are very eager to work. When winter comes it still would be worse with water all freezed up grub short do we have to see our children suffer." They advocated remaining at Funter Bay until their children were healthy enough to return, as there was no doctor on St. George Island over the winter.[87] The women concluded with their signatures and a statement: "We all have rights to speak for ourselves" (fig. 5). Haretina Kochutin, the mother who lost her three-day-old baby on the *Delarof*, signed first. The signatures represent an empowered collective of Native women, mothers, aunts, and grandmothers.

Another way in which Unangax̂ exercised control was in securing seminary contracts by selecting, contracting, and paying for a priest. In February 1944, John Misikin, John Hanson, Condrat Krukoff, Iliodor Kozoloff, and Logan Mandregan delegated for St. Paul Pribolobians, requesting that Father Makary Baranoff return with them to the island as their priest.[88] Pribolobians agreed to provide food, subsistence, and an eight-hundred-dollar annual salary to Father Baranoff. During Russian colonization in the eighteenth and nineteenth centuries, Russian traders and settlers introduced and established the Russian Orthodox religion as an institution.[89] Indeed, with the action of selecting and paying for a priest, religion offered sustenance, hope, and a form of autonomy at the camps.[90]

Oral histories tell of how practicing religion remained central to Unangax̂ exercising their spirituality. In an interview in February 2016 with the Kashevarof family, Andronik, Elekonida "Ella," and their daughter Bonnie Mierzejek reflected on the importance of religion. When asked, "How do you think Unangax̂ kept a positive community during World War II?" Bonnie

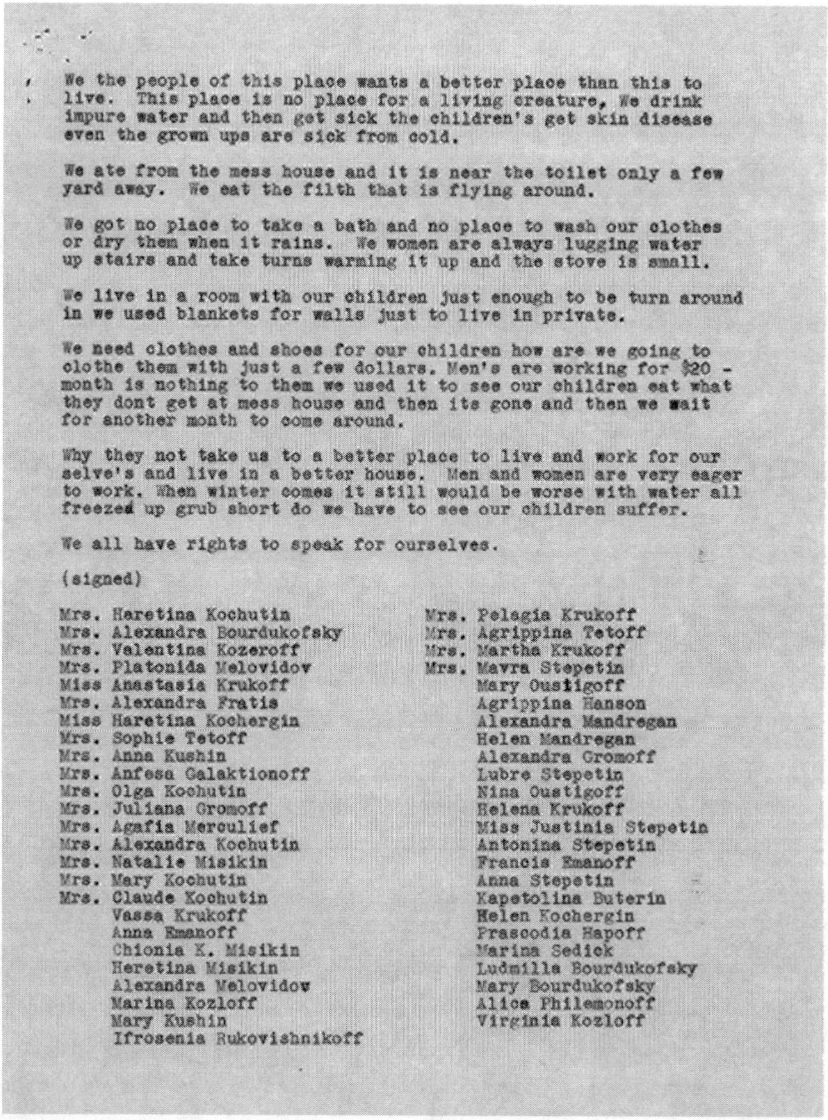

We the people of this place wants a better place than this to
live. This place is no place for a living creature, We drink
impure water and then get sick the children's get skin disease
even the grown ups are sick from cold.

We ate from the mess house and it is near the toilet only a few
yard away. We eat the filth that is flying around.

We got no place to take a bath and no place to wash our clothes
or dry them when it rains. We women are always lugging water
up stairs and take turns warming it up and the stove is small.

We live in a room with our children just enough to be turn around
in we used blankets for walls just to live in private.

We need clothes and shoes for our children how are we going to
clothe them with just a few dollars. Men's are working for $20 -
month is nothing to them we used it to see our children eat what
they dont get at mess house and then its gone and then we wait
for another month to come around.

Why they not take us to a better place to live and work for our
selve's and live in a better house. Men and women are very eager
to work. When winter comes it still would be worse with water all
freezed up grub short do we have to see our children suffer.

We all have rights to speak for ourselves.

(signed)

Mrs. Haretina Kochutin
Mrs. Alexandra Bourdukofsky
Mrs. Valentina Kozeroff
Mrs. Platonida Melovidov
Miss Anastasia Krukoff
Mrs. Alexandra Fratis
Miss Haretina Kochergin
Mrs. Sophie Tetoff
Mrs. Anna Kushin
Mrs. Anfesa Galaktionoff
Mrs. Olga Kochutin
Mrs. Juliana Gromoff
Mrs. Agafia Meroulief
Mrs. Alexandra Kochutin
Mrs. Natalie Misikin
Mrs. Mary Kochutin
Mrs. Claude Kochutin
    Vassa Krukoff
    Anna Emanoff
    Chionia K. Misikin
    Heretina Misikin
    Alexandra Melovidov
    Marina Kozloff
    Mary Kushin
    Ifrosenia Rukovishnikoff

Mrs. Pelagia Krukoff
Mrs. Agrippina Tetoff
Mrs. Martha Krukoff
Mrs. Mavra Stepetin
    Mary Oustigoff
    Agrippina Hanson
    Alexandra Mandregan
    Helen Mandregan
    Alexandra Gromoff
    Lubre Stepetin
    Nina Oustigoff
    Helena Krukoff
    Miss Justinia Stepetin
    Antonina Stepetin
    Francis Emanoff
    Anna Stepetin
    Kapetolina Buterin
    Helen Kochergin
    Prascodia Hapoff
    Marina Sedick
    Ludmilla Bourdukofsky
    Mary Bourdukofsky
    Alice Philemonoff
    Virginia Kozloff

FIG. 5. Petition by Unangax̂ women protesting conditions, October 10, 1942. National
Archives, 2641505.

reiterated to her parents, "What kept you guys happy during World War II? How'd you survive that? Funter Bay? What kept you guys together?" To which Ella replied, "Religion"; Bonnie responded, "Yes, their faith"; and Andronik agreed, "Yeah." Ella explained, "Father Theodosy came with us, very strict priest," and that the Funter Bay dining hall held church services. In addition, Andronik explained that the St. George community made improvements to the Funter Bay camp, and they cooked meals together.

According to Andronik's testimony, sharing grief with a religious leader from the Russian Orthodox Church provided emotional support. He reflected with deep sadness, "One worse thing that I've ever seen in my life in Funter Bay was . . . when we start [to] bury people in graves. I still have that in my mind. It was very hard to [under]stand what they were doing . . . we put the coffin in." Here, Andronik paused before he continued, "[We put the] coffin down in the grave so it was only about four feet. And when you put it in there, they had to step on the coffin, because the grave was full of water. All full of water." Ella sadly recalled, "Yeah," as Andronik continued. "And even the soil that they're supposed to put, it was full of water, they'd just put it on there." The damp earth from the rainforests in Southeast Alaska made burials all the more difficult. Andronik reflected, "It just hurt. Father Theodosy used to cry, seeing that was worse. I was only about fifteen, sixteen years old when I was an altar boy at that time. That was . . . ," Andronik paused again before continuing, "very hard to get, very hard to get it out of my mind, put those people in grave. That was the worst-est one I ever went through when I was a young boy. Father Theodosy, boy he was in terrible condition, crying too." While seated at the dining room table drinking tea, with Russian Orthodox icons lining the mantelpiece, the Kashevarof family ended their interview by singing the hymnal "Yakko Plan" in the Slavonic language.

During an interview in February 2016 at his home in Dutch Harbor, Nicholai Lekanoff (Unangax̂) described a twist of fate when the military rejected him from enlisting and cited that he needed to care for his two younger sisters at the camp.[91] Nicholai's daughter, Patricia Lekanoff-Gregory (Unangax̂), an artist in Dutch Harbor, assisted with his interview. Nicholai was born in 1925 in the Unangax̂ village of Makushin. Remembering Japan's bombing of Dutch Harbor in June 1942, he had tried to visit his brother at the hospital. Their parents had died before the war and as the eldest brother Nicholai provided for his family. Amid relocation, he moved from Wrangell to Burnett Inlet to eventually Ketchikan where he worked for the Ketchikan Spruce Mill. He laughed detailing that he had never worked with trees since the Aleutians are tree barren. With his job he escaped the camp conditions. He explained, "We were down in Southeast [Alaska] two and a half years. I didn't stay that long there though. I spent most of my time [at] Ketchikan Spruce Mill." With a somber tone, Nicolai reflected that those with no jobs remained in the camps.

Oral histories provide personal testimony illuminating many forms of Unangax̂ resistance that occurred in daily life. Rather than coerced total reliance on the government, Unangax̂ evacuees sought jobs, supported their communities in any capacity that they could, and worked on home improvement projects amid dire circumstances. For example, Larry Chercasen's father and uncle worked in the neighboring towns of the Ward Lake ccc camp where his father held multiple jobs in Ketchikan and on the Annette Island base. He explained, "My father worked quite a bit. He was a carpenter, and he built on a base called Annette Island down in Metlakatla. . . . He could sell his skills because he was a skilled carpenter."[92] With his father working long hours, Larry shared that he often felt lonely: "He was usually absent, at work, you know. But there were times when he was off work when I stuck with him, but I can remember times being home by myself. One time I had the measles, and I was very sick in bed there, we had bunk beds. And I remember laying there in the bunk, and my aunt fortunately looked after me." Larry's aunt took care of him often, and Larry went to Ketchikan whenever he could, describing, "I stayed with my aunt and uncle and sister. They lived in a house downtown. Uncle Frank was a cook in Ketchikan." While relocation brought extreme disorder to Larry's childhood, his extended family navigated the camps as best as they could, often creating linkages to relatives in nearby towns.

Similar to both Larry Chercasen and Nicholai Lekanoff, General Jake Lestenkof, in a November 2014 interview, described his grandparents escaping Funter Bay by finding jobs in Juneau. Jake was born in 1932 on St. George Island. He described the *Delarof* boat as "very, very bad. Very crowded, yeah there were hardly any food. And it was a ship from hell."[93] About Funter Bay he explained, "But the place became infamous because of the bad treatment and the bad weather, no medical facilities, no schooling because the teachers couldn't stand it and they left. . . . The teachers even left." When he was ten years old, Jake's mother died. He recalled, "I lost my mom. Losing a mother is a traumatic time; it is more traumatic I think if you are in strange surroundings."[94] With deplorable camp conditions, his mother's passing, and a lack of educational resources, Jake's grandparents moved to Juneau. He explained, "when the teachers left Funter Bay, my grandfather and mother decided to take me to Juneau for that winter. The winter of '42–'43 so that I could attend school." In the decades after the war, Jake brought change to the BIA when he worked as the Alaska area director. He also served in the Korean War and the Alaska National Guard.

Return to the Land

"Awal tingin kidul haqachx̂iinax̂. With God's help we'll be back." Alice Petrivelli's taatax̂ (adax̂ is the Unangam Tunuu word for "father," although Russians adopted this word, changing kinship terms in an attempt to assimilate Unangax̂) told her this during relocation.[95] Alice first said this phrase in Unangam Tunuu, which Dr. Moses Dirks (Unangax̂) of APIA graciously transcribed, and then she translated it into English. Although the US military restored the Aleutian Islands from Japan's control following the recapture of Attu on May 11, 1943, the government returned the Pribolobians and Unangax̂ to their homelands in the successive years of 1944 and 1945.[96] In 1944, Pribolobians returned, non-coincidentally, in time to harvest seal pelts for the US government. Yet the navy and BIA argued about which branch would pay to return Unangax̂ to the Aleutian Islands, so Aleutian Unangax̂ remained in the camps until 1945.[97] These colonial bureaucracies fought against each other to avoid paying for Aleutian Unangax̂ return, and yet the same overarching federal government financially profited immensely from Pribolobian sealing labor. As chapter 2 details, some Unangax̂ families chose to remain in Juneau rather than return to the Pribilofs, and some intermarried with Tlingit in the postwar years.[98]

Attuans encountered yet another fate in which they have not returned to their ancestral land. In 1946, they left the POW camp in Otaru, crossed the Pacific to Seattle, and then journeyed back to Alaska. The US government refused to return Attuans to their home island, which was littered with wartime debris polluting the ecology. Building what will be analyzed in chapter 2 as "survivance alliances," Attuans joined Unangax̂ from Atka, where they resettled with their island neighbors. In exercising equilibrium restoration, in this case returning to Attu in whatever capacity possible still today, the tribal nonprofit Atux Forever educates the public on relocation and plans pilgrimages to their home island.

Unangax̂ resettlement on their home islands—the Pribilofs and most of the Aleutians—goes against the settler colonial project of removal, exhibiting unrelenting Indigenous determination to negotiate the demands from removal with refusal of complete federal control. Some federal archives indicate potential plans for permanent removal, as one Alaska Indian Service letter specified: "Killisnoo and Burnett Inlet are located in very good fishing areas which would be suitable permanent resettlement locations."[99] Unangax̂ took control of their future not only by continually advocating for their return to home but also through asserting their mobility and creating new contacts and work opportunities. Despite government regulation, camp boundaries remained relatively fluid. Unangax̂ relocatees worked in the neighboring towns of Juneau, Ketchikan, and Annette Island to improve their condition. In doing so, they resisted government oversight.

Indeed, wartime imperial occupation and settler occupation worked in tandem to encroach upon Native lands. Upsetting settler colonial plans for permanent removal, when Unangax̂ came home to the Aleutians, tensions heightened between Unangax̂, white settlers, and US servicemen. Reportedly, white settlers in Unalaska did not want Unangax̂ to return. As Don Foster of the Alaska Indian Service explained, "There is a two-fold reason for this attitude; namely, they are definitely anti-Native; and secondly, the property owned by the Natives in Unalaska is in the best residential part of the town."[100] Certain colonial officials in power tried to retain the Aleutian Islands for white settlers. For example, Foster stated that "US Commissioner, Jack Martin, at Unalaska is a bad one; and he is doing everything he can to make the situation there unbearable and either squeeze the Natives out or run them out by any means possible." Alongside settler colonial attempts to replace Natives from Unalaska, military occupation impacted social relations of the Pribilof Islands. In St. Paul, for example, the military regulated activities such as shows, dances, and social events due to conflict between servicemen and local Native people.[101]

When they returned to their home islands, Unangax̂, including teenagers, asserted personal autonomy and equilibrium restoration by resisting imposed government regulations in the most mundane circumstances. In June 1944, government agents sought "more rigid control of the younger [N]ative boys" of St. Paul who continuously ran unattended trucks until their batteries died.[102] At this time, blubbering operations continued to profit the US government, and Native youth did what they could to stall these operations.

In the many decades after the war, military debris contaminated the Aleutians. World War II relocation brought significant ecological changes to Unangax̂ land and waters. Al Wright (Athabascan), a serviceman from the US Army who was stationed in the Aleutians, reported that after the war his superiors instructed him to dump barrels of oil and an entire CAT into the Bering Sea.[103] These items polluted the Aleutian streams, waterways, and soil. As Alice Petrivelli relayed, following scorched earth tactics, the US Navy burned the village of Atka, forcing Atkans to physically rebuild their homes. In fact, three Unangax̂ villages remained abandoned after the war. This included the Attuans who reestablished their community with the Atkans.

Alice's interview in the film *Aleut Story* describes how one of her children did not believe the story of Unangax̂ internment since they never learned about the subject in school.[104] Pedagogical erasures, not only of histories of Indigenous and immigrant captivity under US empire but also the general omission of Unangax̂ internment from the broader narrative of Japanese American incarceration, perpetuate misunderstanding of this era. In all honesty, there should also be more teaching on Japanese American incarceration, and the two should be taught together. In recent years, scholarship in Japanese American studies includes references to Unangax̂ (Aleut) relocation as well as public education programs coordinated in partnership with Tadaima Japanese American Memorial Pilgrimages, organized by Kimiko Marr and Julie Abo.

Unrelenting Japanese American and Unangax̂ collaboration in seeking restitution from the federal government resulted in a US apology and an attempt for amends. After hesitation, President Ronald Reagan signed the Civil Rights Act of 1988, formally apologizing to Japanese Americans and Unangax̂ for wartime internment and providing a monetary settlement from the federal government. For eligible Japanese Americans, restitution included $20,000. This amount hardly covered lost possessions, businesses, household items, educational opportunities, and gaps in labor experience. For Unangax̂, payments included a mere $12,000 to eligible survivors; $1.4 million for church restoration projects in Nikolski, Unalaska, Akutan, St. George, and St. Paul after significant vandalism by the military; a formal apology; and the establishment of a $5 million Aleutian Pribilof Islands Restitution Trust to benefit Unangax̂ and their descendants.[105] While there is likely some government explanation for the varied payments between the two groups, it may also be interpreted as further efforts by a colonial government to create dissatisfaction and thus divide coalitions among marginalized groups. Other requests by Unangax̂ have not been met, such as financial support to develop resources to raise public awareness on Unangax̂ relocation; a cleanup of wartime debris on the islands, including metal contaminants as well as hazardous waste from fuel and battery waste and detonated munitions; and protection of the camps as historic sites.[106]

A majority of Unangax̂ and Japanese American survivors died prior to the government apology. Alice reflected, "And when we got our reparations they didn't even," and here she paused before continuing, "because the elders had passed on they didn't get nothing, which I thought was not right." Reading through the names of Unangax̂ survivors who gave testimonies for reparations, Alice explained how all these people had passed on. Even with reparations, wartime trauma emanates, and no monetary value can fill this void. Money will never buy back Larry Chercasen's childhood and the devastating day when he walked around the Ward Lake CCC camp and found that three of his closest childhood friends and cousins perished from epidemics. Money will never erase the trauma of the measles epidemic that Alice witnessed at the Killisnoo camp where she as a teenager was responsible for providing care for dozens of sick Atkans, the pneumonia that almost claimed her sister Vera's life, or the image of her uncle's corpse after a fishing accident in Killisnoo. Money cannot mend fractured families, government neglect, and stolen wages from Indigenous and Japanese American laborers.

Remembering together and instructing the future generations on the history of wartime atrocities are important components of Indigenous futures. The descendants of Unangax̂ relocation camp survivors make intergenerational pilgrimages to collectively remember and witness the relocation camps. In a return trip to Funter Bay in the 1990s, Andronik Kashevarof explained that Unangax̂ restored the crosses at the graveyard where Father Paul Merculief held funeral services. Andronik's daughter Bonnie, who taught fifth grade at the time, brought her students from St. George to Funter Bay. Bonnie explained that she never formally learned about Unangax̂ relocation in school, and she recalled her childhood with hushed conversations on the topic: "I would hear them talk about it in Aleut and I could understand Aleut pretty well." Bonnie relayed how her older brother never heard the stories about evacuation, but she heard some stories: "You could see sadness in their eyes . . . when they think back about how many people that were lost and what not." She detailed that while standing in the Funter Bay graveyard with her fifth-grade class, "I was just standing there, and I just felt this sense of loss when I was there." Bonnie's trip reveals intergenerational healing from pilgrimages to the camps where educating the youth meant ensuring a future for Native people.

"It's okay to look back, but don't stare." Larry Chercasen's sage reflection offers a powerful message on moving forward. Just before the Japanese military invaded Attu and Kiska, Larry's mother died in childbirth. Larry's infant sister Lucy survived by drinking canned milk and because of the care provided by their Aunt Anna. Upon returning to Nikolski, they discovered that American GIs trashed their home. Larry's father filed for a reimbursement from the government for damaged household items. While visiting the National Archives in College Park, I found a photograph of Larry's father's house showing broken furniture that barricaded a doorway. This destruction of his home occurred in the alleged name of safety. For Larry's father, a carpenter, rebuilding his home for his son meant dismantling the barricade, assessing what items could be salvaged, and replacing others. Readapting their home environment meant that physical marks from the former military occupation in their home—their most personal space—such as scratches on the floor and damage to the walls, would remain. And yet rebuilding a home formerly occupied by imperial entities on one's homelands is an act of equilibrium restoration: putting your home back in order after ejecting soldiers from your house and islands. Larry shared that he has preached on the subject of moving forward and has refused to allow historic trauma to shape his own future. At one point, while visiting him and his wife, Pat, at their home in Vancouver, I brought a fresh loaf of San Francisco sourdough to go along with Pat's beef stew. I learned that Larry designed and built their home in Vancouver, that he and Pat adopted Native children, and that they hosted Unangax̂ children on weekends who attended the nearby Chemawa Indian boarding school. While he himself lost a large portion of his childhood at the Ward Lake CCC camp, he provided a home away from home for various children throughout his life.

Interviews with Larry, Alice, and Jake, in addition to other interviews recorded by Congress and APIA, as well as scholarship by Unangax̂ academics such as Mike Livingston, Lauren Peters, Haliehana Stepetin, and Eve Tuck, testify to Indigenous survival, adaptability, and the consistent legacy to move forward. Indigenous equilibrium restoration both within the Alaskan relocation camps and after the war was occasionally suddenly achieved, as in the case of Alice's Uncle Bill who banished the BIA's Dr. Bauer. Yet equilibrium restoration is most representative as a continuous process that stems from a concerted effort by community members to bring positive change and to assert not only Native rights but also Native sovereignty alongside a return to their home islands.

TWO
SURVIVANCE ALLIANCE
TRIBAL MUTUAL AID
AND SOVEREIGNTY

"SHE HAD A BEAUTIFUL BIG FIELD OF STRAWBERRIES."[1] This is how Alice Petrivelli (Unangax̂) described a Tlingit elder named Annie Samato (Davis). The US government incarcerated Annie's husband, Harry Samato, a Japanese elder who was born in 1878, when he was sixty-four years old. Born in 1888 in Killisnoo, Annie was fifty-four years old when she witnessed multiple government removals during World War II, including her husband and Unangax̂ relocatees at the Killisnoo camp near her village of Angoon in Southeast Alaska. According to a KINY radio interview with Betty Samato of Angoon, the granddaughter of Annie and Harry Samato, Harry was born in Japan, lived in Hawaiʻi, worked in Seattle, and made his way to a whaling station at Killisnoo where he met and married Annie.[2] As strawberries have a unique history among Japanese American workers, gardeners, and horticulturists, Annie's action of continuing to tend her family's strawberry garden shows significant care and resilience.[3]

Water for Unangax̂ relocatees was a resource that the federal government chose to ignore and a resource that local Tlingit, such as elder Annie Samato, shared, thereby maintaining Native survivability. As archival records emerge in unexpected places, anthropologist Ted Bank found a collection of school papers written by Atkan children in the postwar years. The essays, marked with a teacher's edits and comments, revealed memories of Atkan children about relocation. In one essay, an Atkan child, Oleana Snigaroff, identified Annie Samato as a neighbor who provided clean water to the Atkans. Oleana recalled, "We used to get water from a land across Killisnoo. That's where an old woman lived. Her husband was a Japanese. She had a daughter who was married and had four children. The old woman's name was Samato. We stayed at Killisnoo for three years."[4] In addition to this child's memory, multiple Atkans mentioned Mrs. Samato from Angoon, including Alice, who mentioned that children picked strawberries from her garden.

Indeed, the lives of those incarcerated by the federal government during war intersected on multiple levels; Annie Samato's story articulates this convoluted history of wartime camps that overlapped in her life. Recalling Mrs. Samato and her husband separated from his Tlingit family, Alice explained, "Her husband was in one of the Japanese camps, they took him away. So, she was a really bitter old woman." Mrs. Samato's aid likely came not only from her humanitarian compassion for Atkans but also as a form of resistance to the federal government. When the federal government failed to provide the basic human right to water, Annie Samato provided water to relocatees in a camp who had encountered a similar uncertain fate as her husband.

The scarcity of clean water at a camp underscores federal neglect and indifference toward Native people, and it directly correlated with Native survivability. In 1942, a US government inspector concluded that "no satisfactory water supply" existed at a wartime relocation camp for Unangax̂ Atkans in Killisnoo.[5] This government official advised that Killisnoo not serve as a permanent camp site for Atkans since "groundwater supply in sufficient quantity cannot be found on the island within reasonable distance from the settlement [so] it would seem useless to develop this as a permanent site for the Atka Natives." And yet, knowing of this inadequate water supply for human consumption, the US government continued its plan to relocate Unangax̂ to this makeshift camp at an abandoned cannery building in Killisnoo. Testimony by Henry Dirks, adopted by William Dirks during the war, detailed, "the water they had there at Killisnoo had bugs in it. Some people died from it."[6] Prior to BIA teacher Ms. Ruby Magee departing the relocation camp at Killisnoo, she indicated that an Atkan crew searched extensively for a groundwater source. Yet unlike the BIA teacher who could readily leave the camp or be reassigned, over 880 Unangax̂ remained at these relocation camps where 10 percent of Unangax̂ perished. While death impacted all age groups, infants and the elderly accounted for a majority of those who passed away.

At the neighboring camp, Burnett Inlet, Chief William Zaharoff of Un-alaska asked for a better place to live upon arriving at the camp. Chief Zaharoff explained to Claude Hirst of the Alaska Indian Service that "the water is low and not fit to drink" and the "houses are not fit to live in."[7] Funter Bay had no running water or indoor plumbing; the outhouse at the end of the pier dumped excrement directly into the bay. Unangax̂ hauled water from a nearby stream.[8] In theme with a lack of clean water, in 1943, public health engineer John Hall evaluated the Funter Bay camp for St. Paul villagers, highlighting that "samples of water taken at several times during the past year have indicated pollution." Speaking in language perhaps in line with plausible deniability, he continued, "although no outbreaks of disease have occurred that were definitely proven to be water-borne."[9] Such conditions proved dire to Unangax̂ who lacked water for drinking, cleaning, and handwashing to prevent the spread of rampant illnesses at the camps, including impetigo, measles, mumps, and tuberculosis.

This story of Unangax̂ expelled by the federal government into makeshift camps on Tlingit lands occurred without consent or treaty following patterns of Indian removal from the nineteenth century and the early colonial era. The US Navy never asked permission from Tlingit to relocate Unangax̂; rather, the military acted on the impulse of a colonial authority disregarding Native rights and diplomacy. How could the United States have known whether Tlingit would abide by the imposition of this new population on their lands? What the United States had not realized was that they had unintentionally fostered links between the two Native nations. Local Tlingit individuals such as Annie Samato represented efforts by Native people to foster equilibrium restoration in their homes and towns. Tending to the garden until her husband returned from incarceration, sharing clean water with Atkans, and allowing Atkan children to pick strawberries were not the actions of someone who felt hopelessness but rather those of an elder Native woman who sought to provide and care in whatever capacity possible for a refugee population imposed upon her land.

The formation of Unangax̂ and Tlingit intertribal alliances represented collective Indigenous resistance to US colonialism. Acknowledging the Indigenous ability to survive acts of genocide enacted by Western empire, acclaimed literary scholar Gerald Vizenor (Minnesota Chippewa Tribe) termed the concept of *survivance*, which is "an active resistance and repudiation of dominance, obtrusive themes of tragedy, nihilism, and victimry."[10] Such a concept can be applied to two Native nations who support each other. Here, in Alaska, Indigenous survivance depended on tribal mutual aid that fostered equilibrium between Unangax̂ and Tlingit who navigated the war together. In this manner, tribal aid, and the act of giving or receiving aid, allowed tribes not only to exercise their sovereignty but also to generate equilibrium restoration on a landscape fraught with settler colonial relocations. Tlingit could have expelled or ignored Unangax̂ relocatees, and yet Tlingit did the exact opposite by assisting Unangax̂, thereby going against settler efforts attempting to dictate terms of removal.

Forced relocation by a colonial authority thrust a dire situation onto two Native nations, and yet these nations worked together defying the odds of the settler colonial government's divide and conquer techniques. Tlingit encountered their own challenges during the war, including loss of regular fishing routes due to militarized marine activities and struggles with the influx of military personnel in Alaskan towns, subjecting the Native population to racial segregation.[11] Nonetheless, Tlingit overwhelmingly supported Unangax̂, advocating for Indigenous rights as political activists through the Alaska Native Brotherhood and the Alaska Native Sisterhood but also as a Tlingit nation. The two nations possessed lands on the opposite sides of the Gulf of Alaska, yet their similar experiences of settler colonialism by both Russia and the United States led to shared significant commonalities stemming from their Indigenous resilience in navigating sequential colonizations of Alaska.

Indeed, Tlingit and Unangax̂ asserted autonomy as Native nations in giving and receiving mutual aid. Despite settler colonial efforts to erase its governing presence, Indigenous sovereignty remains intact.[12] Therefore, when Tlingit provided—and Unangax̂ accepted—mutual aid, both nations asserted their sovereignty. Alaska as a case study reveals that equilibrium restoration can mean expanding Tlingit aid and kinship, as was done for the relocated Unangax̂. These reciprocal actions demonstrate decolonial powers from Indigenous exchanges that act independently and without the approval or regard of a settler colonial entity.

The Battle of Sitka

The alliance that Unangax̂ and Tlingit created is perhaps surprising given earlier histories of colonial violences that occurred within various imperial projects. The history of the US military in Alaska, including the establishment of military forts on Native lands, is one of violence.[13] Numerous stories tell of battles between Tlingit and neighboring tribal nations including warfare from settler encroachment and exploitation. The Battle of Sitka that occurred in 1802 and 1804 included Russian Imperial Forces, the Tlingit, and some enslaved Aleut (as this colonial term did not differentiate between Unangax̂ and Sugpiat, it could be either or both) who fought on behalf of the Russians. Illuminating this Russian imperial violence that predated Unangax̂ relocation (1942–1945) reveals historical contingencies of intertribal diplomacy.

Missing explorers mark the first colonizers who visited Tlingit America. In 1741, a Russian Navy vessel named the *St. Paul* sent a party ashore that never returned.[14] As colonial maritime traffic increased, in the mid-1770s, Spanish voyagers conducted expeditions in the region. British voyagers including Captain James Cook continued in the North Pacific and beyond until Cook met his demise in Hawai'i. Meanwhile, across the Gulf of Alaska, Russian fur traders began fostering the transpacific fur trade relying on Unangax̂ and Alutiiq hunters, enslaving them to produce fur pelts for the global market with China.[15] The Russian-American Company sought to establish a permanent trading post in Sitka in 1799. Tlingit, however, did not accept this action. The attempted seizure of land for a Russian business resulted in the Battle of Sitka in 1802. Losing Sitka meant foregoing a valued trading post in Southeast Alaska. And so, in 1804, Russia retaliated. Unbeknownst to the Russians, the Tlingit had prepared by building a fort.

The Battle of Sitka, initiated from conflict in 1802 and resuming in 1804, represents how colonial violence by Russia converged enslaved Unangax̂ and Alutiiq with warfare against Tlingit. On October 1, 1804, Russian fur trader Alexander Baranov led the assault with four hundred Unangax̂ and Alutiiq as the front line on Tlingit land. Yet the Tlingit waited until the Russians approached their fort on Indian River and then fired at the Russian ranks.

When this occurred, Tlingit warriors chased the invaders from the fort known as Shís'gi Noow, and the Unangax̂ and Alutiiq broke ranks and ran for their baidarkas (sea kayaks). After the four-day battle, Tlingit pursued what has been called the Sitka Kiks.ádi (Survival March). The Russians waved a white flag, and not trusting them, the Tlingit fled by foot at night.[16] The Russians interpreted this as surrender and burned the Tlingit fort to the ground. The Russians then constructed eight fortresses to continue the Russian-American Company. All sides suffered casualties: the Russians lost ten including four Alutiit, with twenty-four Russian forces wounded and thirty Tlingit bodies found by the fort.[17]

Lethal US Naval Attacks in the Nineteenth Century

With US occupation of Alaska beginning in 1867 in the post–Civil War era of US expansion, imperial violence followed, replicating violences witnessed by other Native nations in the ever-expanding American West reaching to the Pacific and north to the Arctic. Decades prior to World War II, the US Navy attacked the Tlingit nation, killing several people. In 1882, for example, the Northwest Trading Company killed a Tlingit shaman allegedly on accident. Yet when the company failed to comply with Tlingit customs by refusing to pay restitution with two hundred blankets, Tlingit from Angoon took two hostages.[18] Heightening their response to subdue Native nations at all cost and rejecting negotiations that fit within Tlingit customs, US Navy commander E. C. Merriman pillaged and burned the Tlingit village of Angoon. Many Tlingit retreated into the woods, yet six Tlingit children died from this attack by the US military.[19] That same year in the nearby Tlingit town of Kake the US Navy killed ten people during an attack.[20] Elders from Angoon who witnessed the 1882 US naval attack undoubtedly also observed the World War II era of Unangax̂ relocation on their lands.

Native nations organize, coordinate, and supply national aid. Highlighting this allows for a re-envisioning of tribal nations as fully functioning governments with diverse applications capable of forming alliances and supplying or accepting aid. Depicting Native history as solely combative either before or after colonial contact lends itself to the trope of Indian savagery. Native studies scholar Elizabeth Cook-Lynn (Crow Creek Sioux Tribe) illuminates that anti-Indianism renders Indigenous peoples into savages within the American imagination to denigrate Native sovereignty.[21] Such an understanding of Native nations as humanitarian appears to be complex because Native sovereignty has been diminished by the colonial myth of a vanishing Indian and the trope of savagery, both of which justify imperial goals of US settler colonialism.[22] Tribal mutual aid indeed predates the 1940s and colonial eras. As historian Michael Witgen (Anishinaabe) articulates, Native nations selectively choose various alliances and kinship networks, retaining a fluidity and an infinite number of sovereign tribal alliances.[23] Such an understanding reveals a long history of Native nations of the Americas selecting alliances with nations of their choice.

Killisnoo History and Russian Mission Education

The neighboring towns of Aangóon (Angoon) and Wooshdeidatetl' Seét (Killisnoo), on the waterfront of the Inside Passage, reside only three miles apart and are only accessible by boat and seaplane. Aangóon comes from the combined Tlingit words *aan* meaning "town" and *goon* meaning "cold water spring"; it became anglicized as the name Angoon.[24] Wooshdeidatetl' Seét, which translates to English as "oiled or oily channel" and became anglicized as the name Killisnoo, fittingly possessed a herring plant and whale processing plant. At one point, Killisnoo housed a productive cannery originally built in the 1880s. Many Tlingit acquired their first working jobs in Killisnoo at the fish saltery when the whaling station employed largely white workers and exercised workplace segregation.[25] During cannery times, two hundred to three hundred people moved from Angoon to Killisnoo for jobs to attend the government school. After a fire in 1928 leveled Killisnoo, residents moved to Angoon.[26] The Killisnoo cannery had been vacant ten years prior to Unangax̂ arrival as relocatees. Thus, fifteen years after the fire, the US Navy left Atkans at Killisnoo, the very island adjacent to where the US Navy once attacked Tlingit.

Despite the United States formalizing its settler colonial presence in the early twentieth century in the aftermath of the gold rushes, Russian colonialism persisted through the realms of religion and education. For example, a Russian school in Sitka continuously brought Unangax̂ students to Tlingit lands. These stories about student migrations under Russian schools, and even the US boarding schools that followed, reveal that Native youth are interconnected, constructing their own social fabric as citizens of their Native nations and engaging with diverse Native peoples.[27]

The life of Reverend Walter Soboleff (Tlingit) is an example of entanglements among Russian ancestry, Tlingit, Unangax̂, mission schools, and the towns of Angoon and Killisnoo. Born in 1908 in Killisnoo, Soboleff came from a family dedicated to the Russian Orthodox religion. Soboleff's mother, Shaaxeidi Tlaa (English name Anna Hunter Soboleff), was Tlingit, and his father, Alexander (Sasha) Soboleff, had Russian and German ancestry. In 1896, Walter's grandfather, Fr. John Soboleff, moved from San Francisco to Killisnoo where he served as the Orthodox priest. Reverend Soboleff attended preschool in Angoon, and his family moved to Killisnoo so he could attend the elementary school administered by the US government. Walter then attended the Russian school in Sitka from 1916 to 1917 until its closure from the Russian Revolution. According to Reverend Soboleff, he was the only Tlingit student in a group of otherwise Unangax̂ students.[28]

Unangax̂ children migrated to this region through the means of a colonial entity seeking to indoctrinate Native students, and yet students created their own social spaces within the confines of colonial settings. Children ripped from their families forced into colonial indoctrination seemingly removes the possibility of personal agency, and yet, as historian Matthew Sakiestewa Gilbert (Hopi) identifies, students "turned the power" by Indigenizing their surroundings and generating alliances despite these colonial settings.[29] Such a story shows that while children's friendships seem inconsequential in power, they indeed inform social alliances that have the capacity to carry over to adulthood and to shape a community. Reverend Soboleff is himself evidence that Tlingit and Unangax̂ schoolchildren engaged with each other and generated shared social spaces and perhaps friendships.

Tlingit and Unangax̂ Mutual Aid, Political Support, Friendships, and Intermarriages

Forced government relocation linked Native people to one another, and with Tlingit help, Unangax̂ survived the camps. Alice spoke about the first actions by the Atkans when they landed at the camp: they pooled their money together, bought lumber, and built a boat so they could travel outside of the Killisnoo camp. As there is no one alive today to confer this first wartime encounter between Tlingit and Atkans, we can only speculate how they met each other. Perhaps the first encounter between Atkans and Tlingit occurred after Atkans pooled their money together and built a boat. Or most likely, Tlingit saw the conditions of the Atkans as they landed on the shores of Killisnoo, greeted them, and advised them on where to obtain lumber, a resource that came from Tlingit lands. When Unangax̂ built temporary homes at Killisnoo and Funter Bay, they did so on Tlingit land where Tlingit accepted them as residents not knowing the duration of their stay.

At other camp locations, Tlingit greeted Unangax̂ upon their arrival on Tlingit homelands and strategized to help Unangax̂ survive by supplying food, water, and housing. In Wrangell, for example, when a ship landed, Tlingit chiefs discussed with their villages how they could accommodate Unangax̂.[30] With the Wrangell Institute closed, Unangax̂ relied on food from the Tlingit. George Gordaoff explained in an oral history that Tlingit gave dog salmon as food and that Unangax̂ had to kind of "beg and steal" to acquire more food.[31] As no altercation between Tlingit and Unangax̂ occurred, perhaps it can be inferred that Tlingit knew of food desperation and might have even set out food for easier access. Perhaps Tlingit encouraged the relocatees to harvest subsistence resources. Other stories such as one collected by scholar Lauren Peters (Unangax̂) reveal an oral tradition describing Tlingit in Angoon hunting deer and sharing meat with Atkans in Killisnoo.[32] Alice explained that the Angoon people had given the relocatees fish.[33] These stories indicate a network of Tlingit aid in supplying food and opening their land to subsistence harvesting for Unangax̂.

Alice Petrivelli identified the Tlingit as the reason why her people survived the camp at Killisnoo. She reflected, "The Tlingits, you know, used to have a cannery at Hood Bay, when the Angoon people found out our situation, they stopped by almost every day and gave us fish you know. So that's how we survived." Archival documents corroborate Alice's story about Tlingit providing fish. In autumn 1942, the Alaska Indian Service in Juneau reported to the commissioner of Indian affairs that Tlingit shared fish with Unangax̂ and that AIS then "assisted in obtaining fishing gear, barrels, and salt" for smoking and preserving fish.[34] At one point, when Superintendent Johnston of the FWS corresponded with Donald Gibbins of the Fouke Fur Company on the price of fur seal sales—made possible by Pribolobian labor—he thanked Gibbins for oranges as "the [N]atives certainly enjoy them especially the children" and boxes of Christmas presents for Natives.[35] These items presented as benevolent from a company that profited from Pribolobian labor paled in comparison to the wages stolen from Pribolobians forced into sealing operations by the government and a private corporation. When the US government failed to provide cold weather gear and basic necessities such as blankets, Alice recalled that the Tlingit donated blankets and mattresses to Atkans.[36]

Heavily burdened with surviving inadequate housing conditions at a relocation camp, Atkans had to find their own water. With a lack of government infrastructure following forced removal, Atkans in Killisnoo collected rainwater to sustain their population of eighty-three people. The abandoned cannery building presented a fire hazard with faulty electrical wiring and had only three outdoor pit toilets and one bathtub to serve nineteen Atkan families. Additionally, to obtain drinking water, Atkan men pumped water from the pond and boiled it. During an oral history interview, Alice described how the pumped water brought illness since Atkans possessed no reliable standard for sanitizing it. Alice explained, "What started the sickness was they pumped, the men, there was a pond up there, and they pumped it down there and we were told to boil the water. Some of us did, some of us didn't. And we lost, when we got there we had eighty-three, we lost about sixteen people there . . . mostly elders and babies." The lack of infrastructure for potable water proved lethal. Investigating how the Atkans obtained clean water illuminates interactions between Atkans and the Tlingit nation whose land they resided on.

In addition to water, food, and blankets, Tlingit aid from Angoon included medical care for Atkans. Remembering Tlingit assistance with healthcare, Alice reflected that her older sister Vera nearly died, explaining, "[We] almost lost her, she had pneumonia, she had, we didn't even have aspirin to relieve the pain to the people. We didn't know the (pause) only thing—plant—we recognized was a dandelion. In Atka we could use the plants to help the people. And we didn't have that in Killisnoo, my sister almost died."[37] She detailed how a Tlingit family helped: "Finally Mrs. McClain got some medicine from the Brandy's in Angoon. Got aspirins and everything . . . at that time everybody had measles, that was the beginning of the measles." Alice herself contracted the measles and she survived. The measles epidemic could have easily spread to their town, and yet Tlingit families shared medicine with Alice's sister Vera.[38]

In opening their homes to Atkans, Tlingit families controlled their own land boundaries, thereby upending ones imposed by the US government. In addition to sharing their church with Atkans in Killisnoo, Tlingit from Angoon hosted Atkan families on the weekends and celebrating holidays. When I asked if Tlingit ever visited Alice's family in Killisnoo, she replied, "They helped us a lot, you know holidays, we didn't have church in Killisnoo so we'd go to Angoon . . . we'd stay with the Zubows . . . and my Uncle Bill and them stayed with the Johnsons, you know different families stayed with different people. The Angoon people really helped us a lot." Opening homes shows power of shared domestic spaces, most likely coordinated by Native women. Alice revealed an amusing story about Christmas presents donated by Tlingit in Angoon to Atkans: "Christmas time, they gave us gifts. My brother's name is Poda, P-o-d-a." Here she paused, laughing while explaining, "I guess it sounds like a woman's [name] because he got his present and it was a woman's dress. We think his mother-in-law was the same size, so she got a dress." Amusing annotations aside regarding gendered assumptions about Atkan names, Tlingit provided community support and structure to the Atkans in a capacity that exerted Tlingit aid and exercised their land rights.

The Russian Orthodox Church in Juneau provided a space that fostered Indigenous languages and linked spirituality (fig. 6). During an interview

FIG. 6. Russian Orthodox Church in Juneau, Alaska, 2021. Photo by the author.

with the Kashevarof family (Unangax̂) in 2016, Bonnie Mierzejek, the daughter of relocation survivors Andronik and Ella Kashevarof of St. George, reminded her parents about the Tlingit. She explained, "You sang with them and participated in services with them." This prompted Andronik to recall that his family escaped the Funter Bay camp by moving to Juneau. During this time, Andronik worked as a hired hand at Governor Gruening's house. Remembering interactions with the Tlingit in Juneau, Andronik recalled, "There was a lot of Tlingits in Juneau, and they had Russian Orthodox Church there, and they had their own choir and a priest from St. Paul was in charge." He continued, "The Bishop, priest, moved to Juneau and stayed with the Tlingits and the Pribilofs. So the Pribilof, St. George, St. Paul choirs was running the choir in Juneau too. They had three choirs." Tlingit and Unangax̂ came together to worship in foreign colonial tongues yet uniquely Indigenized the space by claiming it as a multi-lingual congregation. Larry Dirks Sr. (Unangax̂ from Atka) recounted that after learning of the Russian

Orthodox Church in Sitka, he went to church there during the time he worked at the Sitka Spruce Mill.[39]

Through the primarily Tlingit-led organizations of the Alaska Native Brotherhood (ANB) and the Alaska Native Sisterhood (ANS) centralized in Southeast Alaska, Tlingit leaders advocated for alliances with Unangax̂. During an era when the ANB and ANS fought to secure land rights, political rights, and fishing rights, these Indigenous political organizations sent community-wide messages to support Unangax̂. During this time, activists including Elizabeth Peratrovich (Tlingit), Roy Peratrovich (Tlingit), and other members of the ANB and ANS fought to eliminate segregation in Alaskan towns.[40] While embracing Unangax̂ displaced upon their ancestral lands, ANB and ANS activists protested settler laws and ordinances that discriminated against multiple distinct Alaska Native nations.

While the ANB has been commonly associated with political activism for Native rights, the organization also promoted tribal mutual aid. The ANB asked its members to sponsor Unangax̂ families by providing food and winter clothing and offering their assistance and friendship. In a letter addressed to all ANB members dated July 6, 1942, just one month after Unangax̂ arrival, Grand President Roy Peratrovich (Tlingit) explained, "These people came with very little of their personal goods, and living conditions will be extremely difficult for them, especially this Fall and Winter."[41] Calling each ANB member to service, Peratrovich continued, "It is our patriotic duty to offer every aid and comfort to these our fellow countrymen, by gifts of friendship, advice, and assistance. At the present time, second-hand fishing gear of all kinds is needed by them to help them put up their winter food." This "patriotic duty" identified by Peratrovich can be traced not necessarily to US patriotism but rather to an Indigenous patriotic duty in providing tribal mutual aid. Peratrovich's letter calling the ANB and ANS members to service fit the ANB's mission of civic engagement.

A shared labor history provided mutual spaces between Tlingit and Unangax̂ workers. Unangax̂ and Tlingit fished together and worked alongside each other at the cannery.[42] In the 1970s, Larry Dirks Sr. (Unangax̂ from Atka) told a story of his work with Tlingit in Unangam Tunuu to linguist Knut Bergsland, translated by Michael Lekanoff Sr.: "I headed to Killisnoo, near Angoon. There I stayed until we were being taken back. I fished with the Tlingit people there and also once went to Sitka to work at the Sitka Saw Mill. This Mill cut up lumber for which was used in building houses."[43] One can imagine other forms of Tlingit support, such as helping them to secure jobs and patronizing Unangax̂-run small businesses that opened in Southeast Alaska. Prior to the war, Sergeus Golley (Unangax̂) ran a trading post on Atka. Golley then opened a store in Killisnoo. His daughter, Nadesta, explained in a school essay saved by anthropologist Ted Bank, "When dad was down at South Eastern Alaska he borrowed a small house that was part of the old cannery and bought fresh fruits from Juneau and sold them at his small store."[44] Nadesta continued, "To keep his store running all the time Dad later started ordering lots of things." For Golley's store to remain in business, it may be inferred that locals and Tlingit patrons must have supported it. In addition to patronizing Unangax̂ business, the Tlingit helped them obtain money by other means.

Continuing a tradition of art from their home islands, Unangax̂ women made baskets in Southeast Alaska, thus supplementing household incomes. An Atkan child, Oleana Snigaroff, explained in a school essay how Unangax̂ women participated in art sales: "Some women make baskets including [for sale at] museums at Juneau."[45] The Atkan women either found the proper grass to make baskets or perhaps Tlingit women showed Unangax̂ women where to collect grass and popular places to sell baskets, including museums. Tlingit women had sold baskets and berries to tourists along the Inside Passage since the late nineteenth century.[46] Another Atkan child, Tatiana Crevden, wrote in a school essay that Unangax̂ women collected blueberries, huckleberries, raspberries, salmon berries, and thimble berries.[47] Because women like Annie Samato shared strawberries with Atkan children, perhaps Tlingit women shared their berry picking patches with Unangax̂ women. Collecting berries reveals that Unangax̂ women readily accessed vitamin-rich fruits and subsistence resources on Tlingit lands.

Beyond convening as labor and political organizers, Tlingit and Unangax̂ created a voting bloc. In seeking ANB expertise, Unangax̂ laborers tried to learn their rights related to federal sealing operations. As chapter 1 articulates, the FWS forced Pribolobians to harvest seal pelts that profited the US government even during relocation. In response, Unangax̂ labor organizers from Funter Bay met with ANB president Roy Peratrovich.[48] When Unangax̂ learned that Tlingit and Haida controlled their own labor and wages instead of just receiving store credit, they saw their own labor as independent from federal oversight and control. In connecting with the ANB, these labor organizers strengthened intertribal alliances and their own footing to negotiate labor demands with the federal government. During this labor activism, Tlingit activist William Paul urged Unangax̂ to form a Native voting bloc and to vote against Bob Bartlett as territorial delegate due to his alliance with Governor Gruening.[49] Although Bartlett won as elected delegate from Alaska in 1945 and continued a long career in Alaska territorial politics, organizing this vote against the political establishment offered political power to Natives as a united front.

Observing how Tlingit activists interacted with the federal government shifted Unangax̂ attitudes, creating new forms of activism and advocacy against government intimidation. Unangax̂ elders take great care in acknowledging the labor activism and strategizing that the Tlingit provided. Carlene Arnold (Tlingit/Aleut), who conducted an interview with Alice Petrivelli, identified that prior to the war, Atka possessed a brotherhood that primarily served religious purposes.[50] Alice claimed that Tlingit organizers changed how the Unangax̂ organized in politics, explaining, "In Southeast [Alaska] we learned that the brotherhood could do a lot more, so from there we learned that you could fight for your rights through the organization." Alice continued, "the one thing my uncle Billy was chief at the time said the mistake he made was he didn't join the brotherhood in Angoon, Alaska Native Brotherhood, when we were down there." Nonetheless, after the war, someone from St. Paul started an ANB chapter propelling the fight for Indigenous rights.[51] In 1948, Elary Gromoff served as a delegate for ANB from St. George, traveling all the way from the Pribilofs to Hydaburg in Southeast Alaska for the annual ANB and ANS convention.[52] Also in 1948, the Pribilofs became a voting precinct in the same year that the Pribolobians joined the ANB. After this newly formed chapter, the ANB hired lawyers in Washington, DC, to represent Unangax̂.[53]

Fighting to secure healthcare in Southeast Alaska, ANB and ANS activists improved healthcare for Unangax̂ at the camps who were most afflicted by the epidemics. In March 1944, Commissioner of Indian Affairs John Collier references letters from ANB president Roy Peratrovich advocating for Native healthcare and preventing "discrimination against the [N]atives of Alaska."[54] Integrating healthcare would primarily assist Unangax̂ at the Ward Lake CCC camp who went to Ketchikan for healthcare.

Restructuring the colonial nature of its organization to assimilate students, the Wrangell Institute, administered by the BIA, provided a place where Native student alliances flourished. Unangax̂ children, including twenty-four Pribolobian children in 1943, between the ages of fourteen and twenty-one were taken to the boarding school to ease the number of occupants at the camps.[55] In this instance, the boarding school allowed some Unangax̂ children to escape dire conditions at the camps, including impotable water, fish poisoning, and impetigo.[56] One Unangax̂ child, Tatiana Crevden from Atka, recalled that they could not understand when Tlingit children spoke their Native language at school.[57] Such a story reveals Indigenous language retention and also that, for the most part, Tlingit and Unangax̂ children observed and likely engaged with each other in school. An oral history by Lawrence "Larry" Chercasen (Unangax̂) also reveals these childhood alliances. Larry attended school in Ketchikan with other Native students, including Tsimshian students from Metlakatla.[58]

The Tlingit and Unangax̂ alliance is all the more powerful considering that white people in Southeast Alaska did not offer as much aid or serve Unangax̂ in the same capacity as did the Tlingit nation, which organized as a collective and offered aid on their lands. Interactions between Unangax̂ and the white population in Southeast Alaska could be characterized as a mix of minor forms of advocacy and full-scale conflict. While some white people, such as Mary Jane Gaither of Juneau, identified abuse by government officials, other white people in Southeast Alaska brought undue stress to the camps.[59] As an example, the Division of Public Health Engineering conducted night patrols to prevent fishermen from introducing alcohol and "complications with the women"—a euphemism for sexual violence.[60] Although patrolling the waterfront near the camps prevented some fishermen from bringing negative influences, the government chose to provide resources for surveillance yet failed to provide adequate healthcare, food, and potable water. While some stories about white aid to Unangax̂ might be unrecorded, there are many visible stories about Tlingit aid.

In addition to marriages during the war, stories from Tlingit and Unangax̂ elders reveal intertribal friendships, alliances, and marriages that continued in the postwar years. The federal government invested heavily in surveilling Pribolobian whereabouts, even documenting intermarriage between Unangax̂ and local Southeast Alaska Natives during relocation in 1943: "One marriage took place in Juneau. We lose one inhabitant as this girl married an Indian."[61] The government framed this marriage as a loss since an Unangax̂ woman's body absent from the Pribilofs potentially took away from sealing operations. During this time, if a Pribolobian woman married outside the Pribilofs, like in the case of Parascovia Oustigoff Merchenin, government agents claimed, "this family should not be allowed to return to St. Paul Island."[62] Such a statement circulated by federal officials reveals that government agents sought control of all Pribolobian bodies, including their marriages. The government tried to control laboring bodies, physically for capital extraction and reproductively since birthing bodies created more Indigenous laboring bodies in the Pribilof Islands.

Born shortly after the war in 1947, Bob Loescher (Tlingit) grew up in Juneau and later served as the president and the CEO of the Sealaska Corporation. In May 2013, during his interview at the Central Council of the Tlingit and Haida Indian Tribes of Alaska, when I asked if Bob's family knew about Unangax̂ in camps during war, Bob thoughtfully reminisced, "[Mom] talked about people, what happened, and there were . . . places in southeastern Alaska where Aleut people were interned. And our people knew about those people and we tried to help them with food, and visit them and what not in these remote sites that the government placed the Aleut people in."[63] In addition to reiterating his mother's stories, Bob identified how Unangax̂ became members of the community: "And she spoke about those people, and even today some of those people live in our communities, and we know who they are, and they're integrated into our community now. But basically my mother told me about what happened and where those people were living and how they were being treated and what our communities did to help."

For Bob, identifying that the federal government neglected Unangax̂ and then highlighting that Tlingit extended aid to Unangax̂ became part of his family's oral tradition. The intergenerational nature of sharing these stories lends itself to what literary scholars Renée Hulan and Renate Eigenbrod identify as the distinct ways that knowledge is produced and conveyed generation to generation and the ways in which oral tradition forms the foundation of Indigenous societies.[64] Such a concept conveys the power of oral tradition in illuminating the memory of alliances through giving and receiving tribal mutual aid.

Revealing Indigenous social alliances, Tlingit and Unangax̂ women danced together in Juneau during a time when military officials from the Coast Guard forbade the association between Native women and servicemen. Nora Dauenhauer (Tlingit), a prolific author and an advocate of Tlingit language revitalization, recalled that as a young adult she socialized with Unangax̂ women. In May 2013, she and her spouse, Richard Dauenhauer, participated in a joint interview at the Central Council of the Tlingit and Haida Indian Tribes of Alaska. Her memories of shared social activities in Juneau with young Unangax̂ women contrast the deplorable conditions of the camps. Nora explained, "I met some of [the Unangax̂]. Mostly by dancing. The girls would come and dance and I don't remember the guys . . . they came to town and then they left."[65] Her story offers a glimpse of how some Native women created joy and recreation during these times of darkness during relocation. In this manner, Native women created social networks to support each other.[66]

During an oral history interview, an elder from Angoon who elected to remain anonymous described her childhood friendships with Unangax̂ children relocated at Killisnoo. This elder recalled, "They were just more kids to play with. Yeah they talked about home, nothing dramatic. They missed their homeland. But they were made to feel welcome; they always came to town [in Angoon]. We went to the movies with them."[67] This memory fills in more details from Alice's stories; by identifying that in addition to Tlingit and Unangax̂ attending church together and Tlingit hosting Unangax̂ families in their homes, Atkan children participated in numerous other recreational activities with Tlingit children in Angoon.

Intermarriages between Tlingit and Unangax̂ occurred in the postwar years, highlighting marriage bonds and solidified kinship networks. Some elders married Unangax̂ tribal members whom they met at boarding school. Charlotte McConnell (Tlingit) from Juneau explained that after the war, she met her Unangax̂ husband at the Mt. Edgecumbe Native boarding school in Southeast Alaska. Charlotte explained how her husband conveniently fit within marriage regulations: "I met my husband, Alex Fadaoff. And I know I can't get in trouble because he's not an eagle or a raven, he's a Aleut! I have four children by him and so they're half Aleut and half Tlingit, and I call them Tlineuts."[68] Charlotte laughed sharing the term of endearment in which her children occupy multiple identities from two tribal nations.

Native Alliances Withstanding Time

Despite challenges from US settler colonialism that brought varied forms of violence to marginalize Native sovereignty by, for example, physically relocating Unangax̂ across the Gulf of Alaska onto Tlingit lands, Tlingit and Unangax̂ facilitated intertribal friendships and survivance alliances. Examining friendships and alliances between these two nations offers a story of collective Indigenous empowerment and an explanation for a higher survival rate of Unangax̂. These stories about friendships are primarily evident from oral histories.

During a follow-up meeting with Alice, I brought a copy of Roy Peratrovich's letter from 1942 mentioning the ANB aid to Unangax̂. When Alice saw Peratrovich's letter encouraging the ANB to supply assistance to Unangax̂, she explained, "I didn't know he did that. I knew Angoon did."[69] Alice knew that Tlingit from Angoon chose to help Atkans, but until that point she had not known that the ANB notified all its members to aid Unangax̂. Reading through the names at the top of the ANB letterhead, Alice described knowing the elected officials on a personal level: "I knew Peratrovich, Paul, Andy Hope, Cryril Zuboff, my sister used to babysit for [him] our first year we were there." Exhibiting a flood of positive memories from this era, she reflected, "ANB, the Tlingits were wonderful. My sister was friends with Cecelia Kookesh. We were family friends with the Johnsons . . . we spent the night with them for church. They lived in a big white house in the center of town. We stayed with the Johnsons from Hoonah, the Tlingits, and we'd walk home after church." Peratrovich's letter to the ANB and Alice's memories of Tlingit from Angoon demonstrate the power of Indigenous alliances and community support during times of significant hardship. The stories of friendship between the Tlingit and Unangax̂ nations offer a narrative of collective Indigenous survivance directly supported by Indigenous nations.

After the Battle of Attu in May of 1943, when Unangax̂ soldiers and the US military recovered Attu Island, the lives of Tlingit and Unangax̂ nations continued to intersect. Activism leading up to the passage of the Alaska Native Claims Settlement Act of 1971 (ANCSA) brought Alaska Native nations together to jointly petition the government for Aboriginal land rights. Unangax̂ remain invited guests at the biennial Tlingit Celebration. According to anthropologist Rosita Worl (Tlingit), one year, Tlingit gave a song back to Unangax̂ that had been sung to them generations prior during the Russian colonization era. Still today, Tlingit, represented by Worl and allies including C. W. Smythe at the Sealaska Heritage Institute are working together with Martin Stepetin Sr. (Unangax̂), representatives of other Unangax̂ communities, and the Juneau-Douglas City Museum through the Funter Bay Working Group to develop interpretive panels. These panels depict forced relocation from the Pribilof Islands and internment at the Funter Bay dilapidated cannery site, which has recently been placed under the management of the Alaska State Parks through special legislation introduced by this group.

In the decades after war, Alice brought two daughters to Killisnoo on a pilgrimage. When they visited Angoon, Alice and her daughters met up with Betty, the granddaughter of Mrs. Samato (Tlingit). Here, concentric circles of colonialism emerge. Various Alaska Native and Japanese Alaskan identities intersected in Annie Samato's strawberry garden where alliances formed, linking Native peoples together through a shared history of tribal mutual aid transcending time and spanning intergenerationally as well as Alaskan geographies.

THREE
WAR ON UNANGAX̂ SOIL
THE BATTLE OF ATTU,
NATIVE NATIONS,
AND THE US MILITARY

AT THE OUTSET OF WORLD WAR II, the Unangax̂ nation and other Indigenous Alaskans resided between the three global empires of Japan, the Soviet Union, and the United States. They had a choice about which empire to ally with, and in making this choice, they strategized about which alliance might allow them to best protect their communities and homelands while reacting to rapidly changing events on the ground. One pivotal event took place in 1941 when a Japanese warship landed on the westernmost Aleutian Island of Attu and measured the island and its harbor. Mike Hodikoff, the chief of Attu, told US wartime correspondent Corey Ford that Japanese naval officers had spoken to him. He then detailed sexual violence directed at Attuan women by members of the Japanese Navy: "J*ps come to our village two–three years ago, rape the old women. Women too old to have kids, but they have them for J*ps."[1] Undoubtedly, these actions of sexual violence by the Japanese Navy shaped how Unangax̂ chose not to ally with the Japanese and instead turn to another empire for defense.

Across the Pacific Ocean, Japan was colonizing East Asia extending to the South Pacific as well as the North Pacific.[2] On June 3, 1942, Japan bombed Dutch Harbor some 650 miles northeast of their base at Paramushiro in the Kuril Islands. A surprise attack on June 4 to 7, 1942, intended to divert attention from Japan's assault on Midway.[3] On June 7, 1942, 2,500 Japanese troops invaded Kiska Island, where a mere ten US military personnel surrendered.[4] Next, Japan invaded Attu, where forty-two Unangax̂ lived alongside the white BIA teachers Charles Foster Jones and Etta Jones, who had moved to Attu in August 1941.[5] When the Japanese arrived, they shot an Attuan woman in the leg, which a Japanese doctor tended to. Because Charles Jones operated the radio on the island, the Japanese interrogated and tortured him, trying to find out if links existed between the United States and the Soviet Union. Japanese soldiers then concentrated Attuans and Etta Jones by taking them to a POW camp on Hokkaido. Within the month, the US Navy responded by evacuating the remaining Unangax̂ from the Aleutian Islands to relocation camps in Southeast Alaska.

US servicemen lamented the Aleutian williwaws—squalls that brought non-stop rain—and they expressed confusion about why they were defending peripheral islands at the edge of US empire. Yet, to Unangax̂ servicemen, the Aleutians represented their homeland and US militarization meant a chance to reassert their people's Aboriginal rights and land title. Some critics might deem such an act as being "colonized," but upon closer examination, Indigenous alliances with the US military reveal layered complexities linked to Indigenous identities, power, and hope for land reclamation. Such a concept of sovereignty existed in other geographies such as the Philippines and Guam where Pacific nations chose to accept alliances with the United States to defend themselves from Japan's imperialism.[6] Atrocities including the Nanking Massacre of 1937 in China and Koreans forced to serve in the Imperial Japanese Army, including Korean women and girls as military sex slaves known as "comfort women," evidence this empire that Pacific nations sought to escape.[7] The US military offered an alternative means to secure Native lands from colonization.

During Japan's occupation of the Aleutians, Indigenous equilibrium meant restoring Native lands through reinvasion and reclamation. Asserting oneself as an Indigenous soldier with an agenda of land reclamation meant representing one's tribal nation within the construct of the US military. Other dual citizens and non-citizens served in the US military, including American Indians from the contiguous states, Mexicans who served in hopes of acquiring citizenship, and incarcerated Japanese American Nisei. The United States, like Japan, had servicemen from a variety of national backgrounds. While it is true that by enlisting and serving in the US military Alaska Natives were emboldening the very colonial structure that would oppress them, such a concern remained tangential to the foremost desire to maintain Indigenous lands from invasion by Japan. At this time, Japan represented the most powerful empire of the Pacific world. When the Pacific War reached the Aleutian Islands in 1942, Native men responded by allying with the United States.

The Battle of Attu from May 11 to May 30 in 1943 is one of the lesser-known battles in World War II history, and yet it is the only battle fought on the North American home front. During the Battle of Attu, Native men provided essential combat intelligence to the US military, and the Unangax̂ nation led this reinvasion. Native servicemen saw this as a chance to restore the Aleutian Islands not to the US military but, more importantly, to Indigenous Alaskans. They allied with the United States utilizing the military to make this happen. As historian Ryan Hall articulated about the Blackfoot nation, "Blackfoot history illuminates how Indigenous people creatively managed colonial geography to their own benefit, to great consequence."[8] Borrowing this concept, Alaska Native nations allied and managed the US military as a means to assert land reclamation.

Native men, and more specifically Unangax̂ men, provided essential skills to US special intelligence in the recapturing of Attu Island. Native people chose to ally with the United States to fight fascism, and they did so by centering an Indigenous agenda that allied with operations by the US military. The social history of Native veterans and an Indigenous military history are made possible through oral testimony that supplies Native reasons for military action. Oral histories from Alaska Native veterans show that the armed forces linked Alaskan tribal geographies within the common backdrop of US military service. Native men chose military service and selected to serve as experts of the Alaskan landscape. This chapter follows the stories of Unangax̂ servicemen, identifies the racialized identities of Native servicemen who continued to assert their Indigenous identities, and highlights the concept of dual patriotisms in which Native men served their Native nations and the United States to reclaim their homelands.

From the beginning of the Battle of Attu, Unangax̂ servicemen changed their status from being Indigenous peoples dispossessed by the multiple empires to war heroes whose expertise facilitated the reclamation of their Indigenous homelands from enemy invaders. Unangax̂ servicemen reclaimed Attu alongside US troops, playing a critical role in the recapture of Attu. Alongside the reconnaissance platoon known as Castner's Cutthroats, Unangax̂ men landed on Beach Red beginning the Battle of Attu. At nine o'clock in the morning on May 11, 1943, Commander Colonel Frank L. Culin sent the Alaska Scouts and Unangax̂ men on two landing crafts.[9] One commanding officer on Adak identified Unangax̂ as "the best sailors in the world," praising their navigation skills of isolated harbors during variable weather conditions.[10] Due to the rocky landing area, the Japanese never suspected this area could be invaded. Unangax̂ boatmen moved as close to shore as possible before transferring to plastic dories rowing to Beach Red. After the landing, Colonel Culin sent Unangax̂ to check the surrounding hills while six boatloads of troops followed the destroyer toward Beach Red.[11] In total, 12,500 US soldiers outnumbered the less than 2,500 Japanese soldiers on the 377.4 square mile island.[12]

According to military historian Galen Rogers Perras, the Battle of Attu ranked as the second most costly battle in the Pacific, second only to Iwo Jima with the number of losses relative to the number of troops.[13] The United States suffered 3,829 casualties with 549 killed, 1,148 injured, and more than 2,000 soldiers incapacitated from frostbite and cold weather injuries, which required over two hundred army men being sent to San Francisco for hospitalization.[14] An estimated 2,351 Japanese soldiers died, and the US military captured only twenty-nine Japanese soldiers as prisoners of war.[15] During one of the first mass banzai charges of World War II, Japanese servicemen committed suicide with handheld grenades rather than surrender as US prisoners of war.[16] Japan's high casualties stemmed not only from their ratioed servicemen but also from receiving no backup defense.[17] It is unknown how many Japanese soldiers wandered into the mountains; in autumn 1943, the US military captured three more Japanese soldiers who descended from the mountains and snuck to the US camp to steal food. US servicemen kept Japan's remaining supplies, marveling at their stationery and their cold weather gear, looting these items. As a final act of dehumanization of an enemy, some US servicemen took bone fragments from Japanese soldiers' bodies.

After the Battle of Attu, the botched invasion of the neighboring island of Kiska resulted in friendly fire. Unbeknownst to the allied US and Canadian military forces, on July 29, 1943, Japan had loaded all 5,100 Japanese soldiers from Kiska disappearing in the fog.[18] On August 15, 1943, the allied invasion of Kiska resulted in over three hundred casualties from Japanese mines and friendly fire amid thick fog cover.[19] The military outfitted these GIS so poorly that over a thousand servicemen developed severe frostbite and gangrene, and they needed toes and feet amputated in San Francisco, as the Alaskan territory lacked major hospital infrastructure and personnel. Loaded on a ship with a secret mission, the soldiers had been outfitted with tropical weather gear rather than subarctic gear. Those who changed their socks even once were spared from the worst foot amputations. Alongside the damp cold, severe weather from the fog meant that the US and Canadian Forces blindly shot at each other. One oral history from an Athabascan elder describes that her brother had been in combat and that he hid in a fox hole.[20] While in hiding, her brother only recognized an allied soldier by speaking Athabascan together. It is possible this event occurred during the botched invasion of Kiska. To date, the mishap of invading Kiska remains a quiet narrative.

While perceived as experts of the Alaskan terrain on their homelands, Native combat soldiers still navigated their racialized identities as Indigenous men. During the Battle of Attu, Simeon Peter Pletnikoff, nicknamed "Aleut Pete," from Nikolski in the Aleutians, served as one member of a sixty-eight-man platoon in the 1st Alaskan Combat Intelligence Platoon known as the Alaska Scouts (fig. 7).[21] During World War II, he earned eight decorations and received distinction for his service in the Alaska Scouts in addition to many awards.[22] Despite his numerous medals—the Combat Infantryman Badge, Bronze Star Medal, Good Conduct Medal, American Defense Service Medal with Foreign Service Clasp, Asiatic-Pacific Campaign Medal with Bronze Service Star, World War II Victory Medal, Presidential Unit Citation, and the Honorable Service Lapel Button—that highlight his essential combat skills in the recapture of Attu, Pletnikoff's Indigenous identity at times put him in danger.

Due to Pletnikoff's Indigenous identity as distinct from a white male

FIG. 7. Simeon Peter Pletnikoff, also known as "Aleut Pete." "He fights on home ground en route to Attu." Photo courtesy of Dr. Michael Livingston.

identity, US soldiers confused him as a Japanese enemy spy. According to Pletnikoff, "I had a heck of a time. Out on the front line the Americans would get a hold of me to the Provost Marshal for impersonating a US soldier."[23] Pletnikoff responded by asserting his Native identity: "What's the matter with you guys? I'm an Aleut." Other Native men encountered similar issues due to their physical features that resembled specifically Japanese identities. After the Battle of Attu, Private First Class Lee Dowd, "a half Indian," approached another soldier at Massacre Valley for a cigarette match. The white soldier tried to choke him to death and explained, "I thought [he] was a J*p."[24] This racial slur, "J*p," dehumanized not only Japanese soldiers but also Japanese Issei and Nisei Americans and evidently applied to Alaskan Indigenous servicemen mistaken as Japanese by US soldiers. Such a story reveals the effectiveness of US propaganda in the years following the bombing of Pearl Harbor.

Soldiers circulated and saved "Japanese hunting licenses," which appropriated an image from Southeast Alaskan Indigenous art to depict an eagle fighting the Axis world leaders (fig. 8). Prior to Alaskan invasion, Lieutenant General Simon Bolivar Buckner of the Alaska Defense Command had written to Major H. H. Arnold: "Now that we have an open season on J*ps and no bag limit, I am very anxious to have an opportunity to enjoy the delightful spectacle of seeing bubbles come up where a Japanese ship went down."[25] The fight against Japan included religious differences as well. Buckner (or Colonel L. E. Schick, who delivered his speech on KFAR radio in Fairbanks) scribbled out parts of a speech that he delivered celebrating the 141st anniversary of the US military academy in 1943. Parts of one sentence were crossed out: "Our immediate duty here is the extermination of ~~slant-eyed~~ vermin" followed by the Japanese being "~~barbarians~~" and requiring "~~a good Christian burial~~."[26] The main message of the speech on fighting alongside the Royal Canadian Air Force remained.

In other regions of the Pacific, Alaska Native servicemen utilized their resemblance to the Japanese to pass behind enemy lines. Jimmy Reed, an Iñupiaq Marine who fought at Tawara, Saipan, and Tinian, looked so racially ambiguous that he was able to cross enemy lines, only to find allied troops slaughtered. No one on the Japanese side even fired at Reed behind enemy lines. When Reed returned to US lines, the men opened fire because they

FIG. 8. Japanese hunting license, n.d. Courtesy of the Wing Luke Museum, Seattle, Washington.

thought he was Japanese. They stopped firing only when Reed approached closer, and his uniform showed his US affiliation.[27]

Despite forms of discrimination that Native servicemen encountered, such as the case of Pletnikoff when his peer soldiers accused him of being a Japanese spy, dual patriotisms informed a Native experience where Native men shaped their time in the service to create patriotism(s) that fit their Indigenous identities. The Indigenous experience of Indigenous patriotism(s) represented plural patriotisms that were entangled and sometimes separate. Historian Paul C. Rosier claims that during World War II, American Indians possessed a "hybrid American patriotism" in which they "imagined an American nationalism that drew upon rather than destroyed their values."[28] Such a concept shows that Native servicemembers saw US military service as a malleable space capable of existing for Indigenous means. The story of Pletnikoff and his dual patriotisms to the Unangax̂ nation and to the United

States, and his dual identities as an Unangax̂ member of the armed forces in a combat intelligence platoon, reveal that Native men came to terms with their identity that bridged military service with Indigeneity. Indeed, as historian Kenneth Townsend relays, Alaska Native men in the military, like American Indians, served their communities while they carried their Indigenous racial identities.[29]

To understand dual patriotisms, it helps to uncover the motivations of non-white soldiers who chose to serve an empire through military service. Historian Robert Jefferson uncovers Black American motivations while serving in segregated military units during World War II as "far more complex than we have ever imagined."[30] In a similar regard, historian Stephen Kantrowitz argues that African American military service during the nineteenth century and the Reconstruction years presented an opportunity for African Americans to define their own citizenship in a white and corporate America that budged only when pressed against by adamant insistence.[31] From a global perspective, examining the role of African soldiers in establishing German colonization, historian Michelle Moyd illuminates that people "negotiate [. . .] working for organizations and institutions that, as a matter of course, employ violent and coercive methods."[32] These scholars highlight that non-white marginalized populations had a multitude of personal, social, political, and economic reasons for allying with colonial militias.

Native men responded to invasion by enlisting in the military and working in special operations units known as the Alaska Scouts and the subgroup called Castner's Cutthroats. Both the Alaska Scouts and Castner's Cutthroats represented servicemen who wore no uniforms and who conducted missions with independence. As a combat intelligence detachment, Castner's Cutthroats formed on November 19, 1941, under Colonel Lawrence Vincent Castner. What began with three men expanded to a platoon of sixty-six men and two officers.[33] The military selected men in these platoons based on their survival skills and their ability to navigate the Alaskan landscape. Castner's Cutthroats gained a reputation as a collective of scrappy outdoorsmen, dog mushers, hunters, and survivalists.

Unangax̂, Iñuit, and Indians, alongside white settlers including hunters, trappers, and prospectors, made up this reconnaissance platoon of Castner's

Cutthroats. These units, which featured Alaska Native men's survival skills, paralleled special missions like those of the Navajo code talkers and the Tlingit code talkers.[34] During Japan's occupation of the Aleutian Islands, Castner's Cutthroats worked as intelligence reporters in Kodiak, on the Pribilof Islands, and secret bases on the Aleutians at Cold Bay, Umnak, and Dutch Harbor.[35] While hiding in mountainous and volcanic terrain, the Cutthroats lived off the land by hunting, trapping, and fishing. As resourceful outdoorsmen, they reportedly rendered seal fat to make oil for their guns, and they steamed wood in subzero temperatures to make dog sleds.[36] Draven "Buck" Delkettie (Athabascan) served in Castner's Cutthroats helping in the recapture of Attu at ground zero.[37]

One has to wonder how Unangax̂ men felt providing combat intelligence to the US military while their families remained confined to camps in Southeast Alaska. Perhaps their feelings were similar to Japanese Nisei soldiers who served in the segregated 442nd unit while their families remained at concentration camps in the US heartland. In serving the US military while their family members were incarcerated, both Unangax̂ and Nisei likely tried to speed up the process of freeing their families from the camps. Perhaps military service or patriotism equated to a measurable outcome that an individual could volunteer or provide that might lead directly to a more hasty return to normal un-incarcerated life, restoring equilibrium in their households with a measured end to war. Each individual had varying motivations, including Japanese American "No-no boys" who rejected US military service while incarcerated.[38]

Remembering the names of Unangax̂ servicemen who restored their home islands through US military service illuminates specific Native contributors who changed the outcome of war in the North Pacific. Henry Swanson, from Unalaska, a World War I veteran, patrolled Unalaska Bay, transported a mapping crew around Unalaska Island before the bombing of Dutch Harbor, assisted in selecting outpost sites in Unalaska and Adak, piloted vessels that delivered supplies for the Battle of Attu, and instructed GIs while transferring them by boat between Aleutian bases.[39] John Nevzoroff, from Atka, navigated with Adak's Port Commander Carl "Squeaky" Anderson.[40] Paul Gundersen from Nelson Lagoon enlisted in Cold Bay on

December 19, 1942, and served in the Alaska Scouts at Attu and Shemya. Chester Bereskin from Unalaska served in the Alaska Scouts, as did Akutan's traditional chief Luke Shelikoff. Ralph Prokopeuff, from Atka, served in Adak and Anchorage. Herbert and Bill Hope from Unalaska served in the navy. While stationed overseas, George Fox from Unalaska died in Italy in 1944. Vincent Tutiakoff from Unalaska provided the military with knowledge on Aleutian survival. Major General Edward G. Pagano, from Unga, served in the army in the South Pacific where he invaded Okinawa as a member of the 96th Division and then received a Purple Heart. In 1982, Pagano became Alaska's first Native adjutant general of the Alaska National Guard.[41]

Some Unangax̂ men left their wartime relocation camps in Southeast Alaska by joining the military. The FWS, with sealing profit motives in mind, tried withholding Unangax̂ from the Pribilof Islands from enlisting in the draft while relocated, yet the Juneau draft board enlisted them anyway.[42] Here, colonial bureaucracies butted heads, and Unangax̂ men could use one branch of government to navigate oppression from another branch. A few of those who did included Luke Shelikoff from Akutan, who left the Ward Lake CCC camp by enlisting in the army, and William B. Hope, who left Burnett Inlet and Wrangell Institute by enlisting in the navy.[43] According to the official log from St. Paul Island in May 1944, thirty-eight Native soldiers from St. Paul aided the war efforts.[44] On July 1, 1944, the Alaska Territorial Guard rolls from St. Paul listed seventy-four men enrolled with one officer, and the data at St. George listed thirty-eight men enrolled with two officers.[45]

Alaska Natives and American Indians from the contiguous states fought in the Aleutians and received recognition. The National Park Service identified twenty-five Unangax̂ men who joined the armed forces, with three who participated in the US invasion of Attu Island and received Bronze Star Medals.[46] Staff Sergeant Peter N. Jackson (Hoopa) received an Air Medal for his service in the Aleutians in the 11th Air Force; Jose P. Venevedez (Isleta Pueblo) received a Purple Heart for his service in the Aleutians; John Crowder from Oklahoma received an Air Medal for his service in the Aleutians; Staff Sergeant Irving Jumping Eagle (Lakota from Pine Ridge) received an Air Medal for his service in the Aleutians; and Private Gabe Neiss (Lakota from Rosebud) was wounded in action in the Aleutians.[47]

Elder Native men, while too old to enlist, also provided combat intelligence to troops. One such elder was Simeon "Nutchuk" Oliver, who lived in New York. While dining at a restaurant, he heard a newsboy announce "Dutch Harbor bombed!" As an Alaskan, he immediately returned to Alaska to help.[48] Nutchuk was born in Chignik in 1902, to a Yup'ik mother and a Norwegian father who was a fisherman and trapper. After his mother died in childbirth following the birth of his sister Christine, born two years after him, he became an orphan at the predominantly Native orphanage known as the Jesse Lee Home in Dutch Harbor. Before he enlisted in the army, Nutchuk was a concert pianist and anthropologist. He conducted anthropological research alongside Smithsonian expeditions, including the 1938 expedition to the Aleutians led by Ales Hrdlicka.[49] Nutchuk is known as the composer of the song "Aleut Lullaby." During the war, Nutchuk directed his talents toward military intelligence, where "he served as a G-2 intelligence officer at Fort Richardson and was assigned special responsibilities for the Aleutian Campaign."[50] In addition to his autobiographies *Son of the Smoky Sea* and *Back to the Smoky Sea*, Nutchuk wrote a book for the army on how to survive the Aleutian Islands.[51] He also instructed soldiers on emergency food foraging in the Aleutians.[52] Continuing to serve Native people of the Aleutians, Nutchuk became the school teacher on Atka after Attuans returned from the POW camp in Japan.[53]

One would suppose that after the culmination of the Indian Wars in the late nineteenth century, and centuries of Indigenous resistance to the US government, American Indians would resist US military service. Indigenous engagement in US imperial projects is indeed complicated since Indians from the continental mainland served with the US Army as well as fought against the army and settlers during the Plains Wars. Yet somehow, across all racial categories, American Indians demonstrated the highest rate of military participation during World War II.[54] Alaska Natives fit a pattern of Indigenous peoples across the United States who collectively fought fascism. During World War II, 25,000 American Indian men across the country enlisted and another 40,000 American Indians served in civilian employment for national defense.[55] John Collier, the commissioner of Indian Affairs, boasted that nearly 100 percent of Native men cooperated with the

Selective Service Act. Even states that denied Indigenous voting rights into the 1940s, such as Arizona, Utah, and New Mexico, had tribes with over 70 percent of their men in the service.[56] In 1945, 21,767 Indians served in the US Army, 1,910 Indians served in the US Navy, 121 Indians served in the Coast Guard, and 723 Indians served in the Marines.[57] An estimated 5 percent, or 550 Native persons, died in the service during World War II, and 700 were wounded.[58]

Indeed, some American Indians served in the US military during the war, continuing family legacies of Native men in the service during World War I and dating back to the Indian Wars against and alongside the US Army and settlers of the 1860s. Brummett Echohawk's (Pawnee) phrase relays a sentiment of adaptation: "Instead of eagle feathers, I wear a steel helmet. I carry an M1 rifle instead of a bow and arrows. Instead of drawing on a buffalo hide or shield, I will draw on notebook paper. And, like the warrior-painter of old, I will tell and draw of battle . . . as I live it . . . as I see it."[59] Of some of the Native men who received recognition for their efforts overseas, Lieutenant Richard Balenti (Cheyenne/Haida) in the navy received a Purple Heart, an Oak Leaf Cluster, and an Air Medal for his service in the Pacific; Lieutenant Francis S. Harper (Athabascan) received an Air Medal and three Oak Leaf Clusters for serving in Europe, where he was also a POW in Germany in 1944; Private First Class Herbert M. Bremner (Tlingit from Yakutat) received an Award for Valor for his service in the Netherlands; and Lieutenant Bertram Leask (Tsimshian/Haida) received a Distinguished Flying Cross and a Purple Heart for his service in the Mediterranean.[60]

In remote areas of northern Alaska, such as on the Diomede Islands located in the Bering Sea between Siberia and Alaska, Iñuit men tried to serve in the US military. When Iñuit from Big Diomede Island arrived on Alaska's shoreline in Nome to register for the draft, the US Army informed them that they resided on Soviet territory rather than on US territory.[61] Such actions to enlist by the Iñuit from Big Diomede show that sovereign Indigenous nations tried to ally with the United States—and that in doing so, they saw themselves as coming not from Soviet territory but from Iñuit territory over which they themselves exercised sovereignty.

As Native commitment to the war effort indeed had financial dimensions,

FIG. 9. Al Sahlin's war stamps from elementary school. Photo taken in Nome at Al's kitchen table, 2015. Photo by the author.

when Native tribes purchased war bonds, they exercised sovereignty in selecting to invest in another country. When tribal organizations purchased US war bonds as a collective, rather than as individuals, they exercised actions of sovereign nations. In 1944, Harold Ickes, the secretary of interior, reported that American Indians purchased at least $2 million in war bonds. John Collier estimated the Indian commitment to the war effort at $50 million.[62] In Alaska, the Office of Indian Affairs in Juneau reportedly sold $110,646 worth of bonds to local Natives alone; adjusted to today's inflation rate, this represents over $1.87 million.[63] When Alaska governor Ernest Gruening visited St. Lawrence Island in 1942, the village tried to commit its entire treasury from fox skins and ivory sales of $1,500 toward the purchase of war bonds.[64] Tribal sovereignty was thus displayed in selectively investing in and supporting a partner sovereign.

Elders still remember the war bond stamps that they saved as mementos. Al Sahlin (Iñupiaq) grew up in Nome and later served in the Alaska National Guard during the Cold War. Inside a small container mixed with vintage family photographs, Al saved his ten-cent war savings stamps and fifty-cent defense stamps. As it was common at the time for even children to support the war effort, Al purchased these stamps from his teacher to help fight fascism (fig. 9).[65] After June 1942, financial contributions paled in comparison to the military sacrifices made by Native servicemen when Japan's military invaded the Alaskan coastline.

Wartime Alaskan Perspectives: Stories from Veteran Elders

Oral history interviews illuminate Native motivations for serving during wartime Alaska. Stories by veteran elders show that Indigenous Alaskans appropriated military service and fashioned a patriotic identity that fit their Indigenous identities, countering the assumption that Native people passively absorb colonial institutions. The military never indoctrinated Native soldiers; rather, Native soldiers proudly served on their own terms. Stories from elders show that Indigenous identities informed each individual's motivations for protecting Alaska and the US home front while shaping their Indigenous wartime experiences.

Arnold Booth, a World War II army veteran, was born in 1919 in Metlakatla. His father was Tsimshian and his mother was Tlingit, and he grew up speaking the Sm'algyax language.[66] As a teenager, Arnold cleverly escaped an arranged marriage by his grandmother by seeking help from the church to attend school at Greenleaf Academy in Idaho. While in the army, Arnold saw many Indigenous lands across the Pacific Rim, including Australia, the Philippines, and Papua New Guinea. Using the GI Bill, Arnold obtained his degree from Oregon Pacific College. He later returned to Metlakatla where he taught and coached basketball for thirty-one years. When he taught students on Alaska's only Indian reservation, Arnold never began US history with Columbus; instead, Arnold instructed students to tape off portions of the classroom throughout the year to signify the shrinking of Native lands.

Just as Arnold's Native identity shaped his pedagogy as a teacher, it also shaped his experiences as a buck sergeant in the army. Wearing civilian clothes, Arnold encountered anti-Indian discrimination that contrasted his time in the service. Arnold remembered a restaurant that refused to serve him and another American Indian serviceman until they changed into uniform: "During the war, when I came back, I had an Indian friend. . . . [We] went back down to have a snort before we had our big dinner. We got kicked out. We were Indians. We went back home, put on our uniform, walked in." Here, Arnold laughed recalling how the restaurant then accepted their patronage: "they didn't tough us." Military uniforms afforded Arnold and his friend equal access to a restaurant that otherwise excluded Natives. This story reveals how allied war efforts provided Native servicemen with some social equality at businesses. Accordingly, Arnold could not procure transportation from Seattle to Ketchikan until he changed into uniform: "I came into Seattle and I couldn't get onto the steamer they were all booked with tourists. . . . I went back down there and got a GI haircut, took my uniform and had 'em cleaned and pressed, put it back on and walked through, 'How much does it cost to get home to Ketchikan?' I got a good deal right off [laughs]." While Arnold mused about newly afforded equality at restaurants and more accessible transportation, he expressed grief when he related his experiences overseas in Papua New Guinea and the Philippines. His superiors sent him in first, putting him in harm's way. According to Arnold, "They'd let me go in first." Arnold relayed that his superiors would say, "the Indian will know how to do this, the Indian should do this." Perhaps this was because of the stereotyped view of Native men as scouts and warriors, or this treatment shows prejudice in valuing Arnold's fate less than that of white servicemen, or perhaps a mixture of both.[67] Divergent treatment of Native soldiers put them into life-threatening situations, such as in Arnold's case when his superiors sent him on the front line before they sent white servicemen. Military superiors and fellow soldiers premised their treatment of Native soldiers on racialized identities that stemmed from myths of noble savagery.[68]

Although Native servicemen partook in integrated military units and received equal pay to whites, anti-Native discrimination infused interactions that in turn informed social hierarchies. In contrast to African Americans who experienced segregation in the military until 1948 when President Truman issued Executive Order 9981, American Indian and Alaska Native servicemen participated in integrated units. And yet, as Arnold's stories

FIG. 10. Replica of the flag that hung in Arnold Booth's house.
Photo by the author.

illustrate, Native servicemen experienced degrees of social exclusion from other servicemen that resulted from their distinct Native identities. Arnold explained that some men in the service "wouldn't sit next to me, 'cause I was an Indian." He specified this treatment as geographically specific: "I was surprised when I got out of the service though, that some of the men from the South wouldn't sit next to me. Wouldn't even talk to me. This was the military police. Major Harding found out, he wasn't a hard guy to talk to. But, boy I was much darker." While it is important to not idealize the northern contiguous United States as a haven from racial inequality, American Indians identified the southern United States as particularly hard to navigate with racialized identities.

At the juncture of opportunities and challenges for Native men in the service, equilibrium restoration emerged as Native servicemen navigated the war while maintaining the goal to restore and protect their homelands from

Japan's further invasion. Arnold's stories reveal pride in his service, and yet his stories cannot be disentangled from ways that outsiders perceived him as an Indian soldier. As a Native man in the army, Arnold paradoxically gained certain privileges afforded to whites while also encountering forms of anti-Indigenous discrimination that were structurally similar to anti-Black discrimination. Arnold navigated these tensions of discrimination and newly afforded privilege. These varied degrees of integration occurred during a time when the United States toted racial unity through propaganda while the American home front maintained Jim Crow and segregated armed forces.[69] During Arnold's interview at his daughter Roxee Booth's house, the flag of an American Indian superimposed upon the US stars and stripes hung on the wall, illustrating how servicemen like Arnold grappled with their commitment to Indigenous nations while in the US military (fig. 10).

Born in 1924 in Metlakatla, Conrad F. Ryan Sr. (Tsimshian) attended the Wrangell Institute boarding school from 1942 until 1944, at which point he joined the US Army.[70] Conrad had deferred his service because of a tuberculosis (TB) epidemic: "Dad got me deferred for six months so I could keep going to school. TB went through town, lot of people died. I had five brothers and sisters that died. I was the only one left. It was hard." In 1944, Conrad joined the army with an abbreviated thirteen weeks of training instead of twenty-three or twenty-six weeks. From there, the US Army sent Conrad to Adak on the Aleutian Islands where he worked night shifts guarding buildings called tundarinas that stored military supplies. He described that while stationed in the Aleutians, Henry Brendible (Tsimshian) from Metlakatla obtained passes to visit Conrad on Adak.

Conrad's stories reveal that segregation directed at various American minorities existed in a variety of formats. Racial minorities recognized these treatments of injustice and saw such actions as emblematic of a racial hierarchy. Conrad remembered military segregation directed at African American servicemen also stationed on Adak in talking about segregation on the base: "Our job was shipping and tundarinas [large Quonset huts with supplies]. There were thirty-six pool halls, we used a jeep to guard it, there were four floors for a gym, eight theaters, two in the tundarinas, two in the Coast Guard, two in the colored section, they wouldn't mix with us."[71] In somewhat contrast to this oral history, in another Alaskan geography—Athabascan territory in Interior Alaska—a letter in the archives by government teacher Oscar Drake of Tanacross identified that soldiers visited the Native village each Friday to dance and also that "another group of soldiers, a medical corp, all colored except the Captain, are also frequent visitors to the village during the week and on Friday night."[72] Here, there is evidence that Black soldiers indeed engaged with Native communities in different Alaskan geographies like Tanacross, even when other regions had military officials who enacted strict anti-Black segregation in social settings.

For Conrad, military segregation proved akin to anti-Native segregation that he had experienced in Ketchikan. Conrad reflected, "I don't know why they did that. They always tell us to stay away from that [segregated] theater. It's the same way they treat us [the Natives]. In Ketchikan we couldn't use the restroom, we had to go down to Jim's Café." Conrad then described Native segregation in Alaska, "Our food was pretty cheap. They put us up in the corner, you walk in the Coliseum in Ketchikan, any hotel wouldn't allow you only [the] New York [Hotel in Ketchikan]. Lot of us didn't stay in town since they hate us." According to Conrad, financial interests brought greater equality to Native people. Conrad thanked activism by Elizabeth Peratrovich (Tlingit) for passage of the 1945 Alaska Equal Rights Act, which fined businesses that discriminated against Indigenous patrons: "They found out we had money. Peratrovich is the one that got the Natives to be equal. She was real good. She had a good speech; it went right down to my heart. She opened doors for us. After WWII it became equal."[73] Here, Conrad identified the importance of Native women's vocal activism and also the watershed of World War II in Alaska.

Earl Wineck's stories about the Alaska Territorial Guard (ATG) in Palmer and his military service in Alaska offer a unique glimpse of integrated schools and military service where soldiers forged social bonds. On a winter day in Anchorage with temperatures hovering at ten below zero, Earl shared stories at the Alaska Veterans Museum about his time in the army. Earl served as a teen member of the ATG in Palmer before he was stationed in Adak through the army.[74] Born in 1927, in Paavola in northern Michigan to a Finnish American family, Earl spoke Finnish as his first language. Earl's family moved to the Palmer colony in 1936. His father helped to build the Kodiak naval base in 1939 and Fort Richardson in 1940.

The Native servicemen at Fort Richardson supplemented their meals at basic training by snaring birds. Earl explained, "We were starving when we were in basic training, they were workin' the heck out of us . . . the guys in our hut . . . would snare a spruce hen or a ptarmigan." Native men shared their food with the others: "They'd cook up us ptarmigan or a spruce hen once in a while, we'd all have a little meat, you know." At this point in the interview, Earl's wife Rebecca remembered how Native men cooked the game meat in their helmet, to which Earl laughed and replied, "You got a helmet which is metal on the outside then you got the helmet liner which you wear. So, you take the liner out, and you got a pot you know. All you need is water and some heat." He reflected, "I mean, they were pretty resourceful guys." Earl recalled amusing times with Native men in the army, including Henry from basic training: "Henry taught me all the bad words, you know, in Yup'ik."

Stories by Alfred "Al" Wright (Athabascan) offer a lens to see how Native men from other Alaskan regions interacted with Unangax̂ resettling on the Aleutian Islands. Al was born in Tanana Crossing in 1925 and grew up in Nenana and Minto. Before joining the army in 1944 at age eighteen, Al worked heavy machinery in Interior Alaska. He attended basic training at Fort Richardson before being transferred to Fort Ord where he experienced, in his words, brainwashing: "Actually what they were doin' was, I didn't know it at the time, but they were just brainwashin' us to get into the war."[75] Al laughed recalling his eagerness to go to battle, "they had us really brainwashed," and with a more serious tone, he explained, "They showed a lot of movies, you know, and then they did everything to make you hate the enemy, you know." At Fort Ord, Al missed being sent behind enemy lines by one day. He recalled, "They sent a lot to England to go over enemy lines in Germany. . . . I had a couple friends that never came back. I missed that by one day."

Al's fate in the army relied on a ship with a secret destination that departed Prince Rupert. Crowded conditions, saltwater showers, and chronic seasickness followed. Al explained, "We had bunk beds . . . in the boat, you had to climb up the bunks to get to the top. Everybody tried to get to the top because somebody'd get sick on the top one and then everybody would get sick all the way down." Equipped with tropical weather gear, Al articulated, "We were supposedly going out to the South Pacific or Philippines, but they wouldn't tell us where we were goin'. So, we were out for ten days and then the boat turned around and headed back for Alaska, and we didn't know it turned around. And we ended up in Adak, in the Aleutians."

Al's time in the Aleutian Islands overlapped with Unangax̂ return to the islands from wartime relocation by the US Navy and government. Al remembered when Unangax̂ returned to Atka: "They all came on one boat. And there was one kid, when they landed them, and there was a tree that some GIS had imported from some place. . . . And it wasn't a very big, just a spruce tree only about four or five feet high. And this little Aleut kid came over there and he says, 'Huh, damned tree,' he says, 'I got a good mind to pull it up.'" The Unangax̂ boy saw how militarization changed his land and how the planting of a non-Native tree represented ecological imperialism and Indigenous displacement of the land.

Al's stories about Atka highlight alliances forged between Al and the Atkans in addition to environmental pollution by the military. The military base resided about a mile from the Atka Native village. According to Al, "[Unangax̂] were just starting to move back in when I got there. And then we were startin' to move everything out of there. And we had, I was loadin' these barges with equipment and stuff and they were haulin' 'em out to sea and dumpin' them overboard. To get rid of it." Al defied these military orders, choosing to aid Unangax̂: "I finally left them [Atkans] about two hundred barrels of fuel . . . there was a brand new D6 CAT that geeze I hated to bury it, they wanted me to bury it, the boat they were dumpin' stuff flat, and so they had to get rid of this gas, and why couldn't they just give it to those people, you know? But they didn't do that . . . they didn't want anything to come back [to] the US from overseas cause it would interrupt the manufacturers' business." Al buried a CAT for Atkans: "I took and dug a hole just as small as I could to get the CAT down in, and then I got a big heavy tarp and covered over the top of it, and then I buried it with mostly moss. And leveled it off a little bit but I was real careful to get on top of it, you know, the hole after I buried it." Al told the Atkans about the CAT, in hopes that they could utilize the equipment that the military sought to destroy.

Native servicemen found ways to support one another and to provide aid even within the confines of a colonial institution such as the military. Al's stories about a friend from King Island who helped him with economic stability and Al's willingness to help the relocated Atkans with equipment, oil, and a CAT illustrate how Native people supported one another, informing interpersonal alliances. When military orders segregated the servicemen from the Atkans, Al nonetheless forged alliances with Atkans. Al recalled, "I was movin' the oil out I was supposed to, you know, crush all the oil barrels and bury them. And then I'd take and send some down to their village cause the guy who was runnin' it he never went up there where we were workin', and so I'd send, you know, a couple of truckloads of oil to the village instead of burying it, and so they ended up with I don't know how many thousand gallon[s] of fuels." In giving oil to the Atkans instead of burying it, Al helped preserve some of the ecology as well. Al recalled financial hardship in the army eased by a Native friend who helped him supplement his income by carving ivory. He explained, "That's when that guy from King Island taught me how to carve the ivory. And he had a bunch of tusks, and so I carved ivory." Although several decades later Al couldn't remember his ivory instructor's name, he specified, "He'd send me ivory, his folks from King Island would send it to him, and then he'd send me some all the time." Al sold these ivory bracelets as souvenirs for ten dollars to GIS who mailed them to their girlfriends in the states. The object, ivory tusks, passed from an Iñupiat family in King Island to their son in the service, to his Athabascan friend (Al) who carved the tusks, to white soldiers, to (presumably) many white women in the contiguous states. More valuable than the ivory was the knowledge bestowed upon Al pertaining to the art of ivory carving. What a gift to teach a friend this trade.

Born in 1927, to an Iñupiaq mother and Norwegian father who worked in the mining industry, Holger "Jorgy" Jorgensen was raised in Haycock and Koyuk. As a teenager, Jorgy joined the ATG in Haycock, and because he knew Morse code, he quickly experienced promotion to sergeant (fig. 11).

When his older sister accepted a waitress job in Nome, Jorgy's whole family moved, and he joined the ATG there. While in Nome, Jorgy partook in the famous Dream Theater sit-in as a planned episode of activism with fellow mixed-race Iñupiaq teenager Alberta Schenck.[76] The two teenagers forced integration of the Dream Theater in 1944 as part of a Native movement to end racial segregation in Alaskan towns. Jorgy's dedication to fighting for equal treatment in Nome during the war years matched his steadfast commitment to military service on Alaskan terrain.

Migrating to South Central Alaska during his wartime travels, Jorgy attended boot camp at Fort Richardson in Anchorage in 1945 and then became a member of the reconnaissance platoon known as the Alaska Scouts. While in the Scouts, Jorgy ventured on multiple missions to rural Alaska by dogsled and boat. Jorgy's knowledge of the Alaskan landscape aligned with the military's mission to find sounding areas in northern Alaska and to map the Yukon-Kuskokwim Delta in 1946. Before that sounding mission, the

FIG. 11. Holger "Jorgy" Jorgensen's Alaska Territorial Guard promotion certificate, 1943. Courtesy of the Jorgensen family photo collection.

FIG. 12. Holger "Jorgy" Jorgensen (center) and two Alaskan Scouts snowed in for days while on a mission. Jorgy explained that the Scouts stayed in the tent until the storm passed. Courtesy of the Jorgensen family photo collection.

Scouts fished from the Cook Inlet region for an entire summer to preserve meals for wintertime. With two other scouts, Jorgy embarked on his journey around the Seward Peninsula. They cached food along their route, mushing along the coast and stopping through Native villages for days at a time to allow their dogs to rest. When the Scouts stopped in towns, the locals held dance parties. Jorgy claimed that some of these Native villages held jitterbug dances for multiple days straight! Native people also held traditional dances. On a more serious note, Jorgy also remembered severe storms in the Arctic that inhibited dogsled travel for days (fig. 12).

After completing his sounding mission around the Seward Peninsula, Jorgy's next mission involved mapping the Yukon-Kuskokwim Delta near Bethel with an eight-person mapping crew.[77] This crew included Sergeant Story, the Huhndorf twins (Fred and Philip), and a Latino soldier named

Perez. Jorgy held a mapping tool, and he recalled, "We did the mapping on the ground. We'd park the boat and bring our gear up, and we did the mapping with, we called 'em 'alladays,' and what they were was something like a transit." During this time, Jorgy found three Japanese bomb balloons. As historian Ross Coen highlights, Japan sent these bomb balloons across the Pacific to instill fear on the American shoreline, yet due to extreme weather, these bomb balloons proved ineffective.[78] Lieutenant General Emmons commanded bomb disposal of the balloons and that any tags be sent to headquarters with detailed reports.[79] Jorgy remembered, "And of course we never found a live one, but we found a lot of these balloons with the nylon rope, and they had really good nylon rope, and we confiscated all the rope off those balloons. Cause, that nylon rope was very, very strong and good, and we used it." Taking fabric, like appropriating resources from the US military to defend an Alaskan homeland, represented ways that Indigenous men's actions shaped an outcome of war in favor of Native land maintenance.

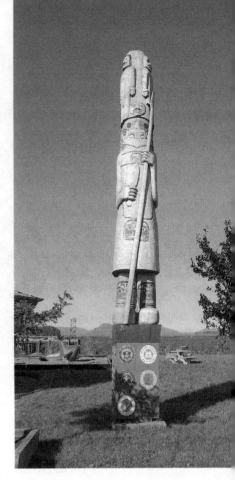

FIG. 13. Totem pole honoring veterans in Metlakatla, October 2017. Photo by the author.

Emblematic of Native appropriations of US military service, fostering an Indigenized service to fit the needs of Native nations, various tribal and public venues have generated memorials for Native servicemen. In Metlakatla, a totem pole honoring veterans marks the shoreline (fig. 13). Similarly, the veteran's exhibit at the Metlakatla Clinic showcases vintage photographs of Metlakatlans, both men and women, who served from World War I up to recent years. The display also shows the continuation of wars throughout the twentieth century.

Many Native organizations including tribal libraries, research centers, museums, and the Alaska Federation of Natives (AFN) have recognized Native service during World War II. In 1998, AFN dedicated its annual convention to Native veterans.[80] In 2017, the Aleut Corporation created a digital archive complete with names, photographs, and short biographies of Unangax̂ servicemen from the eastern Aleutian villages.[81] And, in 2023, AFN curated an exhibit about Native military service. These commemorations demonstrate that military service continues to thrive within an Indigenized identity.

Stories about GIS from the contiguous United States tell an entirely different narrative of Aleutian occupation than those of Unangax̂ and Alaska Native servicemen. Many servicemen from outside Alaska despised the weather, high winds, and mud. Cartoon artists for *The Adakian* military newspaper satirically depicted the GIS as lonely, homesick, cold, windblown, horny, and bored. For Unangax̂, particularly those in the service, they cherished the maintenance of their home islands while they waited for their families to reunite in the Aleutians. Unangax̂ largely dictated the terms of their military service in selecting an alliance to the United States. The Aleutians were a geographic juncture where Unangax̂ could have selected to build alliances with Japan, the initial invaders during the war; the Soviet Union, which Alaska Natives associated with a history of forced labor during the Russian fur trade; or the United States, which offered a newer opportunity to define cross-national relations. At this moment in history, Unangax̂, like other American Indians, allied with the United States because military service presented a way to restore Alaskan homelands while asserting sovereignty.

FOUR
THE ALASKA
TERRITORIAL GUARD
THE INDIGENIZED
GUERRILLA PLATOON

AT ALASKA'S NORTH SLOPE, a place where whales migrate at summertime, and where Iñuit have lived for over ten thousand years, World War II reached the Arctic. Along this northernmost coast, Irene Itta, a young Iñupiaq mother, carried a loaded pistol and extra bullets as she guarded her town of Utqiaġvik (English name Barrow). From eight o'clock in the morning until eight o'clock in the evening she stood on top of a tower while holding and breastfeeding her baby. With the uncertainty of imminent invasion by Japan, she wanted to watch over her town's coastline, reflecting, "We hear seven Japanese planes are coming to bomb [Utqiaġvik], but they freeze and have to turn back."[1] Irene recalled the great blackout of 1942, when the town residents used reindeer skins to cover light seeping from the cracks of their houses. During this time, a guerrilla platoon known as the Alaska Territorial Guard (ATG) requested the help of women from the Barrow Mothers Club to assist with guard duty. With her husband Miles Itta stationed in the US military in Nome, and baby Martina resting inside her parka, Irene volunteered to watch for enemy planes while the men from Utqiaġvik went whaling.[2] In doing so, women like Irene served key roles in defense, allowing Iñupiat to retain their tradition of whaling by maintaining their subsistence lifestyle that keeps their nation alive.

Irene's story, along with those of other women in the ATG, challenges an assumption that Native men were the only ones who served the military on Alaska's landscape. Rarely do we think of war as conjuring images of a young Iñuit mother holding a baby in one arm and a pistol in the other. But women guerrillas defended Alaska, just as they did the Philippines, as shown by historian Stacey Anne Baterina Salinas.[3] In other regions, Soviet women organized and joined what is known as partisans. Women had different reasons for engaging in partisan activities, although their primary goal was to drive out an invader.[4] Irene's story illustrates Native women's motivations for volunteering, even in short episodes, in the ATG. She also expressed pride in her service. "No one knows about it," Irene asserted. "It was never in the papers, not on the radio. I always tell my son, when I die, I want a special ceremony. I want a flag, I want a salute, with the guns, because I served my country in the territorial guard." Guarding is not an insignificant action but rather an assertion to prevent Japan's invasion, otherwise interpreted as pre-planned action to restore equilibrium given the threat of attack.

It would be easy to essentialize Irene's story into one of patriotism during the war. Many sources document Alaska Native patriotism to the United States during World War II.[5] More than exhibiting patriotism to the United States, however, Irene's volunteerism represented a mother who protected her town and ensured that her community's Indigenous subsistence lifestyle of whaling continued during the uncertainty of war. Her story also suggests that Native communities refashioned a colonial organization like the military and amended the ATG platoons to fit their community needs. The ATG therefore represented an Indigenized organization appropriated from the colonial institution of the US military. Irene reflected, "I did it so the people can have a safe place to go." Irene's story reveals that the contributions by Native women during the war proved essential to this strategy. In addition to substituting as scouts, some women joined the ranks of the ATG. Other Native women supported the war effort by designing cold weather gear for the US Army, literally outfitting this military that Native nations chose to ally with while profiting from their sewing skills and using skins from Indigenous sustainable hunting measures.

As this chapter highlights, the ATG as an organization was chosen, designed, and implemented by and for Indigenous Alaskan communities during the war. Several factors indicate that the ATG represented an Indigenized organization, such as inclusion by age with the elderly and youth, relatively fluid gender enrollment that proved particularly high in some towns, the maintenance of the subsistence lifestyle that propelled physical and cultural survival during US colonization, and Unangax̂ participation after relocation. For Alaska Natives, equilibrium restoration meant selective allyship with the US military, accepting their guns on Indigenous terms, and appropriating the US military to fit an Indigenized agenda. Here, equilibrium restoration did not mean defying the US military but rather using the organization and tools provided by the US military to protect Native lands from Japan's invasion. This understanding of the ATG restructures our understanding of Indigenous agency to show that Indigenous peoples appropriate colonial structures, like the US military and guns, all while asserting their political sovereignty. Ultimately, the Indigenized nature of the ATG threatened US colonial efforts to control Alaska through the military. Because of anti-Native discrimination by military officials, the US military disbanded the ATG in 1946. Yet, even with the termination of the ATG program, the ATG laid the foundation for Indigenous volunteerism in the Alaska National Guard in the decades that followed, where "Iñuit Scouts" (formerly called "Esk*mo Scouts") persisted as an entity into the Cold War.

The war represented the first time in Alaskan history that the United States and Indigenous Alaskans allied with each other on a nation-to-nation basis.[6] After Japan's invasion of the Aleutian Islands of Attu and Kiska in June 1942, the US military supplied guns to Native peoples to prevent further coastal invasion by Japan. While it is important to highlight that the United States supplied guns to Alaska Natives, it is equally necessary to understand why Alaska Natives chose to accept guns from the United States and to build an alliance with the United States. Truly, the ATG formed once Indigenous people accepted the format of the guerrilla platoons in creating an organization that fit the needs of Native people on their homelands.

While they primarily fought to secure their homeland, Native scouts have historically played a prevalent role in expanding US empire across the American West. As Indigenous peoples are sovereign and they possess the authority to wage war and to ally with other militaries, Indigenous nations elected to serve in the US military as scouts to defeat or thwart an enemy. During World War II, Alaska Natives scouted for the US military to prevent Japanese invasion on their homelands.

Using the ATG as an organizing structure to link Native nations across the landscape, Alaska Natives protected over 5,200 miles of Alaskan coastline. In July 1944, records show 287 officers and 4,427 enlisted volunteers in the ATG.[7] In total, 6,000 joined the ranks of the ATG, and they patrolled the coastline.[8] As experts of the Alaskan territory, Iñuit, both Iñupiat and Yupiit, accounted for a high percentage of the ATG.[9] The exact number might not be available by tallying the names from Major Marvin "Muktuk" Marston's book *Men of the Tundra*. This is because a village roster might also include a white teacher or BIA employee and their race was not labeled on the roster. Additionally, the roster did not contain names like Irene Itta's, those who volunteered but remain unlisted in official documents. In other regions of Alaska, like the Palmer colony north of Anchorage, a larger membership of Euro-Americans made up the ATG. For the purposes of understanding the Indigenous adoption of colonial structures, this chapter focuses on the experiences of the ATG within predominantly Native communities.

Iñuit chose to join the ATG because they saw Major Marston as an ally to their nations. Initially, Marston appointed colonists including white missionaries, teachers, and storekeepers as leaders of the ATG. Observing failures in organizing under white leadership, Marston re-evaluated his position. Major General John Schaeffer (Iñupiaq) from Kotzebue joined the Iñuit Scouts in 1957, and he articulated that Marston recognized his flaw in originally assigning white leadership during World War II, explaining, "[Marston] fired most of them [the previous white leaders] and appointed the real leaders. He put the Natives in charge, and he built armories so the men had a place to meet."[10] As an institution, the ATG became successful and widespread because Iñuit found Marston to be an endearing alliance and they chose to accept the ATG within their own communities.[11]

Members of the ATG had special assigned tasks across Western and coastal Alaska. ATG outposts spanned terrain inaccessible by roads where only dog-sleds provided access. Duties of the guerrillas included aiding the army in evacuating civilian populations, providing access through mountain passes and river crossings, arranging food in designated caches, reporting sightings of Japanese planes, identifying Japanese bomb balloons that crashed on Alaskan shores, and capturing enemy invaders.[12]

Indigenizing the Alaska Territorial Guard

Native nations seized the opportunity to adopt the ATG as an organization, after recognizing Marston as an intermediary who met them on Indigenous ground and on Iñuit terms. This is contrary to an assumption that privileges a narrative identifying Marston as a white leader of Iñuit scouts. ATG members came from Native villages, fishing villages, mining camps, homesteads, trading posts, and from the army, and Marston identified this as his "Guerrilla Plan."[13] When Iñuit met with Marston, they exercised their diplomacy. For example, ATG organizer Samuel Davis bestowed gifts when meeting with Marston, indicating a relationship of diplomacy between Iñupiat and Marston (fig. 14). These exchanges represented a contract between Native leaders like Davis and Marston who acted for the US military while physically don-

FIG. 14. "Muktuk" Marston (left) with Alaska Territorial Guard leader Samuel Davis (right), ca. 1945. Otto Geist Collection, box 5, folder 85, UAF-1964-098-N. Courtesy of the Archives at University of Alaska Fairbanks.

FIG. 15. The age of Alaska Territorial Guard members ranged from a youth member marching in front to elders following in formation. Vern Brickley Collection, Anchorage Museum, B1998.014.1.2648.

ning clothing made by Native women. Highlighting Marston's adaptability, Iñupiat endearingly called Marston "Muktuk Marston," as he could eat as much maktak (whale blubber) as Iñupiat in Point Hope. Few white men had accomplished this feat during a time when settlers and colonizers deemed Indigenous foods as too gamey for Western tastes.[14] Marston served as an intermediary who recognized and valued Iñuit on their own terms. He complied with Native people by feasting on maktak with them, wearing cold weather gear made by Native women, and accepting a playful nickname.

ATG ranks accepted US citizens aged sixteen and older, although at times included younger youth. Reportedly, a fourteen-year-old boy from Wales enrolled, as did a twelve-year-old from Haycock. Governor Gruening himself wrote that when he toured Iñuit nuna (land), he enlisted a boy after observing the boy carrying four ptarmigan draped from his rifle.[15] In addition to teenagers, the elderly joined the ranks of the ATG (fig. 15). A photograph

FIG. 16. Two elderly men carve harpoons as an Alaska Territorial Guard guardsman observes. Notice the ATG badge on the carver's parka sleeve. "Alaska Territorial Guard two men sitting on ground working on a harpoon/spear." Herb Hilscher Collection, Anchorage Museum, B1999.014.246.

of elder members of the ATG taking a break to carve harpoons is evidence that drills and membership in the ATG aligned with maintaining customary activities (fig. 16).

Inclusion by age and gender reveals that the ATG fit an Indigenous framework. While women's names do not account for 50 percent of names on the ATG rosters, stories such as Irene Itta's reveal that Native women played a key role in the organization. As historian Lael Morgan argues, the "kashgee," a traditional meeting hall for men, allowed Iñuit to seamlessly adopt the ATG within their communities.[16] Undoubtedly, Native women coordinated their own spaces, deciding whether to support the ATG or to share information with one another, like how to formalize contracts with the United States to sell Arctic clothing.

As an example of the role of women leaders in the ATG and Marston's acceptance of this gender inclusion, Margaret "Megee" Panigeo (Iñupiaq) served as the ATG sergeant in Koyuk until the army discovered her gender and dropped her from the official roster.[17] Originally from Utqiaġvik, Megee attended school outside Alaska, returning to teach in Utqiaġvik, Wainwright, and Gambell.[18] Marston identified Megee as the sergeant and also the best English speaker in town who acted as a translator between English and Iñupiatun.[19] Marston could not have simply named Megee as the ATG sergeant; the town must have endorsed her in choosing to follow her command. To thwart the army from discovering her gender, Marston enrolled her as "M. Panigeo." By concealing her gender from the army, Marston complied with the Indigenous-led organization to retain Megee as the ATG leader. However, when the army discovered that the "M" stood for "Margaret," they struck her from the roster. The removal of her name shows how colonial structures attempted to control Indigenous organizations and nations, in this case by devaluing Native women's inclusion as recognized leaders in their communities. One must wonder if—even with her name dropped from the roster—the town of Koyuk continued to recognize Megee Panigeo as the ATG sergeant, which they likely did without care for Western documentation on the matter.

As the postal worker who ran a dogsled team, Laura Beltz Hagberg Wright (Iñupiaq) navigated the landscape and weather with knowledge of a network of Iñupiaq communities. No man, neither Native nor settler, possessed this same knowledge. Laura, a mother from Haycock, reportedly "handle[d] rifles better than any man."[20] Marston recalled that when he traveled through Candle with Iñupiaq guide Samuel "Sammy" Mogg (from Nome), Laura asked if they wanted ptarmigan for supper. She then stepped outside her doorway, shot three times, and retrieved eight ptarmigan.[21] Marston reported that during shooting practice with the ATG, Laura shot forty-nine bull's-eyes out of fifty. In addition to mothering four children (at that time—she would have six total), Laura administered the mail route between villages by dog team, she snared rabbits, and she caught fish for her dogs. While it appears her primary role as a mailcarrier served the US government as an employee, she acted as a powerful link in generating Indigenous information networks between Native villages, which proved essential to maintaining homeland defense. In later life, she would be best remembered for designing parkas and patenting Laura Wright Alaskan Parkys.[22]

In towns such as Kotzebue, Iñupiat women were at least 25 percent of the ATG. According to the official roster, out of 109 enlisted in the ATG in Kotzebue, at least twenty-nine are women's names.[23] More than merely a list, the names of the women from Kotzebue supply further evidence of gender inclusion in the ATG. Such numbers indicate that Iñupiat rejected the US practice of only enrolling men as scouts. Women's names listed on the ATG roster in Kotzebue include Dora Adams, Mabel L. Berryman, Hazel Flood, Rosa E. Francis, Eva Glover, Kate Green, Laura Gregg, Annie M. Hartman, Priscilla G. Hensley, Dora Hess, Pauline Howarth, Susie Hunnicutt, Gertrude Ituk, Jess[i]e May Lee, Blanche Rose Lincoln, Olivia Neville McClellan, Ida S. Morris, Margaret Ella Quinn, Norma R. Reich, Isabelle Riley, Lydia G. Savok, Annie Curtis Scott, Genevieve Nancy Sheldon, Edna V. Todhunter, Irene Todhunter, Laura O. Washington, Evelyn Weber, Rachel C. Wilson, and Martha G. Woods.[24] Perhaps Kotzebue was one of the only places that actually listed women participants on the roster; there might have been other Alaskan villages with women scouts, but those women were not listed on the official roster, including the likes of young mother Irene Itta who guarded the shoreline during whaling season on behalf of the Barrow Mothers Club.

The military valued Native women's labor and practical fashion, allowing Native women the opportunity to integrate their traditional knowledge and a unique skillset for profit while maintaining the subsistence lifestyle. Poorly equipped for the Arctic, the US Army relied upon Native women who designed cold weather gear fashioned after traditional Iñuit clothing. With the knowledge passed down from generations of Indigenous women, special care went into each item. For example, Native women chewed fabrics to soften hides to make them durable in an unforgiving Arctic climate. Over five hundred Native women made mittens, mukluks, moccasins, snowshoes, and cold weather gear.[25] The Associated Press reported that over two hundred Iñuit women produced 5,000 sealskin parkas for the army valued at over $100,000.[26] Adjusted to today's inflation rate this equates to $1.69 million in contract labor.[27] In February 1940, army officials contracted with the Nome Skin and Sewers Cooperative Association (NSSCA), an organization owned by Alaska Natives under the Indian Reorganization Act, and requested eighty reindeer parkas and forty-eight pairs of mukluks for cold weather gear.[28] In August 1940, the army contracted another 6,396 mukluks, 365 reindeer parkas, 150 sealskin trousers, and future orders of mittens, snowshoes, caps, and fur socks.[29] By 1941, officials recorded 115 trousers made by the NSSCA, as well as 150 parkas, 2,100 mukluks, and boxes with socks, mittens, and caps. World War II army veteran and ATG veteran Holger "Jorgy" Jorgensen (Iñupiaq) described that his mother made clothing for the NSSCA, such as mukluks, sealskin pants, parkas, and mittens, sold to the US military.[30]

These contracts represent not only business exchanges but also total military reliance on Native women for Arctic gear that no one else could have manufactured. In addition, the contract relationship with Native cooperatives organized under the Indian Reorganization Act reveals that the federal government and the military recognized the sovereign rights of Alaska Natives. In this setting, Native women's labor provided the basis of these contracts agreed upon by sovereign Native nations and the US military. Additionally, the furs and skins could only be produced by Indigenous hunting practices. When hunters in the community supplied meat and animal skins, women processed furs fashioning Arctic gear.

Cold weather gear could be taken anywhere, and items made and designed by Native women allowed a mobile Indigenous identity to flourish. As an example, one Native serviceman brought his mukluks overseas, holding them as a mnemonic device. Richard Frank (Athabascan) was born in 1927 from Minto, and he followed his older brother enlisting in the US Army Air Force at the age of seventeen.[31] He later advocated for land claims and helped found the Alaska Native Veterans Association. During his send-off from Minto, an elder woman gave him a special item. While enroute to Anchorage for basic training, he opened the gift and found handmade fur-lined moose-skin mukluks. Those mukluks gave him a sense of purpose, belonging, and comfort from home. During challenging times, Frank held his mukluks and he recalled, "I just look at them." The handmade mukluks signify community support for Native men who left for the unknown while carrying along their Indigenous identities. Such is the power of traditional craftsmanship, where in addition to being expert seamstresses and designers, Native women indeed supported Native servicemen emotionally through these mnemonic devices.

Far from completely invisible, Native women's presence, like that of Irene Itta, emerges in other contexts, even when they are not photographed or documented. For example, in a photograph of Samuel Davis and Private Felix Bolt handshaking and collaborating on training between the ATG and the formal structure of the US military with the armed forces, Native women are absent but their unique skills as parka and mukluk makers are front and center (fig. 17). Private Felix Bolt, who appears to be wearing all Western gear and a military uniform, wore mukluks made by Native women. Davis, a leader of the ATG, dons a Western hat, pants, and sunglasses rather than ilgaak (Iñuit snow goggles), yet he sports a sealskin parka and mukluks. The foot attire and cold weather gear worn by these two Iñuit men in the military would not have been possible without Iñuit women. The photo actually highlights the behind-the-scenes nature of Native women's contributions to the war effort, much like the story of Irene Itta whose name is absent from the official ATG roster.

In addition to supplying cold weather gear and volunteering for the ATG in their communities, some Native women held the power to authorize ATG formation. Mrs. Billie, a medicine woman from Teller, held the power to approve or disapprove of village activities. With such power, Mrs. Billie decided whether the ATG could fit within their community. Accordingly, when Marston visited Teller, he gave Mrs. Billie a bottle of perfume to gain her favor.[32] This story shows that in certain communities like Teller, Native women held authority that white men, like Marston, recognized and valued. Thus, Mrs. Billie held power over not only the community but also military officials like Marston. There are likely other towns where medicine women held power in deciding the fate of the ATG and village activities.

Just as gender enrollment in some villages proved more fluid than oth-

FIG. 17. Two Native Alaska Territorial Guard leaders meet to collaborate on training, July 1945. "A16 4-889-45 Samuel Davis, the [N]ative host of the Naluka-taq, greets Pvt Felix Bolt, the Alaskan Dept representative whose job it is to train the [N]ative men at Point Hope in military tactics. Felix Bolt is a [N]ative of Wainwright." Photo by Walter T. Smith, Vern Brickley Collection, Anchorage Museum, B1998.014.1.11939.

erwise recorded, the organization of the ATG proved fluid too. Native men molded the ATG to fit migrations in accordance with the subsistence lifestyle. While some ATG units drilled daily, others retained flexibility. This variation highlights that each ATG unit organized according to the unique needs of their community. In Chaneliak, for example, ATG activities ceased during hunting or fishing season.[33] As in other regions across Alaska, the subsistence lifestyle and survival remained central and prioritized above ATG activities.

Native men adjusted the expectations of the ATG headquarters in Nome to form an organization that fit their community's needs. Alex Okitkun (Yup'ik), a member of the Chaneliak ATG, wrote letters to Otto Geist of the Nome headquarters to transfer ATG units. In April 1946, Okitkun wrote about the Chaneliak ATG: "After this Easter is over I think it will be very few men here and will be hard to do anything as they have no food. All men are going out seal hunting and some are going to work in cannery very soon I understand to let you know that I am going to fishing in south mouth of Yukon will be gone for June and July. I do my best in our A.T.G."[34] Okitkun indicated a pattern where ATG members dispersed for jobs and subsistence migrations, yet members reconvened after subsistence activities. The ATG functioned secondary to the baseline of community survival.[35]

Other Native men utilized their ATG service to gain financial support from the federal government for their families. Robert Mayokok (Iñupiaq), from Wales, is perhaps best known as an artist. In December 1946, since he struggled with tuberculosis as a single parent, Mayokok stepped down as ATG captain.[36] He pleaded to the governor for medical assistance highlighting his previous role as an interpreter: "Whenever government people come and needed interpreter I always glad to give my service free. I with the government do likewise and help me and my family." Mayokok tried holding the government accountable in assisting him as payment for his previous work as an interpreter. Here, his ATG service provided leverage for him to advocate to the government that they listen to his case and consider supporting his family.

As further evidence that Alaska Natives accepted the ATG as more than a military institution, the ATG organized community celebrations for Native social life. In Nome, the ATG had a baseball team that met each Friday evening; hosted dance parties with live music; and held Fourth of July races and activities, Christmas events, and the traditional Iñuit blanket toss (fig. 18). Native people danced, drummed, and sang at military bases in Fairbanks and Anchorage, thereby claiming the space as an Indigenized one (figs. 19–21). In her book *Sound Relations*, musician scholar Jessica Bissett Perea (Dena'ina) identifies the centrality of music in expressing Indigenous government, delving "into histories of Iñuit musical life in Alaska to amplify the broader significance of sound as integral to Indigenous self-determination and resurgence movements."[37] Historian Jenny Tone-Pah-Hote (Kiowa) articulates that "expressive culture" including song, "regalia, adornment, figural art, and dance" provided an avenue to exercise autonomy and to

FIG. 18. Native girl participates in the Iñuit blanket toss. Vern Brickley Collection, Anchorage Museum, B1998.014.1.1336. (Image has been cropped.)

FIG. 19. Native men take center stage at a USO social event in Fairbanks, wearing uniforms and mukluks. "Esk*mo Native Dances," "taken at the 'Native USO' in Fairbanks," February 23, 1944. Courtesy of the Alaska State Library, Evan Hill Photo Collection, ASL-P343-627.

FIG. 20. Native servicemen dance at the USO in Fairbanks. Notice the Indigenization of this space where they took the drum from the Ladd Army Airfield and used it to sing their songs. "Esk*mo Native Dances," February 23, 1944. Courtesy of the Alaska State Library, Evan Hill Photo Collection, ASL-P343-632.

FIG. 21. Native women dance at the USO in Fairbanks. Their dances appear to blend traditional dances with the jitterbug. "Esk*mo Native Dances," February 23, 1944. Courtesy of the Alaska State Library, Evan Hill Photo Collection, ASL-P343-633.

preserve Native nationhood.[38] While Iñuit dances at the Ladd Army Airfield and the USO look performative in nature, they marked an expression of Indigeneity, Native rights to occupy space, and Native nationhood despite swiftly expanding colonization on their homelands. The inclusion of both Iñuit men and women in the dances shows that Native people kept their traditions and social structures intact. This occurred during a time when some village missionaries banned Native dances outright, such as in Unalakleet.

Yet alongside the story about Alaska Native acceptance of the ATG and an Indigenous social life within the ATG, a parallel story exists regarding US military officials who held biases against the guerrilla platoons made up primarily of Native people. Perhaps the public displays of Indigeneity indeed challenged the overall colonial structure of the military that at least historically—based on the Indian Wars—sought to render Natives into passive colonized subjects rather than sovereign nations with allied militia who exerted themselves on urban and militarized Indigenous landscapes.

The Indigenous Organization Confronts Racial Biases

At the very top of the Alaska Defense Command, General Simon Bolivar Buckner opposed the status of the ATG, and he held racial biases against not only Indigenous peoples but also African Americans in segregated platoons in Alaska. Alongside anti-Indigeneity, he espoused anti-Blackness. He feared that African American troops would settle in Alaska after the war and "interbreed with the Indians and Esk*mos and produce an astonishingly objectionable race of mongrels which would be a problem from here now on."[39] Buckner's father had served in the Confederate army. He showed no restraint objecting to interracial dating—a pattern also displayed by other US military commanders around the world during and after World War II. While he relied on both the ATG and the segregated platoons of African American servicemen in Alaska, Buckner vocally opposed minority servicemen. According to Governor Gruening, Buckner welcomed the ATG initially so it could cover guard duty and not dispose of troops Buckner wanted for defensive and offensive operations.[40] Discrimination by military officials indeed impacted the lives of ATG members inducted into the service.

When former ATG member Herbert Lawrence committed suicide, other Native servicemen reported abuse directed at Lawrence from the army and the Alaska Defense Command. Felix Bolt of Wainwright, Eddie Hopson of Utqiaġvik, Fred Katchatag of Unalakleet, James Starbuch of Deering, Bill O'Leary of Fairbanks, and Lloyd Blakenship of Kiana coordinated with Marston in filing a report to the Judge Advocate's Office on behalf of Lawrence. The army refused to pay Lawrence per diem for delays in the weather and ignored him when he complained of severe stomach pain. In addition to this, "he and the other [N]ative instructors had been refused all privileges and confined to their quarters and in many respects treated as criminal suspects."[41] Criminalized and denied healthcare, while alone in his barracks Lawrence shot himself. In his suicide note, he instructed for his war bonds to go to his sister in Mountain Village and for his personal effects to go to his father on the Yukon. Perhaps ironically or indicating the complex relationship he felt with the US military as an institution that levied discrimination onto him, he ended his note with "God bless the army."

Other forms of discrimination directed at the ATG emerged as ATG sergeants were prevented from advancing in the broader US military. According to Marston, certain military authorities held some Native men in boot camp, training them up to three times and preventing privates from the ATG from advancing. Some of these men had been sergeants in the ATG, yet the military kept them perpetually in basic training.[42] Discrimination by white civilians also prevented some ATG units from accessing guns. Some white missionaries, like one white woman who also worked as the postmistress in Wales, feared arming Natives.[43] One has to wonder if she held racial biases against Natives or if Natives had a reason to arm themselves from her presence in town.

With a decision rooted in racial bias, army general Delos Carleton Emmons ordered the ATG to disband in late 1946.[44] Perhaps conveniently, this occurred after the war with Japan. Baffled by this decision and revealing that he recognized the sovereignty Native nations held, at various points calling their land the Iñuit (Esk*mo) empire, Marston resigned, and he declared that colonial exploiters feared Native organization and Native economic independence.[45] Marston's sentiment here proves that he was more of an ally to Native political organization and economic independence than he has received credit for. The Alaskan Department caved to civilian white sources who tried to dissolve the ATG.[46] And yet, after these formal institutional terminations, the ATG evolved into something new that Native nations continued to utilize.

In 1949, Marston helped establish the Alaska National Guard with an encampment at Fort Richardson for the Iñuit scout battalion.[47] The Alaska National Guard's 1st and 2nd Scout Battalions, 297th Infantry consisted of Iñuit volunteers from over sixty-five Arctic and subarctic villages.[48] The Alaska National Guard enlisted Native men who previously volunteered for Alaska's military.[49] These scout battalions hailing from Arctic nations reaffirmed Iñuit commitment to allying with the United States during the Cold War era. The Alaska State Defense Force, which was renamed in 1987 from the Alaska State Guard that formed in 1984, desended from the original ATG. Yet Marston's role in history is more complicated, as he initiated jade mining in northern Alaska, including "hundreds of tons of jade . . . shipped out of the Arctic of Alaska."[50] The history of allyship and colonization during imperialism is indeed complicated, as to date—broadly speaking—Iñuit maintain fond memories of Marston and his legacy of partnership and as an intermediary to the US military and government.

Arctic military training and the establishment of the US military in the Arctic could not have been accomplished without Indigenous incorporation of the military. As both Native leaders and allies like Marston recognized, numerous military projects relied on Indigenous aid. When advocating for Native land claims, Joseph Upicksoun, former president for the Arctic Slope Native Association, highlighted the role of Alaska Natives in the ATG, explaining, "Once upon a time, we had World War II, and the United States was worried about the Arctic. It sent its soldiers up there for defense. They flunked, because the Army didn't even know how to dress or live or survive."[51] The word *dress* here is an implicit nod to the Native women who labored to outfit the troops in the north. Upicksoun underscored how Natives chose to lead the United States in defense: "We were the security of the United States, and we were proud that through the years and today we are the only units in the world who can provide such security." Truly, the army relied upon these alliances with Alaska Native nations.

Oral Histories with Former ATG Members

Oral history interviews with elders from Utqiaġvik, who transitioned from the ATG to the Alaska National Guard, illustrate continued US military occupation into the Cold War with the Soviet Union. In 2017, at the Iḷisaġvik Tribal College's Tuzzy Consortium Library in Utqiaġvik, Wesley Ugiaqtaq Aiken, an Iñupiaq elder born in 1926 from Alaska's North Slope, recalled stories about his youth when he learned how to hunt from family. During his early adolescence, he worked for the BIA as a reindeer herder. For three years, he migrated with the reindeer never seeing his home or family during that time. When he returned to Utqiaġvik at the age of eighteen, he joined the ATG.[52] He described the ATG upon enrolling: "We had no uniform, you know at the time, just wear our clothes and all we had was a rifle. M-1 they call it, with a bayonet, that's all we have, you know for Alaska Territorial Guard." Ugiaqtaq remembered daily drills, recalling, "Our rifle, we just clean 'em up, cut 'em apart, and clean 'em up then put 'em back you know those rifles." From 1953 to 1970, he served in the Alaska National Guard defending the Alaskan coastline and attending annual training in Anchorage.[53] He explained, "In Alaska Army National Guard we go to Anchorage for trainings. Once a year in April, you know we do that every year." He drove officers with a jeep for Company D. Ugiaqtaq's motivations in serving in the military stemmed from his interest in serving the Utqiaġvik community.

According to Ugiaqtaq, his active duty in the ATG followed by his twenty years of service in Utqiaġvik in the Alaska National Guard allowed him to retain a hunting lifestyle to support his family. When asked why he decided to join the National Guard, Ugiaqtaq replied, "I don't know, probably wanted to raise a family." He laughed, then continued, "that's how, hunt. That's why I decided to be a hunter." At the height of his hunting career, Ugiaqtaq served as a whaling captain. He and the other captains had an exceedingly successful whale hunt in retrieving three whales in just one week. When I asked Ugiaqtaq if he still hunts today, he laughed and responded, "I'm getting too old. Ninety-one there, you can't do nothing. You know? Oh, I got lots of nieces and nephews took care of me, gave me fresh meat right to my house and whenever they got some fresh meat. That's how I live now." Just as he took care of the community as a former whaling captain, they watched him as an elder. Before he passed away in 2019, Ugiaqtaq served as a tribal veteran representative through the Alaska VA Healthcare System, where he assisted veterans in securing state and federal benefits.[54] For Ugiaqtaq, Indigenous equilibrium restoration meant using the military to support a Native lifestyle that could not be bound by a forty-hour-week Western job.

In addition to serving the community as a lifelong hunter and whaler, Ugiaqtaq lobbied in Washington, DC, for Native land claims, and he participated in the Barrow duck-in protest in 1961.[55] During this protest, Iñupiat refused compliance with the Migratory Bird Treaty Act of 1918 which prohibited the killing or harvesting of certain migratory birds. This colonial act demonstrated anti-Indigeneity by trying to prevent Native people from hunting on their own lands where these birds represented Indigenous foods for survival. To protest, each Iñupiat man in town shot and presented a bird to the federal agent, thereby asserting food sovereignty and tribal sovereignty. As the federal government could not arrest the whole town, Iñupiat won a revision to the Migratory Bird Treaty Act. Ironically these birds likely even fed government officials. In protesting the federal law, Iñupiat maintained equilibrium where their land, animal, and environmental resources remained under Iñupiat domain.

David Ungrudruk Leavitt Sr. also served in the ATG and the Alaska National Guard in Utqiaġvik. He was born in Cape Halkett in 1929, and when he was fourteen years old, his family moved to Utqiaġvik. Ungrudruk is the grandson of the famed whaling captain George Leavitt, a mariner from Maine who traveled north for commercial whaling at the turn of the century. George Leavitt met and married Ungrudruk's grandmother, an Iñupiaq woman named Nanouk Elguchiaq. Ungrudruk shared fond memories about watching the ATG practice. He laughed when he remembered Sergeant Bert Panigeo marching the ATG into the lagoon: "He go into the lagoon over there, that lagoon over there. Heading that way, really heading, some of them using on the mukluk you know, real dry on the ground. And they go in on the water!"[56] Amused, Ungrudruk continued, "He forgot to two or three march, they forgot it!" Perhaps Sergeant Panigeo forgot the English words to command the unit. Ungrudruk then thoughtfully remembered that Sergeant Panigeo accepted his paperwork to join the ATG at age seventeen. While in the ATG, he learned about the water and how to use his rifle from Eddie Hopson, who was an instructor for the ATG.

Ungrudruk smiled when he remembered Marston. According to Ungrudruk, when Marston visited Utqiaġvik to help with drills, Marston brought a reindeer skin that he would roll out to sleep on the floor of any host house. In 2014, on his Honor Flight, facilitated by the nonprofit national organization that flies US veterans to Washington, DC to visit memorials for the wars they served in, Ungrudruk met other Native veterans on the plane, and according to him they became fast friends after realizing they all knew Marston. Indeed, many veterans recalled Marston with fondness, indicating that Iñupiat accepted Marston as someone to form an alliance between Native nations and the United States.

Returning to their homelands after relocation, Unangax̂ men joined the ATG to protect their lands. Andronik Kashevarof from St. George Island was born in 1927, and after wartime relocation, he served in the ATG. At age fourteen he joined the group of forced laborers who harvested seal pelts to profit the US government. Andronik recalled, "In the sealing, I was a watchman. You watch the seals before they kill them, keep them in one whole big bunch, yeah. There were clubbers, there were skinners, there were pullers, you pull the skin off."[57] When Unangax̂ returned to the Pribilof Islands in 1944, Andronik joined the ATG at age sixteen. He explained, "There was about forty to forty-five men in the ATG that time. Even old men who were in their sixties." Andronik continued, "Yeah, right now I'm eighty-eight. I've seen all my uncles, friends, that were in that ATG Master Guard. One of my friends called it: ATG 'Andronik to Garbage' [laughs]." Native humor is indeed clever. Andronik's daughter Bonnie clarified that his friends teased him because he was one of the youngest members accepted into the ATG on St. George Island. The nickname, "Andronik to Garbage" could stem from jealous peers, or perhaps it tells another story of forms of youth resistance to the military.

Andronik's story about a gun provided by the military again shows that Native people adopted an element of Westernization and repurposed it to suit Native subsistence practices. Andronik recalled, "The guns were 1917. Something like that, it had some kind of small writing on the guns, '1917.' . . . I used to keep my gun polished all the time, hang it to the door just in case. There were three guns there in my house at that time, my stepbrother, my papa, and me." Andronik chuckled, "Oh my mother used to be mad." Andronik and his family never fired the guns in defense; instead, they used the guns for hunting sea lions.

The act of using guns provided by the military for subsistence provides further evidence that Native people appropriated tools of violence from the military. ATG units received guns and ammunition for drills, and some units received limited supplies of World War I–era military equipment. Whether the United States intended it or not, giving guns to Natives symbolized US recognition of Native nations. For Native nations, perhaps receiving guns symbolized a physical contract of forging of alliances between their nations and the United States. The adoption of the gun for hunting reveals Indigenous adaptability in using Western tools to fit Native lifestyles.

Like Andronik Kashevarof, other Unangax̂ men joined the ATG when they returned to the Aleutians from relocation camps in Southeast Alaska. During an interview with Nicholai Lekanoff and his daughter Patty Lekanoff-Gregory, Nicholai shared stories about Unalaska before evacuation, his experience at the camps in Southeast Alaska, and his service in the Alaska National Guard in the postwar years.[58] Born in 1925, in the Native village of Makushin on Unalaska Island, Nicholai witnessed the bombing of Dutch Harbor from June 3–4, 1942. Housing damage and the federal government's failure to return Unangax̂ to the village of Makushin resulted in Nicholai's village becoming a ghost town.[59] When he returned to Dutch Harbor, Nicholai joined the ATG in 1946 as a patrolman. He reminisced that he proudly served the Alaska National Guard while living in Dutch Harbor. While it is difficult to identify equilibrium restoration in Nicholai's life, as he survived a relocation camp and could never return to Makushin, Nicholai did indeed select the National Guard likely as a way to prevent further upheaval to his family and community during the Cold War.

After he survived World War II relocation, General Jake Lestenkof (Unangax̂) dedicated his life to military service, the BIA, and Alaskan businesses. Born in 1932 on St. George Island, Jake remembered relocation at Funter Bay. After his mother became ill and passed away, his grandparents took him to Juneau.[60] In 1946, Jake attended the Wrangell Institute boarding school and then transferred to Mt. Edgecumbe High School. While at Mt. Edgecumbe, he took one year off to work as a merchant marine mariner. When I asked what sparked his interest in becoming a deck officer, Jake replied, "I don't know, you know it was probably related to the fact that the islands are very maritime oriented and ships became an important part I think of our lives, because that's how our connection to the outside world and growing up in the Pribilofs was through ships."

In 1951, Jake enlisted in the Marines serving in the Korean War. Upon returning to the United States after serving in a rifle company in Korea, Jake converted to the army when he enlisted in the National Guard and served on active duty until 1974. Jake described his eventual work for the Alaska BIA as area director from 1981 until 1988 and his continued service to the National Guard as a brigadier general and the assistant adjutant general for the Alaska Army National Guard. Jake described his work through the military and the BIA as separate from the FWS that formerly controlled the Pribilof Islands and Unangax̂ labor. Perhaps as an assertion of equilibrium restoration spanning his lifetime, Jake took control of the very bureaucratic organizations that formerly relocated Natives; in doing so, he exercised power in helping to foster Indigenous representation and perspective to these colonial organizations. On the importance of Native education, *Tribal College* reported Jake as stating that "tribal colleges are the gateway for the future of Indian reservations."[61]

Native groups have a legacy of service in the military, and for some individuals this dates to the ATG. Many people remember their fathers, brothers, and relatives in the ATG and the Alaska National Guard. Al Sahlin (Iñupiaq), born in 1933, remembered being a member of the junior ATG in Nome.[62] He explained, "We were the messengers and ammo carriers. 'Hey boy, I need this, I need that.' We ran errands. I was nine or ten years old." Al described that in the junior ATG they received wooden rifles, and they marched and practiced other drills. At age seventeen, Al joined the Alaska Army National Guard in 1951 in Nome. During the Cold War, Al listened to radio reports, and he shared information with G-2 Intelligence at Fort Richardson.

Frank Degnan (Yup'ik), from Unalakleet, served as a lieutenant in the ATG. He later served as the Alaska Federation of Natives (AFN) sergeant at arms, and after being elected in 1951, he worked as the first Yup'ik legislator in the Alaska Territorial Legislature.[63] Chris Wooley and Mike Martz contend that the ATG fostered leadership qualities in Alaskan villages and that ATG members actively participated in Alaskan political movements in the 1950s and 1960s.[64] Frank Degnan's daughter, June Degnan, remembered the time her father returned home with an ATG badge on his shoulder. When June asked her father what the badge meant, he replied, "Alaska's Tough Guy."[65]

Irwin Bahr (Iñupiaq and Sami), from Unalakleet, remembered his father in the ATG and how he and other children observed ATG practice. Irwin recounted, "We were a bunch of kids, you know, following them around town. They were serious about it. It was just comical to us. They were serious and they did a good job, if they thought the Japanese would appear, but they never did."[66] Childhood perspectives, like Irwin's, reflect that children experienced amusement watching the officialness of ATG drills (fig. 22). After Irwin attended Mt. Edgecumbe High School, he joined the Marine Corps in 1955. When asked why he selected the service, he responded, "There wasn't anything here. No jobs at all. And they had the draft, and I didn't want to go into the army, so I went to Marines. Me and my neighbors joined together." Irwin agreed that seeing his father in the ATG encouraged his path into the military, where he trained in California and then served in Kodiak during the Cold War.

Wilfred "Mallak" Eakon (Iñupiaq), from Unalakleet, served in the Alaska National Guard from 1959 to 1965. With endearment, Mallak remembered that the men in the ATG hosted an annual Christmas program: "Christmas program was mostly comical and they'd use broken language to tell their stories. Cause at that time nobody knew much English."[67] Mallak's story suggests that Native ATG members tried to navigate Western customs. Yet oftentimes this immersion with Western customs fully integrated Indigeneity. One year at the Unalakleet Christmas program, an Iñupiaq Santa Claus

FIG. 22. Children sitting on the left watch the Alaska Territorial Guard practice drills in Utqiaġvik. "Barrow 6-30 4-957-45 Alaska Territorial Guard in formation." Photo by Walter T. Smith, Vern Brickley Collection, Anchorage Museum, B1998.014.1.11948. (Image has been cropped.)

broke out into a traditional dance to the delight of the children and families; the missionary, however, stormed out of the building.[68]

Unfortunately, many ATG veterans passed away before recognition of their veteran status was finally granted in 2000.[69] Under terms of a Guard Retirement Act passed by the Alaska legislature, guardsmen who completed twenty-plus years of service in the Alaska National Guard and ATG were eligible for retirement payments of fifty dollars per month paid to those ages fifty-five and older. Each month of payment matched a month of their time in the service. In 1998, just a few years before recognized veteran status, Alfred Qaaġraq Wells requested, "All of us ATGs are old men now and I wish we could get some help through the Army to obtain eyeglasses and hearing aids."[70] Ugiaqtaq described how it took decades for the state and military to recognize his ATG and Alaska National Guard service: "I must've been, you know, private first class when I finally got my discharge papers. I even got a little medal for, you know, being Alaska Territorial Guard. But we never got our discharge papers for, after fifty years, you know."[71] Ugiaqtaq laughed a little while reflecting on this, and he described that he had dedicated over twenty years to Alaskan military defense.

Times are indeed changing, and there are continued efforts by the US military and Alaska Natives to officially recognize former ATG members. In 2017, the Alaska Army National Guard hosted a party for Ugiaqtaq's ninety-first birthday along with two large sheet cakes for the entire Utqiaġvik community; the Guard gave Ugiaqtaq a snowshoe gift recognizing his twenty years of service to Alaska's military. Still, the Native community continues to remember and support ATG veterans who protected their homelands. In May 2017, organized by Mike Livingston (Unangax̂), the captain of the Alaska State Defense Force since 2018, the Alaska Native Heritage Center hosted a discharge ceremony for surviving ATG members. Similarly, the Alaska Office of Veterans Affairs ATG Task Force continues its efforts both to recognize and officially discharge ATG veterans.

Within the public realm, ATG statues coordinated by the Alaska Native Veterans Association's Alaska Territorial Guard Statue Project of 2009 began popping up across Alaska after state grant funding.[72] In Bethel, a memorial park features the ATG statue and the names of each member. In northern Alaska, the ATG statue resides outside city hall in Utqiaġvik (figs. 23 and 24). The grant proposal for the statues planned for eleven bronze statues for eleven communities, and Alaska Native artist James Grant designed the statue. In recent years, tribal members started donating wartime objects and family heirlooms, including ATG parkas, photographs, family oral histories, and scrimshaw artist Steven Foster (Iñupiaq) donated a baleen carving commemorating the ATG to the Alaska Veterans Museum. Here archival preservation and art show how Indigenous peoples commemorate their wartime history.

During the war on fascism and Japan's invasion of coastal Alaska, Alaska Native nations allied with the United States in a way that had not previously occurred, particularly through the ATG. Alaska Native people organized in

FIG. 23. *above* Town Hall in Utqiaġvik, with a whale skull on the left and an Alaska Territorial Guard statue on the right, 2017. Photo by the author.

FIG. 24. *right* Alaska Territorial Guard statue in Utqiaġvik next to a roster (left), 2017. Photo by the author.

military scout units, they volunteered, and they served on their land to preserve their land. As a testament to Native efforts for equilibrium restoration during the onslaught of war, the ATG as a framework became an Indigenized organization. Women played a larger role in the ATG than previously considered. Still today, community members from Kotzebue recognize women from the ATG.[73] As oral histories with Ungrudruk, Ugiaqtaq, and Andronik show, teen membership in the ATG proved prevalent. Inclusion by age and gender of this Indigenized organization upset the greater colonial structure of the US military trying to control the Alaskan territory while using Native help in establishing its presence that continued through the Cold War.

FIVE
RACING AND
ERASING NATIVES
FROZEN JIM CROW
AND ASSIMILATION

"NO NATIVES ALLOWED." In 1940, John Marin, a white man, posted this sign above the Douglas Inn in Southeast Alaska.[1] While Tlingit in Southeast Alaska struggled to cling to their land rights and to secure water rights, they confronted blatant anti-Indigenous discrimination. Such a sign demarcated the space between whites and the racialized position of the Alaska Natives deprived of full access to businesses that settlers had built on top of their ancestral lands. These types of signs, and the policies they represented, create not only a racial boundary but an assertion of colonized spaces that mark Natives as different, excluding them from white spaces. Yet Tlingit never ceded to this exclusion. Continuing their legacy of mobilization, in March 1940, the Douglas Camp of the Alaska Native Brotherhood (ANB), an Indigenous activist organization with chapters across Alaska made up largely of Tlingit, passed a resolution condemning the Douglas Inn while vowing to remove the sign. ANB members stressed, "These 'No Natives Allowed' signs are a gross discrimination against the Native people of Alaska, who as first citizens of Alaska, are entitled to all privileges and rights as citizens of the United States of America."[2] The ANB president of the Douglas Camp, S. A. Stevens, signed on behalf of the ANB committee and sent copies of the resolution to the Grand Camp chapter of the ANB, to the proprietor of the Douglas Inn, and to Alaskan territorial governor Ernest Gruening.

Racial formation in Alaska included not only the removal of Alaskan Indigenous peoples but also the categorization of Indigeneity as a race used to deny Aboriginal title to land. A *frozen Jim Crow*—a term coined by historian Glenda Gilmore to describe Alaskan segregation—existed in Alaska as a tool for settlers to displace Indigenous peoples from their homelands.[3] As geographer Jen Rose Smith (dax̱unhyuu) argues, ice geographies carry connotations of racialized landscapes.[4] Fitting with other terminology on segregation that is geographically specific, I adopt this term in referring to the far north where frozen Jim Crow went alongside settler land occupation and an attempt to strip away Native sovereignty by racializing Natives as second-class US citizens lacking full citizen rights and Aboriginal land rights.

Segregation, boarding schools, and healthcare are all components of settler colonial institutions that seek to dismantle Native communities and sovereignty while emboldening US empire. Alaska presents a case study of how Jim Crow, as a practice of segregating Black people, reached the far north by establishing white spaces separate from Indigenous peoples. As historians including C. Vann Woodward show, segregation was far from limited to the American South.[5] Frozen Jim Crow, like what historian Albert Camarillo identifies as "Jaime Crow" in reference to Mexican Americans, reveals how white supremacy had a hand in Western settlement.[6] In the Indigenous American South, historian Malinda Maynor Lowery (Lumbee) explains that Lumbee asserted their own politics and nation in the face of whites' enforcement of racial hierarchies and Jim Crow laws, policies, and practices.[7]

During the mid-twentieth century, in towns with predominantly white populations, white people barred Alaska Native people from restaurants, certain jobs, and hotels. Other businesses such as restaurants and theaters separated Native patrons into different sections. In addition to these businesses that exerted racial boundaries daily, Native people encountered strict surveillance by the territorial police and the government workers from the BIA, regularly checking Native people during curfews, watching their liquor consumption, and even scrutinizing their homes for cleanliness. Each of these forms of monitoring Native bodies stigmatized them and attempted not only to limit freedom and mobility but also to strangle their inherent tribal sovereignty.

Frozen Jim Crow, which consisted of segregationist ordinances directed at the Alaska Native population, provides a case study to link the fields of racial hierarchies and settler colonial studies. A racial hierarchy is a system that upholds whiteness within an institutional position of power that then informs power relations within society, politics, and the economy.[8] Alaska fits familiar patterns of colonial racialization projects that swept across the United States and its territories. White settlers construct the racial hierarchy through settler colonialism, segregation, and xenophobia. Marginalized groups such as Indigenous people, diasporic people, and migrant/immigrant populations reside on the bottom of the racial hierarchy, and they encounter violence from their racialized identities stemming from removal, enslavement, and exclusion.[9] As ethnic studies scholar Genevieve Carpio illuminates, resistance by marginalized peoples reframes the racial hierarchy setting limitations on the settler colonial reach of power.[10] Applied to this study on Alaska, when Natives exercise sovereignty and practice Indigenous cultural traditions, they actively refuse integration within the imposed racial hierarchy.[11] In the World War II era, alongside enlisting in the US military to reclaim their homelands, as the previous chapter discusses, Native civilians exerted activism to challenge colonial structures and not only to maintain equality in public spaces but also to advance Indigenous politics and governance.

Oral histories illuminate how the racial hierarchy took shape, how it informed settler colonialism, and how settler colonial power created racialization attempting to diminish Native sovereignty. The colonial actions of segregation and assimilation sought to race and erase Natives from the landscape. As oral histories, and Native activists show, in seeking equilibrium restoration by maintaining their Indigenous identities, their multitude of rights, and their land, Native people resisted Western assimilation asserting sovereignty while simultaneously challenging segregation. As such, Native people disrupted the racial hierarchy, thereby exerting change over the trajectory of settler colonial efforts. Refusing settler colonial discourses of equality through assimilation, Indigenous Alaskans defined equality and land rights outside a settler narrative of so-called progress, instead asserting their rights. As this chapter shows, Native land rights and civil rights are entangled and together defy settler colonial expectations of removal, assimilation, and segregation.

Oral histories offer a glimpse to understanding Indigenous resistance to segregation and assimilation within daily life. Elders from rural areas with predominantly Native populations knew that segregation existed in Alaskan cities, and some elders equated discrimination to urban spaces. When asked if he experienced discrimination, Wilfred "Mallak" Eakon (Iñupiaq) who was born in 1938 and raised in Unalakleet, replied, "No, I mostly stayed around Unalakleet."[12] Other elders recalled stories about segregation that they heard secondhand. According to an Iñupiaq elder from Unalakleet born in 1926, who chose to remain anonymous during their interview, "People up in Nome, the Natives couldn't mix with the white people to go to church. That's the only place I ever heard of segregation, that was Nome."[13] Even when they had not experienced segregation firsthand, Native people from rural areas possessed an understanding of the racial hierarchy that existed within cities and discriminated against Native people.

Stories from elders in Unalakleet demonstrate that while some elders from Native villages could avoid the explicit racial segregation that existed in cities such as Nome and Anchorage, elders had family members who experienced frozen Jim Crow. By sharing such stories across generations, they marked segregation as an oppressive affront that infiltrated Native public life as well as home life. Theresa Nanouk (Iñupiaq), from Unalakleet, identified segregation as the abusive pedagogical practices administered by BIA teachers, explaining, "They didn't want children to speak Native. They let them stand facing the wall, so they won't speak."[14] When asked if she remembered separate spaces for whites and Natives, she also recalled that segregation forced her uncle to sit in a separate section at the Anchorage movies. Her uncle's story about segregation in Anchorage indicates that family members shared stories about race discrimination. In another interview with Maryann Haugen (Iñupiaq), born in 1931 in Koyuk and from Unalakleet, she told a story about her relative who visited Nome: "Siuvaq told me they pay the same admission as non-Natives in the movie house, but the Natives went up to the balcony with no chairs. You could stand and watch the movie."[15] Evidently, Siuvaq told multiple family members about his experience with segregation in Nome. Frances Charles (Iñupiaq), born in 1933 in Shaktoolik, moved to Unalakleet in 1941. Frances married Harold

"Siuvaq" Charles in 1949. She detailed Siuvaq's trips to Nome in the 1940s: "He used to go to Nome. He used to work there too, somewhere with miners. He always say when you go to the movies you have to sit in a certain place."[16] From a distance, Indigenous people understood that colonialism stigmatized their people and that it racialized their Native identities.

Numerous elders from a community-based oral history project by Seniors and Sitka Sound Youth (S.A.S.S.Y.) spoke on the issue of racially oriented bullying from childhood. For this oral history project from 1996, Sitka youth interviewed Isabella Brady (Tlingit), who spoke about such matters. Isabella was born in Sitka in 1924, and she later attended college through the GI Bill after serving in the US Navy. She detailed that when she grew up in Sitka, there were two groups: minorities, including Native and Chinese people, and white people. Isabella attended the BIA school, and her youth interviewers wrote, "To get to school she had to stay with a group of Native kids to avoid conflicts with white children. If they were held after class, she would pray for a low tide so they could run along the beach to avoid the white kids."[17] A white elder, Althea Buckingham, born in 1922 in Corvallis, Oregon, moved to Juneau at age ten, and then Sitka at age fourteen. She detailed that "at one time there was a wall that separated one part of town from the other and at night Natives weren't allowed to cross into the whites' side, because there was a remaining fear of Natives."[18] Althea recalled segregated seats at the movie theater and that "many of the military men were racist, and their feelings didn't change when they came to Sitka." Another elder, Bertha Karras (Tlingit), spoke of visiting the Russian part of town in Sitka, which had white people and some Indians. In walking home, she passed through a white part of town where "a bully blocked her way, called her names, and shoved her around."[19] She happened across a white ally when "another girl came and started yelling at him to leave her alone." In this instance, as other elders relayed, the presence of other kids alleviated bullying.

Arnold Booth (Tsimshian), from Metlakatla and born in 1919, shared stories about segregation in Southeast Alaska, in the nearby town of Ketchikan, in addition to in the contiguous states in Oregon. Arnold articulated, "There were signs, 'No Indians Allowed' or 'No Dogs and Indians Allowed.'"[20] Recalling the first time he visited Alaska, Ernest Gruening mentioned a

FIG. 25. Kenneth Booth (left) with Arnold Booth (right) on a steamship, late 1930s or early 1940s. Karen Thompson identified these men: "Both on [a] steamship, as per Arnold, to Chemawa, Oregon. Native Boarding School." Courtesy of Karen Thompson's World War II family scrapbook.

similar sign in the Anchorage Grill: "We Do Not Cater to Native and Filipino Trade."[21] A sign itself represented a physical racial boundary and the creation of white spaces excluding Native and Asian immigrant patrons. Because he was raised on the Native reservation of Metlakatla, Arnold explained, "the only time I felt segregation of course is when I would go into Ketchikan. I had relatives there and they would tell me where to go and what kinds of lines to follow."[22] Here, much like the elders from Unalakleet, Arnold's relatives shared stories with him about how to navigate urban spaces where Native people encountered discrimination.

While Arnold attended the Greenleaf Academy in Idaho, he traveled to Oregon to visit Metlakatlans at the Chemawa Indian School (fig. 25). With this memory he articulated the widespread nature of anti-Native segregation that he observed in the states: "Some of the Metlakatla students went onto

Chemawa Indian School. So, I checked in there to see how it was. And there again the stations, Indians on one side and whites on the other." Arnold detailed, "I thought, this ain't so bad. They used to have signs in Ketchikan. And some of them don't even have a sign; you'd walk in and get kicked out." After a week of visiting Chemawa, he left declaring that the constantly ringing bells exhausted him. Arnold's reminisced, "I don't want to be at a place where the bell rings, I get up in the morning, and the bell rings I stand by for bed, the bell rings I walk down the hall, bare-skinned and what have you." These drills came from Richard Henry Pratt's militarized and assimilationist Indian boarding school program. Even as a veteran, Arnold found the Chemawa Indian School to be more onerous in militarized discipline.

These elders from Unalakleet and Southeast Alaska demonstrate an awareness of their Native identity that meant different things in different places. To be a Native person in a village presented different challenges than being a Native person in a predominantly Western city. As Theresa Nanouk explained, "There was no segregation here [in Unalakleet]. Everyone was good to each other. They welcome whoever comes through here." Cities presented racial obstacles beyond those in rural areas. The elders' collective memories about segregation as told by their loved ones highlight what historian Jonathan Holloway describes as memory that "shapes a consciousness and an identity" of a community.[23] One did not have to experience segregation firsthand to share the feelings of being segregated based on an Indigenous identity. And traveling to other regions, as Arnold did, Native people observed segregation in Oregon.

The Nome Dream Theater and Iñupiat Youth Activism

In 1944, in the historic gold-mining town of Nome, two mixed-race Iñupiat teenagers, Alberta Schenck and Holger "Jorgy" Jorgensen, purposefully upended racial boundaries by sitting in the white section of the Nome Dream Theater. Both teens had white fathers and Native mothers; their mixed-race identities called into question the malleability of racial boundaries marked by segregated spaces. Before the movie began, the theater management walked down the aisle and asked the teens to leave. When Alberta and Jorgy refused, Nome police officers arrived with billy clubs, arrested the two teens, and dropped them off at the Nome jail. Alberta's father, "Whitey" Schenck, posted their bail allowing the teens to return home. This incident did not pass unnoticed in the Nome Native community. The following day, Native people turned out in full force to the Nome Dream Theater, sitting in every seat to dissolve racialized sections. Native activism involved upholding a collective Native identity while physically and economically forcing a diffusion of spaces that adhered to white supremacy.

After integrating the Nome Dream Theater, Alberta Schenck penned a letter to the *Nome Nugget* advocating for Native equality by using patriotic language to appeal to white readership. As a teen, she understood much about the war on fascism and the need to end blatant anti-Native discrimination on the Alaskan home front. In her letter dated March 3, 1944, she identified segregation as "Hitlerism," underscoring that every Alaskan held US citizenship. She made herself relatable to a broad audience of readers by identifying as mixed race: "I myself am part Esk*mo and Irish and so are many others. I only truthfully know that I am one of God's children regardless of race, color, or creed."[24] Her tone of inclusivity called to an audience of people with religious backgrounds and to those who would identify as US patriots when she strategically mentioned Thomas Jefferson and the Declaration of Independence. She learned of the Constitution and Civil War in history class and applied these concepts to her understanding of local politics and society.[25] On an economic level, she stated that each patron paid the same price for the movie tickets and should therefore have equal access to accommodations. Alberta Schenck continued a legacy of Native activists who used patriotic and colonial language—made especially relevant during the US anti-fascism propaganda campaigns of the war—to advocate for equality.

And yet, while Alberta's letter and her actions alongside Jorgy pushed against separation at the theater, as archaeologist and ATG quarter master Otto Geist relayed, segregation continued in practice at the Nome Dream Theater, which he observed in January 1945.[26] Concerned by this, he wrote to ATG coordinator Muktuk Marston explaining that an aisle attendant moved a "full blood woman" from the left side of the aisle and also "a young white man married to what appeared to be a half caste." According to Geist, initially the white man refused, then after a woman from the ticket window asked him to move, he complied before the theater called the police. This story indicates that Native people and white allies continued to encounter discrimination enacted by several employees of the theater who worked with local police to carry out segregation in practice. Geist suggested that Natives from Nome obtain a Quonset hut and a secondhand projector to make their own theater. Indeed, even with continued activism by Native youth such as Alberta and Jorgy, white business owners such as those of the Nome Dream Theater continued to maintain segregation in practice until legislation would curtail discrimination.

Elizabeth Peratrovich and the Passage of the 1945 Alaska Equal Rights Act

During this era when Native people organized and protested segregation in Alaskan towns, activist Elizabeth Peratrovich (Tlingit) served as president of the Alaska Native Sisterhood (ANS), a Native rights organization (fig. 26).[27] The Alaska Equal Rights Act sought to end discrimination in Alaskan businesses. When the act failed to pass in 1943, Native activists including Elizabeth Peratrovich mobilized to pass it in 1945. In seeking social equality and coordinating a Native voting bloc, Native leaders advocated for the passage of the Alaska Equal Rights Act in February 1945. Indeed, Elizabeth Peratrovich and other Native activists within organizations like the ANB and ANS propelled this act to pass. Terminating racial separation and exclusion at Alaskan businesses remained an item of concern for Native leadership.

When Elizabeth Peratrovich spoke on behalf of Native people to end discrimination, she acted as an Indigenous leader using Western platforms, like the legislative floor, to assert Native rights. Several politicians opposed the bill. The *Daily Alaska Empire* provided quotes from Elizabeth Peratrovich's elocution, answering the question posed by the skeptics, "Will the law eliminate discrimination?" In her rebuttal, she relayed, "No law will eliminate crimes but, at least, you as legislators can assert to the world that you recognize the evil of the present situation and speak your intent to help us overcome discrimination."[28] This matter-of-fact tone sought to generate realistic

FIG. 26. Portrait of Elizabeth Peratrovich. Courtesy of the Alaska State Library, ASL-Peratrovich-Elizabeth-1.

expectations that everyone would need to continue advancing equality. Her power with words generated alliances.

During this wartime era against global fascism, Elizabeth Peratrovich's skill in identifying racism strongly impacted the Alaskan territorial legislature. Her speech condemned racial discrimination, addressed housing discrimination directed at Native people in Juneau, and sought to find a more inclusive Alaska to raise her family. The audience watching the Alaska legislature, who filled the hallway outside the gallery doors, and who likely included members of the ANB and ANS as well as Juneau residents alike, roared with applause. The Alaska Equal Rights Act passed this second time around, and Governor Gruening signed it on February 16, 1945 (fig. 27). The photo opportunity reveals Gruening's enthusiasm for the act's passage. He indeed collaborated with Tlingit leaders, Elizabeth Peratrovich of the ANS and her spouse Roy Peratrovich of the ANB, to secure its passage. Citing Elizabeth Peratrovich as the mobilizer for change, a *Tundra Times* news article shows Gruening claiming, "Had it not been for that beautiful Tlingit woman, Elizabeth Peratrovich, being on hand every day in the hallways, it would have never passed."[29]

Outside her speech on the Alaska territorial senate floor, Elizabeth Peratrovich engaged in many other forms of activism ranging from community organizing, to creating intertribal networks, to promoting Native healthcare and wellness on intergenerational levels. As the ANB and ANS were largely made up of Tlingit members, recruiting in other tribal geographies fostered cross-cultural Indigenous alliances and extended solidarities. These orga-

FIG. 27. Governor Ernest Gruening (seated) signs the Alaska Equal Rights Act of 1945 alongside Alaska Native Sisterhood president Elizabeth Peratrovich (second to left) and Alaska Native Brotherhood president Roy Peratrovich (far right). Courtesy of Alaska State Library, ASL-PCA-274.

nizations additionally served as places fostering community wellness and socializing, and thus the ANB and ANS accomplished more than political activism. The ANS organized the junior ANB and junior ANS.[30] Marcelo Quinto Jr. (Tlingit/Filipino, he identified as "Indipino"), a recent president of the ANB, fondly remembered the junior ANB in Juneau where he participated in youth basketball with coach Fred Morgan.[31] Such memories indicate that the ANB and ANS functioned as an Indigenized organization within the Native community that provided structures, like recreation, to support youth. This allowed the Native community to flourish on intergenerational levels. Centering Native health and wellness, Elizabeth Peratrovich advocated for resources for Native women, including government programs that provided workshops to benefit Native women's lives and their households.[32]

In addition to creating ANB and ANS chapters across Alaska by physically visiting towns and meeting with tribal leaders, like the Iñupiat towns of Kotzebue, Selawik, and Deering, Elizabeth Peratrovich fostered relationships with the National Council of American Indians, the oldest and largest Indigenous tribal rights organization. She co-wrote a letter with her spouse, Roy Peratrovich, president of the ANB, addressing the passage of the Anti-Discrimination Bill; they enclosed a copy of the bill perhaps to help spur other Native regions to do the same, and they sought cooperation between the National Council of American Indians and the ANB and ANS, inviting them to their annual convention in Angoon, Alaska.[33]

The Alaska Equal Rights Act banned discrimination at businesses and instituted a small fee of $250 and up to thirty days in jail for business owners who failed to comply. Segregation against the Native population, and other minorities including Filipinos, no longer legally existed at Alaskan businesses. William Paul Jr. (Tlingit) urged Native people to vote out Alaskan senators and representatives who opposed the Alaska Equal Rights Act: Senators Tolbert Scott and Frank Whaley and Representative M. J. Walsh of Nome; Senator Allen Shattuck and Representative Curtis Shattuck of Juneau; Senator Grenold Collins of Anchorage; Senator Leo Rogge and Representatives Alaska Linck and Robert Hoopes of Fairbanks.[34] In listing these names, he made it common knowledge that these men promoted segregation, and they should not return to the 1947 legislature. Here, Native activists attempted to steer territorial politics in a manner that recognized Native rights and civil rights.

Alaska Native Voting Rights History

Alaska Natives did not possess guaranteed voting rights even after the passage of the 1924 Indian Citizenship Act—granting dual citizenship to Native people—until the adoption of the Alaska Constitution in 1959. Historian Stephen Haycox identifies the 1925 Alaska Voters' Literacy Act, which aimed to disenfranchise the Native population by requiring them to speak and read the English language, as similar to Jim Crow in other regions of the United States.[35] Tlingit leaders did not sit idly by; grand president of the ANB Frank

D. Price (Tlingit) wrote protest letters identifying the act as disenfranchizing Alaska Natives.[36] While the Alaska Statehood Act of 1958 would secure Native voting rights, it came with a significant expense in allowing the State of Alaska to select over one million acres of public lands with no oversight on how it impacted Native rights or sovereignty.[37] As historian Jessica Leslie Arnett emphasizes, the narrative about Alaskan Indigenous land rights is told less often, if at all, relative to the narrative of suffrage or civil rights.[38]

In exercising Indigenous governance, Native activists advocated for equal rights in Western spaces, voting rights in colonial elections, and Aboriginal land rights. Writer Peter Metcalfe explains that the ANB and ANS fought for equal rights alongside land rights, water rights, and fishing rights.[39] To focus solely on Native civil rights and suffrage within the limits of colonial elections erases Aboriginal land rights from the historical narrative, thereby muting Native sovereignty. While Native peoples advocated for racial equality in Alaskan towns, they simultaneously mobilized their nations—their governments and political structures as separate entities from colonial government—seeking alliances with territorial officials to protect their land from settler and corporate encroachment.

Although Alaska Natives saw equal rights and sovereignty as crucially connected, Alaska colonists and Western-dominated labor unions that supported equal rights understood equality and citizenship through a lens of assimilation. Even if unstated, this lens assumed white supremacy and carried an agenda of dispossession and elimination. The ANB and ANS Bargaining Agency aligned with local workers unions to form the Alaska Marine Workers Union to protect Alaskan workers' rights from corporate interests.[40] Despite the Congress of Industrial Organizations and the American Federation of Labor demanding dissolution of the ANB and assimilation into the national union, the Indigenous organizations remained intact.[41]

Native mobilization by the ANB, ANS, and the tribal organization of the Tlingit and Haida Indian Tribes of Alaska involved seeking expert legal advice to protect their Aboriginal land claims. In February 1945, the same month that the Alaska Equal Rights Act passed, Andrew Hope (Tlingit), president of the Tlingit and Haida Indian Tribes of Alaska, mobilized tribes in Southeast Alaska to consolidate their land suits as separate from Aboriginal hearings for land title.[42] Months later, in November 1945, activists such as William Paul Jr. (Tlingit) reached out to Alaska's attorney general, inviting him to the ANB/ANS convention to foster dialogue on Aboriginal land claims.[43]

Defining the Racial Hierarchy Alongside Alaskan Colonization

Settler colonialism and capitalism go hand in hand to inform and create a racial hierarchy that bolsters white supremacy. As Puerto Rican studies scholar Ramón Grosfoguel elucidates, a racial hierarchy relies upon race, class, gender, and sexuality.[44] This racial hierarchy structures settler colonial society applied to a wide geography colonized by European countries. Critical Indigenous studies scholars Jodi Byrd (Chickasaw) and Nick Estes (Lower Brule Sioux Tribe) identify capitalism as a key component to the making of US empire and as the antithesis to Indigenous sovereignties.[45] Capitalism involved theft of Indigenous lands alongside the enslavement of Africans for labor to generate capital for America's colonies. As a colonial project, racializing Natives involves erasing Native people from the land while creating a new racial group—for surviving Natives of genocide—below whiteness on a racial hierarchy. In making Natives into a race, settlers could more readily erase Aboriginal land title by seizing "savage" lands. Thus, white settlement directly benefited in placing Alaska Natives along with Indians into a racial category created by, according to historian Alexandra Harmon, laws, institutions, and surveillance.[46]

Assimilation serves a nationalist purpose to erase Natives through Western acculturation, yet it contradicts the racial hierarchy since complete assimilation removes Natives from residing as an inferior racial category to whiteness. On the national level, assimilating Native people aligns with military control and the colonial mission of religious outreach. However, for the mundane lives of white settlers, there is no reason to fully assimilate Natives, since to do so would deny forms of white privilege. Native integration presents a conundrum to white identity; to actually incorporate "savages" would degrade the imagined purity of the "advanced" and "civilized" race.

Assimilation is therefore an unattainable evolving myth of empire that seeks to erase Indigeneity through incorporation.[47] Harmon identifies this contradiction in which US Indian policy tried to solve the "Indian problem" by absorbing Indians into the white population, especially where labor and land was wanted, yet constructed Indians into a distinct race of people with customs and lifeways incompatible with American civilization where US colonial law worked for colonizers.[48]

Native people occupy a unique position of the hierarchy since their very survival challenges the system of colonialism that seeks to remove Indigenous peoples while seizing Indigenous lands and resources. As historian Jeffrey Ostler articulates on genocide history, this occurs while colonizers try to ease colonial guilt by physically erasing Natives from the landscape through physical and cultural genocide.[49] When Native people cannot be erased from the landscape, segregation offers an alternative in structuring and maintaining a racial hierarchy that prioritizes white settlers. However, in the case of Alaska—and we could apply this to even global regions— Native people thwart empire's continuous effort at cultural hegemony and land extraction.

While Alaska Native people confronted segregation in cities on their homelands, the US federal government generated propaganda on Alaskan development that conveniently branded Native people as compliant to Western settlement. Linking the imperial and settler colonial goals of settling Alaska with a white populace, printed in 1944, the War Department created a manual titled *What Has Alaska to Offer Postwar Pioneers?* The manual itself sought "pioneers"—a euphemism for "first" settlers— from postwar servicemen and white families. This publication continued a narrative of erasing Natives from the landscape with language such as "American pioneers wasted the nation's resources and drove the Indians from their lands."[50] For Alaska, colonization meant developing the land as a frontier that included not only settler colonization but also the extraction of minerals, fishing, fur processing, agricultural expansion, and harvesting valuable resources. The Matanuska project of 1935, which occurred on Athabascan homelands, is an example of a prewar federal colonization project. Here, the government brought two hundred families from the Midwest to

Alaska, allotting each family a forty-acre tract of land, a home, a barn, and farming equipment.[51]

Only certain settlers could move to Alaska; colonial officials rejected others including Jewish refugees. In April 1940, the Department of the Interior printed a sixty-one-page report titled "The Problem of Alaskan Development," emphasizing that Alaska held strategic value connecting the United States with foreign Pacific markets and the imperial value of the land's proximity to the Soviet Union and Japan.[52] This report also investigated Alaska as a potential refuge for up to 50,000 Jewish refugees.[53] Voicing anti-Semitism and xenophobia, several settler groups and politicians opposed a plan for Jewish refugees, including the Pioneers of Alaska, the Alaska Miners Association, and politicians Alaskan territorial delegate Anthony Dimond and Ernest Gruening, who at the time was head of the Department of the Interior's Division of Territories and Island Possessions.[54] While the plan died, its existence highlights that colonial officials failed to see Alaska Native people, their interests, and their Aboriginal land title as existing—much like the sale of Alaska in 1867.

Not all federal bureaucrats agreed about Alaska colonization projects, and some sought to establish Indian reservations, which ANB and ANS members resisted. Known to advocate for tribal self-government, John Collier, the commissioner of Indian affairs, rebuked the federal report "The Problem of Alaskan Development" advocating for Alaskan Indian reservations.[55] Governor Gruening opposed Indian reservations proposed by the Department of the Interior, claiming they "will prove primarily disastrous" and "seriously jeopardize" "postwar development of Alaska by veterans of this war."[56] Here Gruening relayed his attitude that he sought white veterans to settle Alaska in the postwar years. The words *Indian reservation* would be controversial among members of the ANB and ANS who saw reservations as akin to wartime incarceration camps where the government relegated Native people to plots of land with poor resources.[57] Indeed, while advocating for land rights, ANB and ANS members resisted the imposition of the word *reservation* to protect their land interests. This shows how Native activists through the ANB refused settler categorization and that they continued to advocate for land rights on their own terms.

Assimilation through Separate Education

Paradoxically, settlers sought to assimilate Native children in schools while segregating them from the white populace. Cultural genocide began in 1875 when Lieutenant Richard Henry Pratt forced seventy-two Indian prisoners into Fort Marion, and instead of killing them—as happened in the past with Indian insurgents—he imposed Western education, religion, and language.[58] Pratt's goal of assimilation to solve the "Indian problem" by "killing the Indian to save the man"—essentially brainwashing—parallels nightmarish themes of oppressive empires from dystopian future novels such as George Orwell's *1984*. In racing and erasing Natives, the settler colonial government waged a cultural, political, and social war to displace Indigenous bodies from their human rights, their lands, and their Native identities. Instead of outright battles over the land, the continuation of US imperialism took the form of attempted cultural genocide through Western assimilation intending to annihilate Native culture. Boarding school graveyards reveal deaths of Native children at colonial hands. Regardless of the ways that Native children fashioned the Western education experience to survive, boarding schools served a colonial purpose of separating Native children from their families and indoctrinating them, alienating Native languages and cultural customs, and homogenizing Indigenous peoples as a race, stripping away Indigenous sovereignty. It cannot be overlooked that Indian education also served another purpose of conveniently segregating Native students from white students.

The 1905 Nelson Act bifurcated Alaskan education system into a dual system in which the BIA administered schools for Native students and the Alaskan territorial schools ran schools for white children and Native children of mixed race who led a "civilized life."[59] As historian Paige Raibmon illuminates, the Davis family case involved a Tlingit family led by Rudolph Walton who attempted to integrate the Sitka school in 1906, but "after carefully reviewing the civilized qualities of each family, District Court Judge Gunnison dismissed the material evidence of civilized life as inadequate."[60] Put another way, a judge from a colonial court determined the fate of Native children through the Nelson Act and their personal interpretation of the word *civilized*. Colonial officials relied on the concept of colonial blood quantum to regulate Native student enrollment. In 1945, the commissioner of education identified that Native children of "1/4 or more Native blood" accounted for 26 percent of the nine thousand students within the territorial schools.[61] By 1946, the BIA branch known as the Alaska Native Service operated seventy-five day schools and three vocational schools for roughly four thousand children.[62]

For white settlers in towns across Alaska, separate education relied on an investment not to assimilate Native people like the BIA's motives but to maintain separation between the races that relied upon perceived health hazards and settler-fabricated projections of Native children as intellectually inferior. In the town of Fort Yukon, in 1939, forty-seven white residents petitioned Governor Gruening to keep the Fort Yukon territorial school separate from the BIA school.[63] Citing the prevalence of TB while branding Natives as "without morals," white residents lamented that Native children possessed body lice and "venereal infected sores on their faces." Similarly, in other regions of Alaska, white residents from Kotzebue and Unalaska wrote protest letters arguing that white children should not attend schools administered by the BIA.[64] In Nome, District Attorney Bingham advised that Native children had no right to attend the public school as "their attendance had a tendency to pull down the quality of the school."[65] Each of these varied examples illustrates widespread settler disdain for Native schoolchildren. Here, young children were caught in a social war instigated by settlers who, for the most part, did not want Native children attending school with white schoolchildren. This occurred while boarding schools tried to indoctrinate Native children to English and Westernization through physical and emotional abuse.

As activists, Native mothers and aunts advocated on behalf of their children for integrating Alaskan schools. In the 1930s, ANS member and mother Amy Hallingstad (Tlingit) helped shutter the BIA school in Petersburg, thereby integrating their educational system. Citing financial grievances, white people in Petersburg petitioned the BIA to reopen the school for Natives. The committee wrote, "Petersburg has opened the doors of its schools to the [N]ative children and is giving them the same instruction in the same classes with her white children. This is a grave mistake, for the two races differ both mentally and socially."[66] Labeling children as transmitting infections, like the treatment of Native women carrying venereal diseases (see chap. 6), the Petersburg petitioners addressed the "problems of health" from mixing schools. Symbolic of the status of Native children as captive to a state, three white men, Geo V. Beck, Robert M.Allen, and Earl N. Ohmer, signed their names asking the BIA to reopen the former jail in Petersburg as a BIA school for Native students.

Coined as the "Alaska school problem," Alaskan school integration distressed white settlers.[67] Other regions voiced concern about tax dollars as a reason to exclude Native students. The federal government and local white residents disagreed on who would pay taxes for Native students to attend territorial schools, ironically located on Native ancestral lands. In the Aleutians, in 1939, white residents from Unalaska condemned the potentiality of Native school integration.[68] Citing racial blood quantum and taxes, they voiced outrage that their school could convert to a BIA school, illustrating how a dual education system intended to assimilate Natives was deemed below the standards and expectations of white families with school-age children. In Kodiak, white residents complained that Natives who owned 40 percent of the city property could not be taxed, citing that 192 out of 282 students were Native. In 1949, the town of Palmer voted to integrate their school with Native students; 113 residents voted in favor of school integration and 52 opposed it.[69] The meeting notes from this Palmer meeting reference a Mrs. Sandvik who identified rampant discrimination, including a story about a Native girl who lived with her who quit school "because she was called 'a dirty squ*w' and another one quit because no one would speak to her." These stories, like the ones of bullying that elders mentioned in S.A.S.S.Y. interviews, indicate that bullying continued and included racialized and gendered name-calling.[70]

In 1947, the Alaska Territorial Board of Education identified the inherent paradoxes of the dual educational system in Alaska that generated second-class citizens. The Board of Education explained that "the dual system of education in Alaska is not conducive to economic, efficient or democratic school management. If full responsible citizenship is the ultimate goal for the Native people of Alaska, then segregation is not the way to achieve it.

Segregation tends to treat the Native people as a race apart rather than directing them toward assimilation."[71] Here, the Board of Education identified a dichotomy between assimilation and segregation. Both segregation and assimilation left zero room for Indigenous identities who chose neither. As oral histories and protest letters written by Native activists show, Native people sought social equality and wanted equal treatment at places of business, and this extended to education.

ORAL HISTORIES ON SEGREGATION AND ASSIMILATION

Oral histories reveal that Native people asserted their own agenda, rather than assimilated, to curb discrimination in the public sphere while upholding their Indigenous identities. Here, in the context of separate and assimilative schooling, restoring equilibrium came from the actions of Native children themselves. As one of the most vulnerable populations, subjected to indoctrination and separation—both from their families and from a white settler population that segregated them—Indigenous children creatively found ways to resist. The abuse these children encountered cannot be understated. The government and missionary schools tore Native kids from their families and mothers, physically beating and shaming them for speaking their Native languages. These colonial actions sought to "educate" Native kids, the word being a euphemism for state-sanctioned child abuse. As we see from the voices of elders and the stories they share, equilibrium restoration in response to separate schools and the boarding school era took the form of intergenerational healing by these elders who themselves returned to teaching Native languages to Native youth later in their lives.

Nick Alokli (Sugpiaq) shared his own stories about the abuse he encountered at the hands of Western teachers. Nick was born in 1936 at the Alitak cannery on Kodiak Island and was raised in Akhiok. During a joint interview in 2008, with myself and Peter Boskofsky (Chignik Lake Village Council) of the Alutiiq Museum, when I asked Nick about racial segregation, he immediately answered with, "I wasn't very old then, in school we weren't allowed to speak our own language. There were times we spoke our own language, we got punished."[72] Nick detailed specific forms of punishment:

"We got hit with a black pointer, and those straps from hip boots. They hit us in our hands. And it hurt, the buckle. And some of them, they had to sit in the corner for I don't know how long. I'd rather get hit then sit in the corner." Without pausing Nick then explained how Native youth restored his passion for his Native language: "That's why I almost lost my interest in my culture and my language because of how I was treated. Changed only about five years ago after I went to Afognak camp, then I seen them kids that wanted to learn, wanted to find out about their culture, so I decided to start teaching."

As Nick articulated, colonial education tried to strip away his language and cultural identity, and yet Native youth—an audience eager to learn about their language and culture—restored his motivation for speaking Sugpiaq and teaching it to younger generations. These actions reveal that in Nick's case, equilibrium restoration manifested through Native language use, and it took decades alongside intergenerational commitment between the youth and elderly. In a similar vein, Karen Lynn Weinberg's documentary *Keep Talking* (2018) illuminates language revitalization efforts propelled by Sugpiat women in Kodiak.[73]

While the tragic stories of the Native boarding school are numerous, so, too, are stories of Indigenous resilience. Native families refused to comply with Western education, and some chose to live off the grid. Here, mobility offered a form of Indigenous noncompliance to colonial orders. Nora Dauenhauer (Tlingit), born in 1927, a renowned Tlingit language translator, instructor, poet, and writer with her partner, Richard Dauenhauer, shared that her family maintained a migratory lifestyle so that Nora could avoid attending Western schools. Nora relayed, "I didn't go to school. The thing my dad did to us, he'd take us out of our home in Hoonah and take us out to camp and all winter we'd stay out in camp while we trapped. And we lived on Native foods. None of us kids went to school."[74] Nora's story provides an example of a Native family that removed themselves from surveillance by colonial authorities. In the 1970s, Nora earned her GED on her own terms. Nora's narrative about her history of education shows that Native families asserted limits on Western education and that some elders returned to Western education on their own terms at later points in their lives.

Carol Brady (Tlingit) shared a story about the Wrangell Institute boarding school that saved her life. Her story about being an orphan and a child slave reveals a much darker history of colonialism in which a colonial structure offered a form of refuge from other forms of colonial violence that manifested in her home life.[75] For Carol, equilibrium restoration meant using the boarding school as a refuge from her life as an orphan and child slave.

Some Native students described that they preferred the Native school over an integrated school with white students, underscoring that a positive Native community emerged at Native schools despite punitive Western pedagogy. Helen Sarabia (Tlingit), whom I interviewed at the Central Council of the Tlingit and Haida Indian Tribes of Alaska (CCTHITA) in 2013, recalled not wanting to attend an integrated school since she preferred taking classes with other Native students. She explained, "We weren't allowed to go to public school." When asked if she would have wanted to go to the public school if she could, she poignantly replied, "No. I wanted to be with my people. I didn't like the way—what I heard, it scared me. Not actually scared me but it unsettled me kind've. I just couldn't believe that they were treated that way. I, you know, it was bad enough that we were told not to speak in school, and I could tell by their faces that they really meant it when you were told. I still remember their names some of those teachers."[76]

Still others, such as Sadie Brower (Iñupiaq) of Utqiaġvik, took it upon themselves to harness Western education and teach Native students as a BIA teacher later serving as a magistrate. Selina (Kasáth and Anshawatká) Everson (Tlingit), from Angoon, served as the president of the ANS in the early 1990s. Selina taught Tlingit language at Harborview Elementary School in Juneau since 2001. During her interview at the CCTHITA in May 2013, she described that she felt like she had a sheltered high school experience while attending the missionary school. She described Native students as the majority: "But being in Sheldon Jackson where we were all Native children, all the way up north: Esk*mo, Aleut, Tsimshian, Haidas, Tlingits. It became a junior college; they changed the laws to allow white[s] and we had one white guy at school. So, I didn't really feel the prejudice [from] other people. My brothers experienced it. They couldn't speak Tlingit on the campus. So they used to jump in the air to say a word in Tlingit."[77] Jumping in the air served as a physical and metaphorical act of resistance in which Native children leapt away from Western language hegemony. Selina, like her brothers, found avenues to continue speaking the Tlingit language, and as an act of equilibrium restoration, they brought language revitalization to their Tlingit nation.

In relaying stories about anti-Native discrimination, Rosa Miller (Tlingit) specifically addressed stolen ancestral lands. Rosa, born in 1926, explained that her family held land title in downtown Juneau. Rosa affirmed this Aboriginal land title: "I am of the Dog Salmon clan and we are the Áak'w Kwáan. The original settlers here in Juneau. Our original village was out at Auk Bay recreation area."[78] She spoke about the separate hospital in Juneau and anti-Native signs: "I remember the signs too back then. 'No Natives.'" When asked where the signs existed, she replied, "Oh restaurants, theaters, things like that. And the schools." Rosa then described how community activism brought positive change. She explained, "We had to sit way back, Natives had to sit way back. Things started to change when Elizabeth Peratrovich spoke on our behalf. They say she did it all by herself, we were all involved, and I keep telling them that . . . she was our spokesperson for [the] Alaska Native Sisterhood." Rosa shared that she is still fighting to claim her family's Aboriginal land. Her grandparents have a deed to the land from "Willoughby halfway down the channel." Here, she relayed, "Okay this is my land. Everything was taken from us. That deed didn't mean anything to them. They say our people didn't have deeds, but they did. I have the papers." Rosa's stories illustrate that there are Native elders alive today who continue to fight for Aboriginal land title.

Colonial Healthcare: Tuberculosis in Alaska

As an epidemic for Alaska Native communities, tuberculosis (TB) characterized many stories about Alaska. One elder discovered TB as the cause of death of her uncle in the service. I met Karen Thompson (Yup'ik/Tsimshian) while arranging a follow-up interview with Arnold Booth in Metlakatla in 2014. When the Metlakatla Inn had no vacancies, Karen generously hosted me. While visiting her home, she shared a scrapbook she inherited from her uncle John Hayward (fig. 28). She thoughtfully explained that he died

FIG. 28. John Hayward, early 1940s. Courtesy of Karen Thompson's World War II family scrapbook.

FIG. 29. The Hayward family, in Metlakatla, who would lose John Hayward to tuberculosis, early 1940s. Courtesy of Karen Thompson's World War II family scrapbook.

FIG. 30. Tsimshian servicemen from Metlakatla socialize: Lawrence Booth Faber (left) in civilian clothes, Daniel Reece (middle), and Joseph Hayward (right), early 1940s. Karen identified these men, and she identified Daniel Reece as her Grandmother Rhoda Reece Hayward's nephew. Courtesy of Karen Thompson's World War II family scrapbook.

FIG. 31. Joseph Hayward (Tsimshian) stationed in the Pribilof Islands, ca. 1940s. Courtesy of Karen Thompson's World War II family scrapbook.

long ago. According to the photographs he took in his scrapbook, John Hayward (Tsimshian) attended Chemawa, and during World War II, he was stationed across Alaska Native tribal geographies from the Aleutians to St. Paul to Nome. The photo collection offers a rich history of Tsimshian men from Metlakatla in the service. And yet, the photos that begin with his time at Chemawa stop with him in uniform. After a follow-up visit to Metlakatla, where I showed Karen how to request John Hayward's veteran record from the National Archives, we discovered his cause of death as TB. A young Native man so full of life, traveling across Alaska in the military, socializing with other Native men in the service, and playfully taking camera selfies using the reflection of a mirror, died too young (figs. 29, 30, and 31). According to Karen, John Hayward likely made the album at the hospital, and after his death his mother received his album.

Such are the stories of many Alaska Native people who have family histories from this era. In the 1940s, TB accounted for 20 percent of the deaths in the Alaskan territory.[79] My own Grandfather Lowell Anagick (Iñupiaq), an ATG and World War II army veteran from Unalakleet, survived TB in the postwar years while my Grandma Betty Anagick (Iñupiaq) snared rabbits to feed their eight surviving children. Remembering this time of hardship, many of my aunts and uncles cannot eat rabbit to this day.

TB devastated Native families, and statistics show high fatality rates in Native villages. Reportedly, the military rejected one out of four Alaska Native men from the service because they had TB.[80] In 1945, 69 percent of all deaths from communicable diseases stemmed from TB.[81] In the Iñupiat town of Kotzebue, in 1945, TB caused 54 percent of the deaths. In Utqiaġvik, a teacher reported that out of thirty schoolchildren between ages of five to six years old who entered school, only six survived.[82] In April 1945, when Unangax̂ returned from the camp at Killisnoo to their ancestral home island of Atka, X-ray reports indicated at least twenty-nine active cases of TB.[83] And yet these statistics do little to tell the stories of fractured families and lives lost too soon, like Karen's uncle John Hayward.

Among the practice of the BIA assimilating Native people through Western education, the BIA provided structure and oversight to segregated healthcare in Alaska. As historians Catherine Ceniza Choy and Adria Imada articulate, coloniality of care existed in other Pacific territories while Western diseases and pathogens attacked Native bodies.[84] Alaska had one of the highest rates of TB globally.[85] In 1943, three thousand Alaska Natives had active cases of TB, and the hospital only had sixty-nine beds.[86] Indeed, medical neglect characterized absent colonial healthcare for Native bodies.

During the TB epidemic, rampant medical discrimination existed against Alaska Natives. Shockingly, hospital workers had a practice of giving used bed linens from white patients to Native patients.[87] Native people also received leftover facilities; for example, the government converted old military facilities, like one in Skagway, into a sanatorium for TB patients. Colonial officials in Alaska only addressed Native healthcare when white people feared Native people could infect them. The government built these TB hospitals to prevent Native people from infecting the white military population.

Banishing colonial healthcare workers who neglected patients provided one way for Native people to restore equilibrium. In 1942, in the Athabascan village of Nulato, each adult resident, fifty-two in total, signed a petition to Governor Gruening to replace Emma Lambert, the government nurse who refused to treat sick patients on a Sunday during a measles epidemic.[88] She also left town before seeing all Native patients. Chief Peter Esmailka of Nulato and four tribal council members demanded a new nurse, identifying that Nurse Lambert neglected them dating back to 1936.[89] The request to replace Nurse Lambert parallels the story that Alice Petrivelli (Unangax̂) shared of her Uncle Bill Dirks banishing the BIA doctor H. O. K. Bauer from the Killisnoo camp when he failed to provide medical care. And while they navigated colonial healthcare officials, some elders spoke of traditional medicine as healing. As Nora Dauenhauer (Tlingit) attests from her interview, a traditional medicine doctor saved her life as a child when she hemorrhaged from a cut on her leg.

Truly, Native people organized to care for their communities, evidenced by the ANB and ANS, which advocated for federal healthcare programs to curb health discrimination. Native healthcare presented a space that could be segregated or integrated, and oftentimes it provided a place for racial boundaries to emerge. Some Alaskan towns provided healthcare to both Natives and whites. For example, the Valdez Chamber of Commerce endorsed a government nurse at Chitina to provide care for both Natives and whites.[90] However, in Southeast Alaska, amid the TB epidemic, activist Roy Peratrovich (Tlingit) wrote letters to build hospitals in Alaska for both races "without prejudice as to race, color or creed."[91] The ANB passed a resolution urging Governor Gruening to call a special session to address the need to purchase army and navy surplus hospitals for tuberculosis treatment.[92] In 1946, Governor Gruening responded by calling the legislature to a special session to create the Alaska Department of Health TB Control. Native people did push back, as evidenced by ANB secretary William Paul Jr., who wrote letters to the territorial commissioner of health protesting racial discrimination at the Sitka hospital.[93] Additionally, William Paul Jr. and Frances Paul oversaw the publication of the Alaska Indian Service and US Indian Service's "Home Care of the Tuberculosis in Alaska" (1947), an informational packet for Alaska Native people on caring for loved ones recovering from TB.[94]

Returning to the story of John Marin reveals that, according to Gruening's autobiography, he changed his name from "Marini."[95] This name change reflects a pattern of assimilation in the United States only granted to individuals adapted to a homogeneous white identity. If John Marin had children, they would have attended the integrated school. John Marin's name change occurred while the US government stripped Native children of their names, forcing the English language and English names onto them. As segregation in Alaska history shows, Native children were never assimilated to be white but rather to be a racialized category on a racial hierarchy that privileged whiteness within settler colonial structures.

In recent years, Alaska history has widely embraced the narrative of Elizabeth Peratrovich, the Tlingit activist and president of the ANS who propelled the passage of the 1945 Alaska Equal Rights Act with her elocution to the Alaska legislature. This commemoration includes national efforts, evidenced by the US dollar coin issued in 2020 with Elizabeth Peratrovich's image. And yet the focus on racial equality between whites and Natives is myopic since the settler colonial government and white settlers tried to dismantle Native sovereignty. Governor Gruening wanted to deny Alaska Natives their rights to Indian reservations, which would have preserved Aboriginal land title. Gruening believed that securing Aboriginal land rights would somehow privilege Natives as a race. Herein lies the irony of settler denial, in prioritizing civil rights, territorial administrators and government workers could readily seize Native lands in the name of equalizing whites and Natives. Meanwhile, Native segregation conveniently raced Natives into a racial category that remained marginalized within white society. Native activism that addressed racial equality in Alaskan cities perhaps inadvertently shifted attention from the fight for Aboriginal land title. Yet for Native people, they wanted everything. To sustain their Indigenous livelihoods, they secured their land while advocating for equal rights. Native people defied the colonial system that tried to manipulate them into racial categories and the erasure of Native sovereignty.

The racial hierarchy is reliant on settler colonialism that constructs race by bolstering white supremacy and extracting Indigenous resources from Indigenous land. Alaska presents a case study of frozen Jim Crow in which settlers crafted racial categories through settler colonialism. Colonization through segregation, land appropriation, education, and healthcare weighed heavily on Native lives. While Native people confronted segregation and reflected on what racialized identities meant for themselves and their community, white settlers and the federal government both seized Alaska Native lands and resources. Both racing and erasing seeks to strip away Native sovereignty. As oral histories and protest letters illuminate, Native people restored equilibrium by pushing against oppression, and they asserted Indigenized spaces that emphasized their rights to non-discrimination in business, politics, education, and healthcare in tandem with their stewardship of the land.

SIX
WAR AND
SEXUAL VIOLENCE
GENDER, SEGREGATION,
AND IMPERIALISM
IN ALASKA

PROUD OF HER TLINGIT HERITAGE, Carol Feller Brady never felt inferior for being a Native woman. Born in 1927, Carol published her memoir *Through the Storm towards the Sun* in 2006.[1] Her memoir is one of a few Alaska Native women's published autobiographies and recounts her life's many struggles and achievements. Carol is the sole survivor of her family; after her parents passed away, her brothers and sisters died from illnesses, boating accidents, and a house fire.[2] As an orphan, Carol attended the Wrangell Institute boarding school, and as an adult she spent time in San Francisco before returning to Juneau. In recognition of her commitment to Alaska Native people, which included her volunteer work facilitating talking circles for inmates, the Baha'i Church gave Carol the Service to Humanity Award. Through times of significant hardship and perseverance, Carol recalls moments of tenacity and her encounters with an Alaskan racial hierarchy bolstered by US imperial ordinances.

As a Native woman, Carol witnessed discriminatory treatment when the Alaskan military banned her from association with US servicemen during World War II. "We couldn't even speak to our own," she recalled. Military officials even disallowed Carol from associating with those she knew from the Native village of Klawock from childhood. As a teenager in Juneau, she told, "We were walking after a dance with one of the Native soldiers," she explained, "the shore patrolman came and told him he wasn't supposed to be with us." "The servicemen couldn't be seen with us," she recollected, needing to clear her throat upon recalling these events seventy years later.

Native women encountered patterns of discrimination that shaped Alaska's racial formation. Despite these regulations, Carol and her Native women friends circumvented exclusionary orders, and she even dated Thomas "Rosi" Rosinsteine, a non-Native serviceman from Texas. Carol explained that she never allowed separation orders to ruin her spirit: "I never thought of being insulted because I don't know why I can't explain, I just don't feel, I'm sorry, I don't feel inferior." By dating servicemen, Native women like Carol defied gendered segregation that shaped, and was used in attempts to enforce, an Alaskan racial order.

With the arrival of the military, Alaskan society structured around a series of racial and gendered hierarchies in which Alaska Native women's bodies symbolized a racial boundary that various posts in the US military both policed and monitored. This concept builds from ethnic studies scholar Shari Huhndorf's (Yup'ik) scholarship on racial and gendered hierarchies that informed US culture, media, and Native-white relations as well as cultural anthropologist Ann Laura Stoler's concept of racial boundaries imposed upon colonial women's bodies.[3] As a boundary between the two races, both Native women's and soldiers bodies became regulated by certain military officials in regions of Alaska, a part of a boundary that represented race making with an imagined division between white settler society and Indigeneity.[4] Generating Native women's bodies into a boundary between the races objectifies through a dual effort by patriarchy and colonialism that sought control. The enactment of a boundary by officials in the World War II War Department shows not only control of Native women's bodies but also control of soldier's bodies. The US military's policing of interracial sex and marriage between soldiers and Native women shows how the US government wanted to control the behavior of soldiers, yet the persistent efforts to date and marry among Native women and soldiers show that the government rarely managed to achieve that full control. Carol's oral history illustrates equilibrium restoration in which—as hard as imperial officials tried to render her body into a monitored object and racial boundary—she valued her own body while purposefully defying gendered segregation.

Examining the construction of a gendered racial boundary during World War II, this chapter identifies ways that settler colonial society depicted

Native women. Such a study involves an analysis of the Western sexualization of Indigenous women and also—when applying the concept of equilibrium restoration—identifying how Native women balanced these forms of gendered and racialized manifestations of oppression to highlight the social history of Native women who directly combated gender violence. With examples from oral histories and the archives, this chapter aims to pose the following question: How is sexual violence related to settler colonialism and war?

Material culture, vernacular language, and gendered segregation orders reveal a settler colonial power that used Native women's bodies as the primary site to distinguish race between Western and Indigenous peoples. During World War II, Alaska Native women experienced stigmatization through varied forms of violence that sexualized their bodies.[5] As scholars Lynn Stephen and Shannon Speed (Chickasaw Nation of Oklahoma) argue, voyeuristic violence, "media accounts of sexual violence, femicide, and other forms of gender violence" are exertions of state power and settler colonial powers.[6] On endemic sexual violence directed at Indigenous nations in Canada and the United States, which targets Indigenous women and children, Native Studies scholar Dian Million (Tanana Athabascan) identifies sovereignty movements: "This violence also marks a besieged site wherein Indigenous peoples attempt the 'healing' and revitalization of their politics."[7] Evidence of this violence is found not only in oral history like Carol Brady's but also in several forms, including material culture, vernacular language, and military ordinances. These diverse formats reveal violence that fashioned Native women's bodies into a racial boundary. First, Alaskan material culture, which included stationery and military newspaper comics, provided a medium for the Western imagination to exercise violence against Native women that constructed Indigenous women as savage and sexualized objects available for exploitation. Second, racial slurs such as "squ*w" and "klootch" circulated in the vernacular and constructed racial categories defined by Indigeneity and sex. Third, military exclusion ordinances that segregated Native women from servicemen pathologized Native women and sought to eliminate interracial sex and interracial marriage.

Native women represented a racial boundary between Indigeneity and an increasingly militarized Alaskan territory in which Native women witnessed forms of violence that sought to exoticize, stigmatize, and segregate them. Despite this discrimination, oral histories reveal equilibrium restoration exhibited by Native women who protested degradation, resisted violence, and fashioned their own lives. Native women asserted their presence on the wartime landscape by defying and otherwise delegitimizing such boundaries, interacting with whomever they chose. These World War II findings on Alaska history fit what scholars including lead feminist political scientist Cynthia Enloe identify as larger patterns of wider, global, and ongoing conversations about the politics of gender, race, and militarism in which imperial governments sought to control social interactions and a "gendered base system" to control not only soldiers but also the civilian population.[8] Put another way, Alaska represents another example of failed attempts by a military to facilitate imperial projects that included settler colonial efforts to determine who could intermarry and what a postwar demographic would consist of, as many Western governments imagined a postwar landscape as white.

Material Culture

During World War II, stationery and comics helped to establish the visual culture of Alaska that exploited humor and "Indigenous sexuality." Historian Jean Barman, who writes about Western Canada and British Columbia, provides an important scholarly framework for this study on wartime Alaska. Barman articulates that colonial and Indigenous relations relied upon sex and power where "Indigenous sexuality" struck at the very heart of the colonial project."[9] Violent images in cartoons created a colonial gaze that reified white male patriarchy while it exoticized and dehumanized Native women.[10] For example, the stationery "Wacker City (Pronounced Whack-her Sit-ty) Alaska" (fig. 32) collected by soldiers and tourists illuminates the commonplace nature of violence against Native women within material culture and colonial tourism that featured abuse against Native women.[11] This violence paired with Western humor. Humiliation meant more than embarrassment, as historian Jonathan Holloway argues; it served a colonial

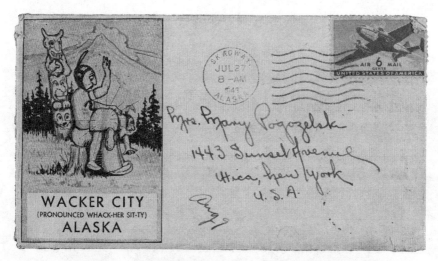

FIG. 32. "Wacker City (Pronounced Whack-her Sit-ty) Alaska" stationery.
Stanley Pogozelski Correspondence, Yale Collection of Western Americana,
Beinecke Rare Book and Manuscript Library.

purpose to "destabilize" the world for individuals to question their position
as "a first-class citizen or a peer."[12]

The town of Wacker City used promotional literature to recruit white
settlers and tourists for settlement through the visual violence of a Native
woman and the landscape. The image "Whack-her Sit-ty" is staged outside
Ketchikan in Southeast Alaska, a predominantly Alaska Native community.
In this case, it highlights violence against Native women by Native men with
the parenthetical caption "Whack-her Sit-ty." Within the frame, a Native man
spanks a Native woman bent over his lap. To argue that this image is merely a
cartoon distorts the powerful messages inherent to its form. First, the image
invokes stereotyped "savage" Indians with a half-naked, big-nosed, and stoic
Indian man featured with braids and one feather.[13] The imagery of a spanking
naturalizes domestic abuse against Native women. A Western audience may
laugh at this production of commercialized abuse exhibited in the image and
even the envelope's caption: "Come to Wacker City—far beyond the limits of
even Los Angeles. This place will make a hit with you!" The envelope's caption
represents a colonial project of settlement and tourism. The caricatured totem
pole is shown pointing and laughing at the abuse, re-affirming the illustrator's

intention of abuse as comical rather than horrifying. These images suggest that physical abuse, or sadistic spankings, against Native women are both natural and acceptable. Such a degraded depiction of a Native woman, and a projected image of a Native man as violent, perhaps gave license to white settlers to feel entitled to occupation of the land.

The "Whack-her Sit-ty" envelope illustrates what historian Philip Deloria (Dakota) identifies as colonial representations that helped to recruit European settlers through visuals that paired Native women with the land that might be conquered.[14] "Whack-her" on the derrière could imply sexual abuse and even rape. The creases on the Native woman's dress between her legs, and the lines emanating from her, exhibit pain. The image objectifies Native women such that the colonial audience can pretend to own, abuse, and laugh at a Native woman's subjective body by what Huhndorf identifies as a colonial and voyeuristic gaze.[15]

Power was derived from the colonial gaze in the "Whack-her Sit-ty" image that reaffirmed layers of patriarchy. Fashioning Native men into the realm of violent racial stereotypes, a Native man might abuse a Native woman, which crafted an Indigenous patriarchy founded on the premise of violence against Native women. All the while, a white audience that purchased the stationery elicits a broader patriarchy in which they may observe, "go Native," as Huhndorf termed, and imagine punishing the Native woman or, alternatively, playing the white savior by supposedly saving her.[16] As another element of reinforcing patriarchy in white society, white men and women could view the image to laugh at, although even if white women who viewed the stationery did not identify with Native women, their position in society remained marginalized to white patriarchy. Yet the white woman audience member, even if deemed subordinate to white men, could imagine herself as morally superior to the Native man depicted as violent and the Native woman characterized as a sexualized object for abuse. Commercialized images of Indigenous people circulated within a colonial market that exercised the ability to punish, humiliate, and mass produce.[17]

The "Whack-her Sit-ty" cartoon represents more than mere humor since it infused power by degrading Native women into a visual "piece of ass," as a powerless and a faceless woman who existed as a body part for sexual

FIG. 33. "Mickaninies Kow-Kow" features a breastfeeding Native mother, 1904. Archived in the Library of Congress Web Archives.

exploitation. Physical abuse, humiliation, and imagined domination of Native women's bodies are an element of the colonial gaze that asserted violence within material culture, like postcards, that World War II servicemen and tourists casually purchased, circulated, and saved as mementos from Alaska.[18] Notably, misogynistic cartoon images called "Tijuana Bibles" also existed during this era, although these cartoon publications remained in the realms of subculture rather than mainstream culture.[19] The "Whack-her Sit-ty" image exhibited an added element of misogyny that relied on race, constructions of savagery, and imagined colonial conquest.

Other postcards depicted Alaska Native women through a colonial gaze that exoticized Native women as fecund and immodest savages while unnaturalizing the practice of breastfeeding. As noted by historian Laura Wexler, through photography, colonizers constructed an imperial gaze that created a distinction between the imagined civilized colonizer and the imagined savage Indigenous peoples.[20] As historian Matthew Jacobson argues, photos of semi-nude women of color perpetuated imperialism and myths of barbarity and contained elements of a "pornographic gaze" that juxtaposed itself to Western "feminine modesty."[21] The World War II postcard titled "Mickaninies Kow-Kow" (fig. 33), collected by an anonymous Navy Seabee, is one example. In this image, a Native woman breastfeeds her baby and toddler called "Mickaninies," perhaps playing off the racialized language of *pickaninn*es*, a word that white people from places including Britain and the United States used to describe Black children, with *kow-kow*, a word that dated to the Alaska gold rush to describe food.[22] The photograph originated from Frank H. Nowell's collection documenting Nome in the early twentieth century.[23]

This photograph of "Mickaninie" and its reproduction as a postcard from 1904 well into the 1940s perpetuated depictions of savagery that critiqued Indigenous people, represented by an Indigenous woman, as immodest to Western standards. The Indigenous woman's body feeding both a baby and a toddler simultaneously displays fecundity, like the Native landscape where capitalist resources may be extracted. Such an image of a Native woman holding a baby, or in this case two babies, is reminiscent of representations of Sacagawea as a mother carrying her infant. Indigenous motherhood plays a unique role in the Western imagination since images of Native women and children likely conjure sympathetic reasons for Western settlers to not seek complete annihilation of the Native population through genocide.

The "Mickaninies Kow-Kow" postcard represents another material object marketed to Alaskan tourists that objectifies Native women's bodies as fecund, indecent, and exotic. The photo itself creates a visual ownership where the imperialist gaze is forever constructed through print culture.[24] Still today, this postcard may be purchased on eBay and Amazon.[25] The real name of the nursing Native woman and her personal story remain unknown; it is also unknown if she ever consented for the photograph to be taken, much less the many reprints, which she herself did not monetarily profit from. The images "Whack-her Sit-ty" and "Mickaninies Kow-Kow" commodified Native women's bodies through a colonial gaze that circulated within the Western marketplace. Deloria argues that stereotypes in material culture influence material events including discourse and ideology that impact federal policies.[26] Such an understanding reveals that these images represented a colonial project that exercised power. This stationery that circulated among

Western hands both constructed stereotypes and distributed a colonial project that rendered Native women into objects of abuse and as fecund.

As a digression from explicit representations of Native women, newspaper comics created a space for Western humor to showcase anxiety related to Native women and sex. Two cartoons from *The Adakian*, an Aleutian military newspaper, referenced implicit sexual relations between Native women and servicemen in the Aleutians. In one such comic, the humor played on the anxieties of interracial dating as represented by a white woman on the US homefront (fig. 34). Oliver Pedigo, a comic artist stationed in the Aleutians, depicted a white woman sitting on a couch, holding a letter, and saying to her friend, "He's in the Aleutians and he says he doesn't fool around with the Native girls."[27] The intended humor of the comic contains several interpretations, yet all interpretations that an audience member may obtain derive from a male perspective that contrasts Native women to white women. One interpretation from this comic plays off a white woman's

FIG. 34. The comic reads, "He's in the Aleutians and he says he doesn't fool around with the Native girls." *The Adakian*. Yale Collection of Western Americana, Beinecke Rare Book and Manuscript Library.

FIG. 35. The comic reads, "You mean there ain't even no Native women?" *The Adakian*. Yale Collection of Western Americana, Beinecke Rare Book and Manuscript Library.

naiveté in imagining that her serviceman boyfriend would never connect with local girls. Another interpretation is that this white woman's serviceman boyfriend doesn't desire to fool around with "Native girls." The third interpretation, and perhaps the most plausible, is that the serviceman wrote to his girlfriend reassuring her that he "doesn't fool around with the Native girls" not because he prioritizes his love for his girlfriend, but rather because the Aleutians lacked Native women altogether since the military relocated Unangax̂ from the islands to relocation camps. In this last interpretation, the humor stems from the serviceman's desire to connect with Native women vacant from the islands. Each possible interpretation of the joke reveals sexual tension on the topic of Native women in the Aleutians.

Another comic from *The Adakian* played on the intended humor of Native women and interracial sex (fig. 35). In the comic, the image of an overweight serviceman with gifts that include perfume, panty hose, and pearls has the caption, "You mean there ain't even no Native women."[28] The serviceman in the cartoon is suggested to trade Western feminine goods for sexual favors from Native women. In this sense, the man in the frame fashioned himself into a sugar daddy. The joke's humor derives from the thwarted expectation of an overweight serviceman who poorly speaks English unable to fulfill his desire to access Native women while stationed in the Aleutians. These comics from *The Adakian* show that even with the absence of Native women, due to Unangax̂ relocation, Native women occupied the minds of servicemen in the Aleutians. Sexual access to the "exotic" Indigenous women overseas or away from the contiguous states could be a "perk" of military service that US serviceman often expected or even demanded on many foreign and colonial fronts during war. The representation of the serviceman as overweight lends itself to the trope of the mockable "squ*w man" who deviated from colonial Western masculinity. This is no coincidence, particularly since many comics in *The Adakian* referenced women and sex, yet these two comics in particular reveal a sexual tension by servicemen who desired contact with Native women.

Vernacular Violence

Images from material culture that depicted Native women as sexualized objects through acts of violence, like spankings from Native men and sugar daddies who wanted to give gifts in exchange for sexual favors, matched racial slurs directed at Native women. Other scholars have shown that language infuses colonial power. Applying the example of Natives in colonial New England, historian Jean O'Brien (White Earth Ojibwe) argues that language describing Natives as "extinct" generates settler power to mentally remove and "replace" Natives from the landscape.[29] Decolonial scholar Frantz Fanon argues that racial slurs generate a white gaze that denigrates while creating a social hierarchy.[30] One Native literary scholar, Beth Piatote (Nez Perce), has taken a stand to disrupt the naturalization of a racial slur and to highlight the violence associated with it by censoring "*sq—w*."[31] The word *squ*w* dates to white colonists of the 1600s who co-opted the Algonquian language word for women applying it to all Indigenous women. As US empire accelerated westward, the term extended. Historian Andrea Geiger traces the words *Siwash* (adapted from a Chinook word) and *squ*w* as derogatory terms used pejoratively in the 1880s North Pacific.[32] *Klootch* is another term appropriated by white settlers from First Nations vernacular used to describe Native women of the Pacific Northwest. Terms such as *squ*w* and *klootch* evidence colonial power where settlers used language to construct racial categories that depended upon race and gender.

Published in 1943, Joseph Driscoll's *War Discovers Alaska* contains a glossary with common vernacular constructing racial categories in accordance with race and gender.[33] Driscoll's definition of *Natives* as "Alaskan [A]borigines, Indians, Aleuts and Esk*mos, looked down upon by whites" shows that he either observed said treatment toward Native people or he projected this bias himself. Other definitions in his glossary fit tongue-in-cheek humor, such as when he referenced "line-girls," "fishburners" as sled dogs, and the "Morningside" mental institution hospital in Portland, Oregon, for those who spent too much time up North. Nonetheless, racial slurs in his glossary crafted a racial hierarchy that relied on language that stigmatized Indigenous peoples. The terms he chose to include disparaged Indigeneity in accordance by gender. For example, Driscoll made a point to define *klootch* as an "Indian squ*w" and *klutch* as a "squ*w man," otherwise known as a white man married to a Native woman, made popular during Pacific Northwest settlement. Similar to the "Mickaninies Kow-Kow" postcard, Driscoll's definition of *Chena fever* as "pregnancy" linked Native women to fecundity. Driscoll's glossary perpetuated vernacular violence, which often relied upon humor. White supremacy used colonial language and misogynistic humor as a way to enact a settler hierarchy.[34]

Archival collections reveal that racial slurs circulated in casual conversation by settlers, rendering Native women the punch line of a joke. For example, a weather station report by the military dated in 1945 announced a new service club in Nome with a "klootch" room, otherwise known as a game room with two pool tables and two Ping-Pong tables.[35] Here, the word *klootch*, formerly used to describe a Native woman, described a men's lounge for entertainment. As another example, in a letter dated in 1945, Beulah Marrs Parisi, a white woman, described Alaskan food that she mailed to

FIG. 36. Four servicemen mock Native women in a performance. A painting of a nude woman hangs in the background. Umnak Island, June 8, 1944. "Quinn singing the song 'Squ*ws along the Yukon.'" Photo by Jack Hunt, Vern Brickley Collection, Anchorage Museum, B1998.014.1.11605.

family. Parisi relayed, "That <u>herring</u> that you received was really salmon and called <u>squ*w candy</u>."[36] The joke is that white settlers perceived Native women to eat salmon like candy. The whimsical nature of "squ*w candy" shows that colonial humor infused daily language. According to anthropologist Rosita Worl (Tlingit), stores in Juneau and Anchorage sold "squ*w candy" until the 1970s and stopped only after Native activism compelled sellers to cease.[37]

The word *squ*w* circulated not only in casual conversation but also in musicals by white servicemen stationed in the Aleutians. White men would, borrowing from Deloria, "play Indian" by using Native women's stereotyped identities to assert a white patriarchal order through performance.[38] In a June 1944 photograph of such a performance, four servicemen don costumes as pregnant "squ*ws" for entertainment (fig. 36). The title of the photograph, "Quinn singing the song 'Squ*ws along the Yukon.' Same as #119 also showing the 'Squ*ws' that he acquired while on the Yukon," references an older white prospector during the Klondike gold rush who presumably had multiple Native wives.[39] This prospector held the stomachs of two men in costume dressed as frumpy, and pregnant, Native women. The intended humor from this performance stems from the depiction of ever-fertile Native women who conceive offspring for colonizers and also from the ludicrous nature of the older prospector as a "squ*w man" with four Native wives. Fixation on Native women's fertility derived from both settlers and the government. As Historian Brianna Theobald argues, the US government has a long history of trying to control Native women's reproduction, dating from the nineteenth through the twentieth century.[40]

The fact that the men dressed as pregnant Native women is no coincidence. The bodies of Native women as represented by white men in costume symbolize white men appropriating Indigeneity as a racial project by literally performing the replacement of Native women's bodies. Historian Katrina Phillips (Red Cliff Band of Lake Superior Ojibwe) identifies that settler performances of Indigeneity are colonial projects of power.[41] As in the comics from *The Adakian*, sexual tensions for Native women in the Aleutians lingered even in their absence. With this "squ*w" performance, white men created a space to showcase impregnated Native women, and the men rendered Native women into a joke that reaffirmed a colonial order through performance. Even though Native women vacated the islands, their imagined position as an object to mock remained a colonial project. The pregnant caricature of Native women is not dissimilar from the "Mickaninies Kow-Kow" postcard featuring Native women's fecundity, but in this case, Native women's fecundity stems from the imagined colonial conquest of white men impregnating Native women.

*Squ*w* circulated with less whimsical connotations and more specifically those of sexual violence. In one archival letter, a captain linked Native women to sex and likely rape or a sex trade. In 1944, Reesly Heurkie wrote to Governor Gruening describing an inebriated Swedish sea captain on the northern Alaskan Kotzebue coast: "He invited me to stay on the ship that night and drink with him then told his officer to go ashore with Vincent and get a squ*w for himself."[42] "Get a squ*w" perhaps indicated consensual relations, although more than likely referenced sexual violence or a sex trade. In this instance, Heurkie discouraged the captain's lewd call for Native women by the ships officer. Yet not all men discouraged sexual violence toward Native women.

Military Ordinances

Along with stereotyped material culture and vernacular language, military ordinances that segregated Native women from servicemen sought to establish a racial boundary that relied on gender. Here, officials in the US military tried to control male soldiers' interactions with civilian women. In this case, colonial and imperial power manifested through segregation and informed a racial hierarchy that discriminated by gender against Native women. The US government and military exerted colonial power by generating Native women's bodies into a racial boundary that relied upon race and gender. Yet, despite ordinances, policing, and likely punishments, the military could not obtain full control over the interactions between soldiers and civilian women. This failure illustrates that US imperialism never obtained complete control of soldiers and civilians on the Alaskan landscape. Non-Alaskan men and local Alaska Native women often managed to exert their own agency, even if only in narrow limitations.

Military orders to segregate Native women, by separating them from servicemen, attempted to lay forth a new imperial policy constructing what an imagined US settler colonial landscape would be. Prior to the 1945 Alaska Equal Rights Act that prohibited segregation at businesses, forms of Native exclusion and separation existed in public venues. Here, all Native people experienced segregation. Yet World War II brought forth a new gendered segregation of Native women. Numerous letters dated between 1942 and 1944 referenced the problem of Native women, venereal diseases, and the solution of racial separation devised by the colonial government. This solution conveniently displaced the Native population from an increasingly militarized and settled Alaskan landscape. Even after the war, archival evidence dated in 1948 reveals that military officials in Alaska prohibited marriages between Native women and white servicemen. Applying legal historian Peggy Pascoe's insights into the relationship between the law and racial formation, these actions by military officials that prohibited interracial marriages sought to uphold white supremacy and generated interracial marriages as unnatural.[43] Borrowing from historian Martha Hodes's theories on the shifting tolerance of interracial "illicit sex," the military's anxiety about interracial sexual liaisons between white servicemen and Alaska Native civilians emerged during particular social, political, and economic circumstances.[44]

Across the globe, including the Alaskan territory, prostitution emerged in conjunction with soldiers altering the social fabric of local communities.[45] As historians Beth Bailey and David Farber articulate using Hawaiʻi as a case study of war, and as Asian American studies scholar Mark Padoongpatt articulates with Thailand as a case study during the Cold War, wherever an influx of troops emerged, prostitution followed.[46] Sex and prostitution troubled Alaskan locals and territorial officials. In the summer of 1942, Mrs. John Birkeland, a concerned resident, admonished Anchorage houses where she observed "thirty-seven soldier boys stand in line on our public street" waiting their turn to visit a brothel.[47] In Haines, a woman named Patay Kelly brought prostitutes to town, and she planned to connect a taxi service directly to her brothel in the summer of 1943.[48]

Both the US Navy and the mayor of Ketchikan observed that venereal disease outbreaks emerged in congruence with burgeoning military bases. In September 1942, C. S. Freeman, the vice admiral of the US Navy, sought to curtail prostitution and venereal diseases near Alaskan naval bases. He developed an outbreak prevention plan that included Kodiak and Seward. In a similar regard, in focusing on the impact of venereal diseases and civilians, Harry McCain, the mayor of Ketchikan, partnered with the army, navy, and Public Health Service to "clean up" venereal diseases with a camp for treating patients.[49]

Yet even amid the Ketchikan mayor's partnership with the military to facilitate treatment camps for prophylaxis, military authorities from Annette Island and Ketchikan blamed women, and specifically Native women, for the outbreaks. Langdon White, a medical director relayed, "The belief that the contacts are chiefly [N]ative girls has induced both army and coast guard authorities to issue regulations forbidding enlisted men to go about in company with [N]ative girls."[50] "Girls" at times described teenage Native girls and at other times referred to Indigenous women. Certain Alaskan territorial officials went as far as to label Native women's bodies as a greater risk of carrying venereal disease than the prostitutes in Southeast Alaska. Despite evidence that brothels corresponded with venereal outbreaks near bases, military officials targeted Native women as the culprits and segregation ensued. Alaska paralleled what historian Jean Barman identified as a colonial project that sexualized Native women as prostitutes.[51]

Other archival records reveal that the military in northern Alaska segregated parts of Nome due to the "complaisant" nature of Native women. An undated article from the war years described, "The army has complained that Esk*mo women are entirely too complaisant and has gone so far as to declare parts of Esk*mo village out of bounds for men in uniform."[52] Such descriptions of "complaisant" Native women are complicated in that they condemned Native women while simultaneously objectifying them. This, in turn, generated forms of patriarchal power that sought to monitor and protect Native women from their own sexuality. Theories by Barman can be applied to analyze this language where "gender, power, and race came together in a manner that made it possible for men in power to condemn Aboriginal sexuality and at the same time, if they so chose, to use for their own gratification the very women they had turned into sexual objects."[53] Don Foster, the general superintendent of the Alaska Native Services, wrote to Brigadier General Philoon about his concern that Native women fell victim to soldiers. Foster described "Native girls": "many of these simple people are easy prey for males seeking to satisfy their sexual appetites; and it cannot be denied, General, that men are generally the aggressors in such matters."[54] This language projected Native women as sexually passive objects and, in true patriarchal authority, excused surveillance and segregation as a means to protect Native women from their own "complaisant" sexuality. Here, colonial officials saw segregation as a preventive measure to prohibit sexual violence by servicemen.

Furthermore, the military ordinances that separated Native women from servicemen to "protect" Native women and to "protect" the servicemen from venereal disease exhibit what gender studies scholar Cynthia Enloe identifies as the adaptability of patriarchy that takes investment by men in power to sustain a system that keeps women in subordinate positions.[55] As Enloe further theorized, relationships between governments depended not only upon capital and weaponry but also on the control of women.[56] In Alaska, this manifested into actions by the military to segregate Native women where decisions informed by the military policy shaped gendered colonial categories.

Conversations on the problem of Native women, servicemen, and venereal diseases heightened, yet the Native community, which included activists and Native women themselves, protested colonial surveillance. Known for its legacy of activism to advance Indigenous rights, members in the ANB opposed military ordinances that sullied the image of Native women. Here, equilibrium restoration can be measured by activism and protest letters from ANB and ANS members who acted in direct response to oppressive measures. Roy Peratrovich (Tlingit), grand president of the ANB, wrote a protest letter to the United Service Organizations (USO) Board of Directors in Juneau on February 16, 1943, articulating, "Regulations prohibit any soldier from publicly associating with Indian girls. The inference drawn is that there are no decent Indian girls, and that the regulations are to protect the soldiers from contamination."[57] Here, Peratrovich identified that military ordinances degraded Native women's moral character. Peratrovich invoked an argument of Native patriotism when he identified that Indian blood spilled for US democracy abroad while Native women experienced discrimination on the home front. Other Native men in the ANB, including Louis F. Paul (Tlingit), wrote to all camps of the ANB and ANS on September 18, 1943, alerting on "Your sisters [. . .] barred from USO activities." In addition to Native women being barred from USO functions, military surveillance extended to mundane interactions, going as far as to regulate a serviceman from associating with a Native girl from his church.[58] Here, Christian influence did not even afford social equality to a Native woman from a congregation.

Alaskan political officials held paradoxical stances on imperial gender segregation and Native land rights. Alaska territorial governor Ernest Gruening supported the Native community to end racial segregation against

Native women. As a nuance, Gruening opposed segregation that excluded Alaska Natives, yet he also opposed Native land rights, and he argued that if Natives wanted equality they should not have reservations.[59] ANB minutes dated January 19, 1942, recorded that Roy Peratrovich read a letter by the governor where he summarized the governor's efforts to do "all in his power to help eliminate discrimination."[60] Such a report by the ANB to its membership shows that the Native organization saw Gruening as an ally on this specific issue, even if he sought to ignore their Aboriginal land rights by focusing instead on racial equality. In May 1943, Gruening wrote to Lieutenant General Simon Bolivar Buckner Jr. at Fort Richardson, condemning the offensive racial separation that stigmatized Native women and urging Buckner to rescind the separation order.[61]

As the strongest advocates for themselves, Native women notified Governor Gruening about the inequality they encountered. While it would seem that Native men including Roy Peratrovich and Reverend Walter Soboleff alerted Governor Gruening on segregation directed at Native women, the ANS deserves more credit than the organization has been afforded. Gruening identified that the ANS in Ketchikan first brought this matter to his attention.[62] One can imagine that key leaders in the organization likely met with Gruening in person in his office where they shared their concerns. As soon as he heard about these orders from the ANS, Gruening sought to have the orders revoked.

Lieutenant General Buckner replied to Gruening expressing fear that interracial sex would "exterminate" the Natives. Buckner allowed his post commanders to make judgment calls that regulated intercourse between their garrisons and civilians.[63] Buckner's next argument supported the colonial myth that Natives vanished through interracial sex: "unrestricted association between white men and [N]ative women has practically exterminated the Aleuts and is rapidly decimating the Indians and Esk*mos. I can think of no better way to exterminate the [N]ative tribes than to encourage their women to associate with unmarried white men, far from home and from white women." Buckner's statement gets to the heart of a colonial project that relied upon Native women as a boundary between the races. According to Buckner, these regulations that separated Native women remained in place, not because Native women threatened to spread venereal diseases, as expressed by military authorities from Annette Island and Ketchikan who public health officials found to be incorrect, but because interracial sex led to interracial offspring. Buckner invoked messaging of Native women's fecundity to caution a perceived problem of interracial sex and racially mixed children.

It seemed that Buckner tried to protect what he imagined as the Native race from colonialism, yet he sought to punish Natives for exercising their Aboriginal rights that restricted settler colonialism. Buckner challenged the BIA when he said, "If the Indians, Esk*mos and Aleuts are to be placed in exactly the same status as the white population of Alaska, there is no reason for the existence of the Indian Service and it should be abolished at once." In contesting Native subsistence rights, Buckner condemned the BIA for representing the interests of Natives, "On the other hand, so long as the Indian Service sponsors regulations giving to the [N]ative tribes special hunting, trapping and other privileges denied to white men, it scarcely appears appropriate that the head of this service should raise the question of racial discrimination." On military bases impacting hunting, in 1946, World War II veteran Arnold Brower (Iñupiaq) wrote to Gruening alongside fifty-seven Barrow residents concerned about jobs; at one point in his letter he made a point of saying, "Smoke and noise has also scared the bear away from the Point area where we used to shoot many of them."[64] Indeed the bases and presence of soldiers affected subsistence activities across Alaska. Thus, in essence, Buckner maintained that his post commanders should discriminate by race and gender when they saw fit, and Buckner sought to abolish the BIA — a government agency that advocated for some protectection of Native rights from settler colonialism. This letter by Buckner shows that he sought to preserve the Alaska Native race according to their blood quantum, yet he paradoxically wanted to destroy Indigeneity by assimilating Natives into a settler colonial society that refused to recognize their Aboriginal rights.

Buckner attacking the BIA is an illustration not only of anti-Indigenous sentiments he held in refusing to acknowledge Native subsistence rights but also of the division of colonial branches of government and the military that actually worked at times to benefit Indigenous peoples. While federal bureaucracy is confusing to navigate, once enough branches are involved, Natives could seize colonizers' words against them to enact change in their favor. Privy to these intercolonial bureaucratic divisions, Native leaders used colonial entities against one another. They did this simultaneously, using the US military to reclaim their homeland, while using the BIA to advocate for and to protect Aboriginal land rights, and while using the territorial government to protect racial equality in urban social spaces.

Native men did not sit idly by as imperial and colonial officials degraded Native women's social reputations; instead, they continued to write letters protesting segregation directed at Native women. Reverend Walter Soboleff dedicated his life to the Presbyterian Church and Native activism. His name is familiar to some because in 2015 the Sealaska Heritage Institute opened a cultural and research center in downtown Juneau and named the facility the Walter Soboleff Building. On June 24, 1943, Reverend Soboleff wrote to Buckner to advocate for Native women's equal treatment. Speaking on behalf of the Tlingit tribe and the Juneau Memorial Presbyterian Church, Soboleff relayed, "The order of which we all are aware of relative to troops forbidden to associate with Native women may have been put into effect with good intentions. The result has been one of abuse and embarrassment. It places the entire Native population under a class of folk as might be termed undesirable."[65] Soboleff called for Native women to no longer be barred from USO functions in Juneau, paralleling Peratrovich's letter describing that the entire Native community experienced humiliation when the military discriminated against Native women.

Efforts by Native activists paid off while propelling further political alliances to those in the colonial government sympathetic to Native causes. On June 28, 1943, Alaskan Delegate Anthony Dimond wrote to Frank Knox, the secretary of the navy, in Washington, DC, on discrimination by the armed forces against Alaska's Indians, Esk*mos, and Aleuts.[66] Dimond suggested that an inquiry be made on the conditions in Ketchikan. He then mailed a blind carbon copy to Secretary of the Interior Harold Ickes, Governor Gruening, Roy Peratrovich, Claude Hirst, and Ruth Gruber. Superintendent Hirst wrote letters to Roy Peratrovich detailing that he and Secretary Ickes worked with the secretary of war and the secretary of the navy to end discrimination against Alaska Native women.[67] A follow-up letter by Dimond to Knox explained that segregation against Native women complicated Allied war efforts that sought to dispel the myth of "master races" and that the military orders should be revoked.[68] Ickes then responded to Knox, underscoring, "Discrimination against the [N]ative Indians, Esk*mos and Aleuts by their white brothers in Alaska is nothing new. To fan this flame with the blessing, as it were, of official sanction, is surely not in keeping with the principles of the cause for which we are fighting."[69] Ickes saw discrimination as unpatriotic in US war efforts, and yet he suggested certain areas in Ketchikan could be labeled out-of-bounds "for the health and well-being of [the local commander's] men." This paradoxical message essentially called for non-explicit segregation measures since it contradicted the war effort, all while keeping geographic segregation intact to limit interactions between military (white men) and civilians (Native women). Here, Ickes shifted the racial boundary from Native women's bodies to the land and urban geography itself.

While the government failed to provide for Native girls who gave birth and mothered without support—government officials responded by incarcerating them—military officials from higher levels of government replied to the problem of segregation with the argument that racial separation protected Native girls. Some schools sought support from the military to regulate race relations and to protect schoolgirls. Acting Secretary of War Robert P. Patterson argued that the superintendent of the Eklutna Native School requested cooperation with the post commander at Fort Richardson to prevent the association between white soldiers and Native high school girls.[70] Other regions of Alaska like the Southeast characterized teen pregnancies as "juvenile delinquencies," and Native girls as young as sixteen and even thirteen years old were incarcerated for having venereal diseases and for being pregnant.[71] The Division of Territories and Island Possessions identified this to be a welfare problem and a direct consequence of war: "Because of the lack of funds [from the Office of Indian Affairs], young unmarried Indian mothers are either uncared for or are classed as criminals and thrown into jails throughout the territory."[72] Enloe identifies other examples of military officials crafting policy that excused patriarchal control over women's bodies.[73] For the remainder of the year of 1943, the segregationist ordinance stood.

The federal government and the war created these conditions of social relations between white military and the Indigenous population, and yet Native women and girls somehow became a problem to be managed through the influx of more settler colonial resources, such as by sending girls to boarding schools or training programs. Homer Stockdale, the government teacher in Unalaska, stated that Native women and girls were not safe due to the presence of soldiers: "It is unsafe for any female to appear on the street after dark or to be left alone in the home."[74] Stockdale wrote that drunk men tried forcing their way into his home when Mrs. Stockdale appeared alone and also that soldiers raped a twelve-year-old Native girl who then irregularly attended school.[75] And yet some Native girls could not access schools and resources, as in a case identified by Karl Brunstad of Kodiak who named Principal Clifton of the Kodiak School: "A young girl, through no fault of her own, was last year overpowered and raped. Mr. Clifton immediately expelled her from his school."[76] Brunstad lamented that Mr. Clifton had refused entrance to several other girls as well. Here, a principal wielded power and authority to exclude Native girls from his school based on his own perception of their sexuality, including when victim of rape.

On the topic of rape, history, and war, previous scholars restructure how gendered/racial/colonial hierarchies are informed by rape and sexual violence. Legal scholar Sarah Deer (Mvskoke) details the importance of writing and speaking the word *rape*: "Because I hope to position rape in a sociopolitical context, I choose to use the word rape to describe all forms of sexual predation as experienced by Native people."[77] In highlighting women's voices, including Indigenous women's perspectives, from early colonial American history, historian Sharon Block argues that rape and sexual coercion were "a gendered act of power" and "never divorced from other hierarchies."[78] As historian Estelle Freedman articulates, "At its core, *rape* is a legal term that encompasses a malleable and culturally determined perception of an act."[79] According to Freedman, "The history of repeated struggles over the meaning of sexual violence reveals that the way we understand rape helps determine who is entitled to sexual and political sovereignty and who may exercise fully the rights of American citizenship."[80]

Also in Southeast Alaska, in the town of Yakutat, concerned teacher Fred

Dimler wrote, "Last Friday night a [N]ative's home was broken into by one of the U.S.E.D. men. A fourteen-year-old girl was attacked, her clothes were torn off and she was cut with a knife. Native men had to force this man out of the house."[81] Dimler identified that the military police had no control over the U.S.E.D. men employed by the Yakutat Army base and that at one point they had also broken the lock off the ANB hall. These stories reveal gender violence that occurred in towns near military bases where neither the servicemen nor employed men of the military bases seemed to face any consequences. Like the Native men activists who wrote letters to end gendered discrimination, it was Native men themselves who intervened to help this fourteen-year-old girl.

Underscoring that Alaska represented an "area for colonization" and "a vacationland" for continental mainlanders, Secretary of the Interior Harold Ickes addressed the issue of "delinquent" Native children and "underground" relationships between "members of the military forces and Native girls" to President Franklin Delano Roosevelt.[82] It appears Ickes was primarily concerned with maintaining Alaska as a plausible postwar settler colony. He also targeted Natives as potentially warding off would-be-settlers: "If Alaska has a large [N]ative population afflicted with poverty and disease, these people coming into constant contact with new settlers will create conditions unfavorable to Alaskan progress." Here, Ickes conveyed a colonial mindset that framed Native poverty and disease as a problem for settlers yet failed to acknowledge how settler colonialism and the imposition of capitalist extraction garnered these issues. President Roosevelt replied to Ickes in May 1944, indicating that "the civilian situation in Alaska has been relatively bad" and that Alaska needed more facilities and infrastructure to navigate the settler colonial relationship between Natives and the military during war.[83] Roosevelt supported the Department of the Interior, and he expressed hope that Congress would do the same.

Stories by Rosa Miller (Tlingit), the chief of the Dog Salmon Clan since 1997, prove that surveillance of servicemen, rather than of Native women, was necessary at times. Born in 1926, Rosa described a close encounter in which she narrowly avoided disappearance. In an interview in September 2014, Rosa explained that one evening around curfew in the 1940s, soldiers grabbed her and tried to force her into the woods. In her words, "[The soldiers] had a few drinks and they treated the Natives, especially the women real badly."[84] While walking home one night, after her friend crossed the street to greet another friend, she recounted, "All I remember they were across the street, and I was walking, and they grabbed me and tried to pull me. There was a little wooded area there." Rosa then specified, "They were pulling me. And I was screaming so Mr. Lighty ran across the street and just then the MPS came. So, they threw them in the bus." Fortunately, her friend Lighty, who paid attention to her screams, and the military police saved her before she disappeared. When I asked Rosa how many soldiers, she replied, "I couldn't remember. I was just screaming I was so scared." Rosa's story demonstrates that perhaps violence was curtailed by surveillance of servicemen, rather than surveillance of Native women.

Going against the racial separation order and the wishes of the Coast Guard, Rosa married David Crockett, a serviceman of Irish American descent. In accordance with Departmental Order No. 82–1943 from the US Marine Corps Headquarters, marriages of navy personnel were made by proxy.[85] Accordingly, "No members of Naval, Marine Corps or Coast Guard forces on duty in any foreign country or possession may marry without approval of the Senior Commander of such forces stationed in that country, possession or area." Rosa's marriage to Crockett provides an example of an interracial relationship between Native women and servicemen that sustained despite racial separation orders. As equilibrium restoration meant balancing Indigenous lives amid waves of colonial violence, proceeding with a marriage to a white man, when colonial authorities disallowed it, upended the colonial structure that regulated interracial sex and marriage.

Similar to Rosa's story about a group of servicemen who tried to drag her into the woods, stories by Ted McRoberts, a US marshal in western Alaska, detailed incidents of harassment, breaking and entering, and rape. Accordingly, in October 1943, ten soldiers cornered a Native woman in a public meetinghouse in the Yupiit Kuskokwim region and harassed her until McRoberts intervened.[86] Other stories by McRoberts, such as one in which Marines from a merchant marine vessel trashed a Juneau restaurant, paled in comparison to what McRoberts described as "drunks, fights, shootings and rape" in western Alaska.[87] McRoberts explained that some soldiers broke into Native homes and raped women: "The [N]atives were frightened of the white soldier and his drunken antics; they seldom resisted in any way. Increasingly, the knock on my wooden jailhouse door became the knock of some scared [N]ative who had been run out of his own home by a soldier who had taken his woman."[88] Perhaps the most horrendous story by McRoberts described the rape of an infant that occurred after a couple left their ten-month-old baby with their GI friend to babysit.[89] The baby had to be taken to Anchorage for medical care. With the GI arrested, a mob in Bethel attempted to invade the perpetrator's jail cell. The military removed the soldier from Bethel and his outcome was never known.

The military's ban on interracial interactions in Southeast Alaska as a mechanism of civilian control ironically advanced Native women's networks of solidarity. Martha Benzel (Tlingit of the Lu'k-nax.a'di Raven/Coho moiety) offered an important perspective about Native women's alliances during the era of gendered segregation. Martha was born in 1923 in Sitka. When the war started, she attended the Wrangell Institute boarding school. She remembered segregation directed at Natives in Southeast Alaska, recollecting, "They had signs, 'No Natives Allowed.' Some places wouldn't let you come in, like restaurants, and the movies you had to sit in the certain areas. And you weren't allowed to date any of the servicemen."[90] When asked if she had friends who dated servicemen, she replied, "Most of them did. They had a way of sneaking around. . . . They found ways. One of them was the couple would go to the movies at different times and then they'd sit together." Martha explained that the USO allowed certain mixed-race Native women to attend functions and barred other Native women. She offered a compelling story about a Native woman who allied with other Native women in solidarity: "Some of the young ladies were part white and they let them into the USO. But one of them said, 'If you can't let the rest of my people come in, I'm not coming.' And she never went in." Martha's stories suggest that Native women supported one another vocally and in practice and that Native women collectively defied discriminatory military ordinances that monitored interracial dating.

Native people indeed established equilibrium restoration by pitting various government bureaucracies against each other to find an outcome that fit an Indigenous agenda. While some captains in the military willingly revoked segregationist ordinances, other captains stubbornly complied. On May 9, 1944, Captain Ralph A. Boaz issued an order to the headquarters of US troops in Juneau revoking the September 9, 1942, memorandum that forbid the association between white military personnel and Native women.[91] Yet, conversely, Captain G. W. MacLane of the Coast Guard hesitated to lift restrictions. MacLane asked Governor Gruening to provide statistics from Ketchikan, Juneau, and Sitka on the percentage of Native women compared to the percentage of white women thought to be carriers of venereal diseases.[92] Here, he used healthcare and the mischaracterization of Native women as venereal to justify Native women's segregation. Such a stigmatization in the name of health is characteristic of what American studies scholar Nayan Shah argues are synthetic boundaries that stigmatize minorities with imagined contagions that are feared to infect an imagined pure white society.[93] The US Public Health Service shut down MacLane's characterization of Native women as venereal. This government institution aligned with Native protesters and challenged military leadership.[94] Like the BIA that stifled full military control, the US Public Health Service also challenged imperial control, showing that bureaucratic branches of the government did and could divide among themselves in favor of outcomes desired by Native people. In writing protest letters to various government entities, Native activists found and leveraged malleable parts of settler colonial government so that they would debate among themselves and then issue orders that favored Native outcomes.

Native people also found allyship with local unions to champion ending racial discrimination directed at Native women. Orvel Holum, the secretary-treasurer of the Ketchikan Industrial Union Council, corresponded with Governor Gruening in April 1944 to promote the end of gendered racial discrimination in town. Mentioning discrimination by the USO against their membership, which extended to Native women, Holum wrote, "One of our members who had been recommended by the policewoman to attend a USO dance at the Army base, was humiliated and embarrassed by the associate director of the USO who publicly told her she was not supposed to go to the dance because she was a [N]ative."[95] Holum's letter reveals not only inclusion of Native women in the local union in Ketchikan but also unwavering support for their cause in ending gendered segregation. Unfortunately, he did not say the name of this Native member, perhaps to protect her identity, but we also do not know who she was or if she herself had requested that Holum write on her behalf. Continuing his letter, Holum stated that the Alaska Steamship Company denied a Native woman customer five times, telling her that "transportation could not be provided because she was a [N]ative and could not share a stateroom with a white woman, also that this was a policy of the company." Here, Holum indicated that a company had a policy of denying Native patrons on the basis of excluding them from sharing rooms with white passengers. Evidently, a woman named Irene Inman rallied white women passengers to ensure this Native woman obtained transportation back to Kodiak where her job with the US Army began three weeks prior. Here, women across racial lines supported this Native woman so she could commence a civilian defense job. Of interest is that it took five times for this Native woman to obtain passage to Kodiak and that no one stepped in the first four times to support her passage on the ship.

Finally following suit, Captain MacLane of the Coast Guard in Ketchikan canceled the ordinance that prohibited Native women from associating with military personnel, yet he issued zoning to limit interracial interactions. While MacLane rescinded his order on July 31, 1944, he issued another proclamation that restricted civilian areas for naval and Coast Guard personnel.[96] In a map of Ketchikan labeled "Restricted Areas," MacLane declared the Native village of Saxman off-limits except for Totem Pole Park and the Mink Farm (map 5).[97] MacLane also ruled hotels, cocktail lounges, and the Unangax̂ relocation camp at Ward Cove as restricted. In doing so, he continued to exercise a level of authority and surveillance by the military in the region to try to prevent interracial unions. The land itself had boundaries, instead of solely Native women's bodies. Meanwhile, in August 1944, Gruening notified Ruth Hampton of the Division of Territories and Island Possession that Captain F. A. Zeusler, who ordered a proclamation at the beginning of the war prohibiting the association of naval personnel with Native women, rescinded his order.[98]

Racial boundaries indeed varied by Alaskan geographies, and oral his-

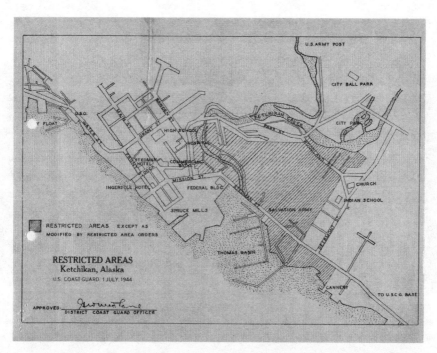

MAP 5. "Restricted Areas," issued by Captain G. W. MacLane to limit servicemen's involvement in Native spaces, July 1, 1944. Courtesy of the Alaska State Library, RG 101, series 79-35, box 462, folder 462-2.

tories indicate the frequency of interracial intimacies. Opposite to the military ordinances enacted in Southeast Alaska, the military in northern and Interior Alaska refrained from exclusionary ordinances directed at Native women. During an interview in March 2015, Holger "Jorgy" Jorgensen (Iñupiaq) described the frequency of interracial dating between Iñupiat women and servicemen in Nome.[99] Iñupiat women and soldiers could be seen closely convening in downtown Nome (fig. 37). Jorgy illuminated, "My oldest sister Martha lives in Fairbanks. . . . Martha met her partner during World War II; he was stationed in Nome. He was from Nebraska." Similarly, Alaskan War artist Henry Varnum Poor wrote about the commonality of interracial couples between Athabascan women and white servicemen in Galena on the Yukon River.[100]

And yet, even with some regions exhibiting non-existent policies on in-

FIG. 37. Native baby held by their mother looking toward a GI in downtown Nome, 1940s. Cora Horton Kendall Collection, Anchorage Museum, B2015.023.51.

terracial dating, the military forbade certain interracial marriages between servicemembers and Native women into 1948. As Pascoe relayed in her analysis of the intertwining of race, gender, and sexuality, "Miscegenation law reached well beyond the South."[101] As a racial project, these miscegenation ordinances extended to postwar Alaska. When the army regulated marriage between Native women and white servicemen, they possessed weapons and bases on Native land while seeking to maintain a racial and gendered hierarchy.

According to BIA records, the army and air force continued to reject marriages between servicemen and Native women. Some archival records show that the air force restricted interracial marriages into 1948.[102] While the air force never prohibited marriages, the organization made it difficult for servicemen to gain approval from their commanding officers. In other words, while no policy explicitly limited interracial marriages, the structure of the military allowed an official to exert his racial biases to allow or refuse to allow an interracial marriage. Here, the colonial project that separated Native women as a boundary between the races came into fruition according to the whim of a commanding officer. As an institution, the military granted a commanding officer this form of authority. And yet other colonial agencies in the federal government remained divided. Jorene Anderson, an employee for the Office of Indian Affairs in Fairbanks, articulated that soldiers, not the military, should select marriage partners.[103] Here, a federal worker representing the BIA in Alaska opposed imperial regulations.

Tensions between the military as an institution and Indigenous peoples as a collective group centered violence and exclusion against Native women. War-era cartoons from newspapers, stationery, and postcards created a commercialized space that garnered objectification and violence against Native women based on the construction of Indigeneity that relied on both race and gender. While material culture and vernacular language provided a space for colonial assertions—and even an outlet for colonial humor—military ordinances that separated Native women from white servicemen as well as orders from military officials that prevented interracial marriages instituted a colonial order disrupting civilian-military social interactions and rendering interracial sex and interracial marriage as unnatural.

Despite colonial efforts by the military that stigmatized Native women as venereal and tried to limit interracial sex between Indigenous women and white servicemen, the Native community, including vocal Native male activists such as Roy Peratrovich and Reverend Walter Soboleff, and Native women, including through the organization of the ANS, prevailed, and they largely terminated the segregationist ordinance enacted by the military. Here, the US government, represented by the World War II War Department and military leaders such as Lieutenant General Buckner, could not shape interactions between soldiers and civilian women as they desired. A full imperial project that dictated sex and relations between soldiers and civilian women could never be achieved as it had been imagined. As savvy activists who knew the multiple layers of the government, Native women and Native men wrote to so many government entities until they found agents willing to side with them against gendered social exclusion by the military.

Even with restrictions imposed upon them, Native women sought whatever they wanted during the war years. Rosa Miller married an Irish American in the Coast Guard despite regulations that prohibited their courtship.

Martha Benzel explained that Native women rejected gendered segregation, and they allied to support one another. And in some cases, while Native women defied discrimination, to some women, like Carol Brady, segregation remained secondary to home life struggles such as rampant deaths in her family and even mundane pleasures such as jitterbugging with friends.

Prevalent forms of violence existed that settlers and the military directed at Native women. Yet, just as colonialism pushed against the Native community by invoking military ordinances that stigmatized Native women's bodies, Indigenous peoples pushed back against colonial powers and utilized divisions in colonial bureaucracy to fit their agenda. Native women and the Native community exercised power through protest, and they reestablished a space of equilibrium restoration.

EPILOGUE
PEOPLE, LAND,
AND SOVEREIGNTY

SOVEREIGNTY INDEED DWELLS in the lives of individuals and erupts into individual actions restoring Indigenous livelihoods. Revealing themselves as role models and positive mentors, numerous elders whom I interviewed facilitated talking circles. Carol Brady (Tlingit) and June Degnan (Yup'ik) volunteered at prisons, Mary Wolcoff (Aleut/Japanese Alaskan) worked with youth on suicide prevention, Selina Everson (Tlingit) and Shirley Kendall (Tlingit) taught Tlingit language at schools, Larry Chercasen (Unangax̂) gave talks to his church about Unangax̂ relocation, Conrad Ryan Sr. (Tsimshian) shared prayers in church in the Sm'algyax language, and my Grandma Betty Anagick (Iñupiaq) worked as a teaching assistant instructing Native schoolchildren. Truly, the names of all the elders I spoke to, their life accomplishments, and the ways that they gave back to their communities in a capacity that upheld community health while bolstering Indigeneity are too numerous to list. Restoring equilibrium within the lives of Indigenous peoples occurs on a holistic level at which you can observe the Native nation pressing against colonialism through the effort of one individual elder to positively impact the community.

These efforts of positive community engagement through verbal expression of talking circles and oral histories indeed fit within an Indigenous theoretical framework. Indigenous scholar Harold Napoleon (Yup'ik) articulates the "Great Death" as colonialism that brought illness, despair/trauma, and violence fracturing families and creating orphan survivors who stitch together pieces of the world.[1] Napoleon identifies talking circles as the only way to recover from this great loss. Listening, speaking, and oral histories are indeed restorative to both the community and individuals. As Western colonialism seeks to remove Native tongues and languages, community-building mechanisms such as talking circles indeed unravel colonial projects while propelling Indigeneity and sovereignty.

Pivoting from healing the people to restoring the land, my own observations reveal how nature is reclaiming spaces formerly occupied by imperial bases. When visiting ruins in Southeast Alaska and the Aleutian Islands, I witnessed how the environment has eroded remnants of World War II to the near point of disappearance. Historian Christine DeLucia calls such remnants of war on Indigenous lands "memoryscapes."[2] On Annette Island in Southeast Alaska, rusted metal peaked through the ground and between heavily forested tree branches. I approached the door of a refurbished Quonset hut where I could hear someone playing old-time music on a radio. In the Aleutians, cement blocks had chipped away to mere rubble where only a building's foundation peaked through the ground while a fox strolled carelessly by.

At Point Davidson, a former base on Annette Island, a gunnery exists as rubble. Here the US and Canadian Forces diligently monitored the waters for Japan's potential invasion. While visiting this location with World War II army veteran Conrad Ryan Sr. (Tsimshian) and Karen Thompson (Tsimshian/Yup'ik), Conrad motioned with his hand toward traditional fishing grounds and the neighboring visible shoreline of British Columbia (fig. 38). The buildings that served as militarized locales of war between empires of the Pacific corroded into the natural environment, and all that remained were buildings that Native people chose to salvage. This paralleled how Native nations actively restore their ancestral lands by reappropriating structures left by colonialism while leaving other portions to decay to rubble. Settler colonialism alongside imperial actions seeks to erase Indigeneity to rubble, yet an analysis of equilibrium restoration shows not only persistence but also reappropriation of colonial sources to perpetuate Native presence and Native futures.

There is a non-permanence of military bases and military sites that seem permanent. Such a concept reveals that even in places where the US military

FIG. 38. Visiting the former gunnery at Point Davidson with Conrad Ryan Sr. and Karen Thompson, 2017. Karen points to where Metlakatlans fished and gathered herring eggs. Photo by the author.

has excluded land access to Natives and civilians alike, such as Hawai'i, the military bases may decompose with time, generations, Native advocacy, and shifts in colonial politics. Like the very premise of history itself, imperial powers are never inevitably foreordained.

In the Arctic and subarctic, I observed Quonset huts reused and reappropriated by Native people who chose to maintain the structure over multiple decades. In the Yupiit town of Bethel, in springtime, snow melted at the edges of unsealed roads. While visiting with my cousin Elizabeth Aarons, who received the Alaska Federation of Natives (AFN) health award in 2022 for her contributions as a nurse in the Alaska Native Medical Center's Oncology and Infusion Center, and Andy Angstman, an avid dog musher, I observed that some Bethel residents had refashioned Quonset huts as sheds next to their houses. In Utqiaġvik, I saw a similar practice of reappropriating Quonset huts for housing and storage. Moving south of Utqiaġvik, to Unalakleet, the southernmost Iñupiat town, my Grandma Betty motioned to Traeger Hill just outside town where the former military base resided adjacent to our family's ancestral village (fig. 39). My grandma told me that back in those days she kept her head down while walking around town to avoid engaging with the servicemen. From the distant view of where my Grandma Betty had gestured, nothing remained visible on Traeger Hill to indicate that a US military base ever occupied this space. The base was gone almost without a trace, other than memories from elders who occasionally reference the location when speaking to their kin. Perhaps portions of the former buildings had been reappropriated by Iñupiat as well. Muktuk Marston's cabin on the North River outside Unalakleet remains in partial shambles. His ashes are scattered on Besboro Island, an Iñupiat region in the Norton Sound.

While some buildings remain in ruins, seeming innocuous to the surrounding ecology, other actions by military occupation have accelerated environmental damage. The stories from Alice Petrivelli (Unangax̂) reveal her continued advocacy for the government to clean up wartime debris on the Aleutians that polluted the land and waterways. My Grandma Betty detailed how the military sprayed Unalakleet in northwestern Alaska to kill mosquitoes. When they sprayed, she would bring her fish inside the house from drying racks to protect her family from contamination by toxic chemicals. Several elders in town, including my Grandpa Lowell Anagick (fig. 40), who used to work on the base on Traeger Hill, died of brain cancer when I was in middle school. My mother told me that Grandpa Lowell shared with her that when he was employed on the air force base at Traeger Hill in the late 1940s and early 1950s, a sadistic white superior forced Iñupiat workers to stand in line formation for several hours until some men urinated themselves.

During World War II and into the Cold War, imperial occupation in Alaska brought poisons to the land and people. To name a few, this included H-bomb testing for the proposed Project Chariot in Point Hope in 1962 and detonations at Amchitka in the 1950s. When I met Iñupiat artist Ken Lisbourne at AFN, before he died of pancreatic cancer, he told me that his watercolor of Cape Thompson with the bodies of people and marine life

FIG. 39. *above* Five generations in our family's ancestral village (from left): Kakarak (English name Lena Williams, also my mother Ella Anagick's namesake), Miowak (also spelled as Mahyuqqiak, English name Marion Gonangnan, my namesake), Apachoalk (English name Martha), and Betty Anagick holding baby Rose. Photo taken by Fred Machetanz in Unalakleet, late 1940s. Courtesy of the Anagick Family Collection.

FIG. 40. *left* Lowell Anagick army photo, 1945. Courtesy of the Anagick Family Collection.

on the shoreline below the red sun represented everyone who died from radioactive contamination by the US government. While Point Hope Iñupiat successfully mobilized in protesting Project Chariot, the US government still brought and buried material from a 1962 Nevada test site to Alaska, contaminating the soil.[3]

World War II, the war that was supposed to end all wars, persisted into a half-century Cold War with Alaska strategic to Arctic defense and offense. The former lend-lease agreement from 1941 to 1945 whereby airplanes passed between the Soviet Union and the United States dissolved. In dropping two atomic bombs on Japanese civilians, the US military flexed nuclear imperial prowess as the Soviets approached imperial control of Japan. As empires that attempted Pacific domination, the Soviet Union and the United States drew the 38th parallel. This arbitrary line created by empires ushered in the Korean War and Cold War where Alaska and the Pacific continued to withstand imperial occupations by these warring empires.

Current demographics and social interactions reveal longer impacts of war in which military mixed with civilian life. Around town, you still meet people who are descendants of interracial unions between servicemen and locals. Some people in Unalakleet, like my Great-Aunt Marjorie Henrietta "Hank" Rhodes, relocated to the Midwest after she married her Hoosier husband Hugh "Ebby" Rhodes, who was stationed in Alaska with the US Air Force in the late 1940s. During two summers of my childhood, Hank and Ebby drove their RV from Indiana to Anchorage along the ALCAN Highway to visit our extended family. This ALCAN Highway, connecting Western Canada and Alaska to the contiguous United States, existed because of the war. Her relationship with Ebby only came from postwar and Cold War Alaskan occupation.

We Are Sovereign Peoples

Returning to the topic of sovereign peoples of Alaska, contrary to what the mainstream media and the government depicts, Alaska Native sovereignty exists and persists. In writing this book, I continually attempted to decolonize my thinking by challenging several assumptions about Native history and Native rights. As I have been indoctrinated by colonial entities since a young age, thinking critically proved essential. Growing up in Alaska, I had two lawyers as divorced parents: my dad a former administrative law judge for Alaska and my mom the only Alaska Native criminal defense attorney. The snippets I heard about Native sovereignty arose from conversations that I had with them where the discussion was strictly limited to a legal interpretation of what colonial law determined to be Native rights. I pieced this together with fragments of information that I heard from the news. I remember asking my parents about Heather Kendall-Miller (Dena'ina Athabascan) and how she argued before the Supreme Court in 1998 on the historic Venetie case.[4] In this case, the Supreme Court determined that Alaska Natives do not possess Indian Country and therefore do not possess the same sovereign status as American Indians who reside on Indian Country.

For many years, I could not understand why Alaska Natives would be treated differently than American Indians by the federal government. As I would learn as a historian, much of this related to the timing of Alaskan colonization. Alaska's so-called purchase by the United States from Russia passed through foreign colonial hands with zero Native voices present. Amid the Indian Wars, by 1871, Congress determined that they would no longer negotiate treaty rights with Indians. Alaskan colonization by the United States occurred in waves aligning with the 1890s Klondike gold rush, World War II, and the twentieth-century oil boom forcing Congress to resolve Native land claims so corporations could access oil.

Yet as a student of Native history, over the years I have learned that just because a colonial court says something, which conveniently extinguishes Aboriginal land title, that does not mean that Native land rights and sovereignty are gone. According to the highest colonial court of law, based on the 1998 Venetie decision, the Alaska Native Claims Settlement Act of 1971 (ANCSA) extinguished Aboriginal land title. Indigenous sovereignty, which exists within the Native nation, cannot be extinguished so easily. Learning this has taken me over a decade of observing community members and listening to conversations within circles of Native activists. Native sovereignty never diminishes as long as Native people survive.

Consequently, before I had the opportunity to delve into academic literature on sovereignty, one Alaska Native activist opened my eyes to the ongoing nature of land claims and Alaska Native sovereignty. When I began my oral history project in 2008 as an undergraduate at Stanford University, I met an elder named Grover "Butch" Riley (Athabascan) from Minto. Upon meeting him in Anchorage, he carried numerous photocopies of a flyer alerting community members to a meeting in a reserved conference room at the Alaska Native Medical Center to discuss Aboriginal land rights. I remember looking at the handwritten flyer and its copies. Butch was the first person I had met who explicitly told me that sovereignty persisted, that he fought for land rights, and that land claims were far from settled. And here he was, like the elders who came before him, using colonial spaces, in this case a federal hospital, as a resource to hold his meeting on Native land rights. Other activists emerged in my life inside and outside Alaska.

Perhaps my greatest lesson on Alaska Native sovereignty emerged when the First Alaskans Institute employed me as a research consultant in 2018 to document eight years of data on their Alaska Native Dialogues on Racial Equity (ANDORE) project funded by the W. K. Kellogg Foundation. Again, here we see Native organizations utilizing Western resources to support positive Indigenous communities. Sovereignty emerged as a pronounced theme in numerous community dialogues on racial equity in Alaska. Sifting through eight years of data from 2010 to 2018 — which consisted of town hall meetings with community centers and partner organizations across Alaska, including over twelve thousand participants — allowed me to see themes related to intergenerational trauma, education equity, and health and well-being. In reading numerous notes referencing sovereignty, it became clear to me that Alaska Native people had not let go of their rights to sovereignty and their exercise of sovereign governments. Native people still exercise their political sovereignty through tribal governments. For example, Bea Kristovich (Athabascan/Yup'ik) served as the traditional chief of the Association of Village Council Presidents for the Yukon-Kuskokwim Delta tribes until she passed away in 2022.

Zooming back out to the broader implications of wartime history, I cannot address US colonialism without a discussion of it reaching across the Pacific, extending from the war in Alaska to Japan. During my time as a graduate student, I visited Japan. From the public history available, I witnessed the atrocities of the atomic bomb that leveled the city of Hiroshima and instantly ended the lives of seventy thousand people in that town alone, mostly civilians consisting of women, children, and elders.[5] Due to radiation poisoning, an additional sixty thousand people in Hiroshima died by November of that year, and another seventy thousand died by 1950.[6] Continually telling this history of mass civilian death—a genocide—followed by the United States overtaking bases across the Pacific and Japan means, borrowing the language of historian Daniel Immerwahr, reconciling that a country that purports to be a republic is indeed an empire that seizes resources from distant lands through colonial violence that manifests physically, economically, and culturally.[7]

Okinawa itself declares sovereignty from the empire of Japan as have Ainu of the Sea of Okhotsk and Hokkaido. I know Alaska Natives who were stationed in Okinawa, and such is the condition of colonialism that paradoxically brings together Native people and those subjected to the projects of empire. And yet these goals of settler colonialism and white supremacy are never met with pure acceptance or ambivalence but rather with resistance and—in the case of Alaska—equilibrium restoration on occupied lands. Global Indigenous sovereignty movements continue even when not covered by Western mainstream media.

Sovereignty exists where people do. Augmenting the voices of Native elders and understanding their roles as cultural educators and as survivors of boarding schools, and how each life represents someone who is an agent of Indigenization, reveals more than just voices but also a collective assertion of Indigenous sovereignty. These voices in history accomplish more than telling a story of war on the Alaskan landscape; they illuminate Indigenous cultural persistence and resistance that continually challenge projects of war that work in tandem with settler colonialism. None of this is preordained; like the contingencies in history, Indigenous peoples exert autonomy and agency wherever they can to restore the land and their sovereignty.

Intergenerationality, Learning from Elders, Death, and Life

No training as an oral historian prepared me for the loss of elders over time. I never expected I would confront mortality on a regular basis. Many elders whom I interviewed, beginning when I was only an undergraduate in 2008, have passed on to the next world. I thought I would have more time with many of them. I pause thinking about wonderful elders whom I connected with over several years. Alice Petrivelli (Unangax̂) passed away in 2015, just a year after I met her. Among conversations about wartime Alaska and relocation camps, off-record we chatted about our mutual enjoyment of travel to Las Vegas and living on the East Coast at various points in our lives. After hearing of her passing, I felt both empty and full at the same time. I continue to feel empty by the loss of our elders and this generation who lived through the war, survived government camps, and advocated to preserve Native lan-

FIG. 41. Jorgy Jorgensen and baby Jada, Fairbanks, April 2017. Photo by the author.

guages. I feel full from having met them, crossed paths with them, and on a few occasions breaking bread over stew and halibut or even at a local diner in Ketchikan or Fairbanks.

Academic history must acknowledge that methods from Indigenous studies, the personal connections, oral histories, and community-based stories of Indigenous nations, are fundamental to the broader field of the humanities. This writing and the website I administer, ww2alaska.com, are my efforts to help solidify these assertions while amplifying the voices of Native elders. Indigenous oral histories are indeed about connecting people, family, and kin.

Over the years, my family and Holger "Jorgy" Jorgensen's (Iñupiaq /Norwegian) family intersected in ways that I had never imagined. Jorgy knew my Grandma Betty Anagick from the time he traveled from Haycock to Unalakleet by dogsled in the early 1940s for a Covenant church conference. In 2015, while visiting my Grandma Betty in Unalakleet, I called Jorgy from her landline; Jorgy and my grandma spoke on the phone after they had lost touch for over seventy years. In 2017, my mom, my daughter, baby Jada, and I traveled to Fairbanks for the Alaska Native Studies Conference. While in town, Jorgy and his daughter Roberta invited us to dinner. At Roberta's house with Jorgy and his son Noel, we went through vintage photographs, and my mom identified a picture of her Grandmother Martha visiting Haycock. We found another photo of our cousin Amelia Lovell, who is a mutual cousin to Jorgy. We had common kin and history in northern Alaska, and here we were one generation later sitting together in Fairbanks. I still remember Jorgy holding baby Jada by a window as snow filled the yard. Both smiled as Jorgy sang in Iñupiaq to her (fig. 41). Just as we linked intergenerational kinship through photographs, Jorgy and Jada sat together sharing an intergenerational and precious moment in time.

Many elders, like Jorgy, notified me of their terminal illnesses. I observed these moments knowing just how special these elders were and how, like watching a baby grow each day, fleeting each moment was in life. What a privilege it was for me to meet so many wonderful elders, to laugh with them, to learn from their stories, and to be given glimpses of what their lives were like during war that changed their lives, and the Alaska that we know, forever.

This community-based project was only made possible by abundant support from Alaskan community members.

Anchorage, Nome, Juneau, Metlakatla, Unalakleet, Kodiak, summer 2008

With the Community Service Research Internship from Stanford University's Center for Comparative Studies in Race and Ethnicity, I received mentorship as an unpaid intern with the First Alaskans Institute (FAI) placed with the Alaska Native Policy Center (ANPC). Gary Chythlook helped me create a flyer for advertising. Dale Smythe, Liz Medicine Crow, and Janie Leaske mentored me at the ANPC. Linda Scott helped me arrange elder interviews at the Nome Eskimo Community. Karlin Itchoak drove Linda and me to historic locations in Nome. The Central Council of the Tlingit and Haida Indian Tribes of Alaska (CCTHITA) provided a room for me to conduct interviews with elders. Chris Bryant, a fellow FAI intern, connected me with his Grandma Barbara Fawcett in Metlakatla. FAI provided an interview location in Anchorage. My Aunt Joan Johnson and mom Ella Anagick helped me to arrange interviews in Unalakleet. Peter Boskofsky of the Alutiiq Museum helped me conduct all interviews with Alutiiq elders and preserve them with radio quality audio at the Alutiiq Museum. My dad, David Stebing, connected me with Judge James von der Heydt. I met with historian Aaron Leggett at the Alaska Native Heritage Center.

Juneau, *May 2013*	Melissa Kookesh helped me arrange an interview room at the CCTHITA. She arranged a few interviews and provided water, tea, and salmon spread with crackers for visiting elders. Marilyn Doyle, director of the Elder Program at CCTHITA, provided me with a list of elders whom I should contact. June Degnan gave me copies of important news articles related to race in Alaska. Richard Dauenhauer gave me a signed copy of one of his books, and Nora Dauenhauer made photocopies of her favorite poems that she had written. Tonja and Mark Woelber took me out to dinner in Juneau. Amy Mount, a graduate student at the Yale School of Forestry and Environmental Studies, traveled with me, and we split a hotel room. My mom, Ella Anagick, hosted Amy in Anchorage for part of her trip. Later in the summer, after attending a conference at Oxford, I took a train to rural England where Amy hosted me in Edale.
Anchorage, *summer 2013*	Maria James, director for the Anchorage Senior Activities Center (ASAC), helped me arrange interviews on site. I visited ASAC multiple times, and I introduced myself at lunch and social events like Bingo night. My dad, David Stebing, put me in contact with Mary Doppelfeld, who arranged an interview with Katie Hurley, the former secretary for Governor Gruening. Mary and I drove to Wasilla to interview Katie. Bob Montague helped me arrange a visit, and we scheduled interviews at the Anchorage Pioneer Home.
Unalakleet, *June 2013*	My mom, Ella Anagick, helped me conduct interviews in town.
Juneau, *September 2014*	Donald Gregory at the Sealaska Heritage Institute (SHI) helped me arrange interviews by calling elders he knew and asking if they were interested in participating in my study. Donald shared herring eggs and seal oil with me too. Before I left Juneau, Donald gave me copper earrings to thank me for connecting with elders and recording their stories. Rosita Worl, president of SHI, met with me to discuss my research, and she shared research data compiled by SHI on race discrimination across Alaska.

Zachary Jones allowed me to use a room at SHI for interviews. Marilyn Doyle, director of the Elder Program at the CCTHITA, helped to arrange an elder lunch visit so I could introduce myself and conduct interviews after lunch. Marilyn also gave me a Tlingit values magnet. Jackie Kookesh, at the CCTHITA, connected me with her cousin Sandy who helped me arrange an interview with her mother, Martha Benzel. Rosa Miller gave me Labrador tea that her son had handpicked. Dorothy Owens gave me jarred salmon. Carol Brady gave me a signed copy of her book, and she hosted me for halibut dinner at her house.

Metlakatla,
September 2014

Karen Thompson hosted me. She drove me to visit historic sites, helped conduct interviews, and hosted a dinner party to meet Conrad Ryan Sr. Roxee Booth helped arrange an interview with her dad, Arnold Booth. Roxee gave me a beautiful Tsimshian doll.

Anchorage,
November 2014

Professor Shari Huhndorf helped me arrange an interview with her family friend General Jake Lestenkof. He is also a friend of my aunt, Gail Schubert. Professor Maria Williams helped me arrange an interview with Alice Petrivelli.

Fairbanks,
March 2015

The Senungetuk family, Ron, Turid, and Heidi, invited me to join them for meals, conference events, and an art show. Harley Senungetuk drove me to campus events, and he hosted an Iditarod watch party. Bill Rimer drove me to oral history interviews with Holger "Jorgy" Jorgensen and Al Wright. Jorgy took Bill and me out to lunch.

Bethel,
April/May 2015

My cousin Elizabeth Aarons and Andrew "Andy" Angstman hosted me at the Angstmans' home. Katie Basile offered to help and provide car rides to/from the airport. Andy drove me around and helped me conduct interviews. Nels and Katie Alexie gave me Luumarvik Fish Camp key chains and mini flashlights. Bea Kristovich gave me blueberry jam.

Anchorage, *May 2015*	I met Jenna Perdew and her son at my niece Citlali Elias's dance class. I showed Jenna my recruitment flyer. Since Jenna worked for Alaska Airlines, she offered to fly her Uncle Larry Chercasen from Vancouver to Anchorage so he could spend time with her family and so he could participate in an oral history interview.
Nome, *August 2015*	I tagged along staying with my mom when she presented on behalf of the Bering Sea Alliance LLC for the US Arctic Research Commission Conference. Sarah Huntsinger, director of the XYZ Senior Center, helped arrange interviews on and offsite. Lauren Otton, of the Nome Eskimo Community, mailed a letter to elders informing them of my research project and encouraged participation.
Unalakleet, *August 2015*	My Grandma Betty Anagick hosted me, took me berry picking, and drove me around town to see Theresa Nanouk. My Aunt Joan Johnson posted my interview flyer at the AC store. Frances Charles taught me some Iñupiatun from a language book. My cousin Charice Johnson drove me to visit Muktuk Marston's old cabin by the river.
Fairbanks, *October 2015*	I attended the Alaska Federation of Natives (AFN) conference in Anchorage and saw Carol Brady who was visiting town. I then flew to Fairbanks for a day to meet with Jorgy Jorgensen. He allowed me to scan his vintage family photographs from World War II.
Anchorage, *January 2016*	Lee Stephan, the Elkutna chief, helped me arrange an interview with his mother, Alberta Stephan.
Fairbanks, *January 2016*	Karen Eddy, director of the Fairbanks Native Association's (FNA) Elder Program, helped me arrange interviews at FNA. My mom's former classmate, Thora "Doya" Ayagiak Watts, invited me to her house to scan vintage photographs of my Great-Grandmother Martha.

Dutch Harbor, *February 2016*	My mom traveled with me to Dutch Harbor. Artist Gert Svarny had us over for tea and cake, and she showed us projects she was working on. Mike Livingston from the Aleutian Pribilof Islands Association (APIA) put me in contact with Aleut elders and Patty Lekanoff-Gregory. Patty helped me interview her dad, Nicholai Lekanoff.
Metlakatla, *February 2016*	Karen Thompson hosted me. She assisted with Arnold Booth's interview, drove me to see World War II historic sites on Annette Island, and hosted a dinner with Conrad Ryan Sr. and John and Barbara Fawcett. Karen let me scan photographs from her uncle John Hayward's World War II scrapbook. Naomi Leask gave Karen and me a private tour of the Duncan Cottage Museum. Barbara Fawcett gave me a jar of her black currant jam. I gave copies of interviews to Duncan Cottage.
Anchorage, *January 2017*	Bob Montague, at the Anchorage Pioneer Home, helped arrange a lunchtime visit. Lucy Whitehead showed me vintage photographs of Anchorage and World War II Alaska. Suellyn Novak helped arrange an interview with Earl Wineck at the Alaska Veterans Museum. Suellyn also gave me photocopies from books on wartime Alaska. Earl donated his army uniform and ATG model plane to the museum.
Fairbanks, *April 2017*	My mom traveled with my baby Jada and me to the Alaska Native Studies Conference. The Jorgensen family—Jorgy, Noel, Roberta, and "Bing"—had us over for dinner, and we went through vintage family photographs from northern Alaska.
Utqiaġvik, *May 2017*	My spouse, Max Guise, traveled with me and Jada to watch her while I conducted interviews with the last two living ATG members: Wesley Ugiaqtaq Aiken and David Ungrudruk Leavitt Sr. Pearl Brower, president of the Iḷisaġvik College, and Kathy Ahgeak, director for the Iñupiat Heritage Center, wrote letters of support for my visit.

Dutch Harbor, *June 2017*	Max, Jada, and I flew together to attend the 75th Commemoration of the Bombing of Dutch Harbor and Aleut evacuation. Pat Chercasen watched baby Jada briefly during my interview with Larry Chercasen.
Metlakatla, *October 2017*	Conrad Ryan Sr. picked me up in town after my ferry landed. Conrad drove his new hybrid car, and he played ABBA music. Conrad took me to lunch at the general store and drove me to the old plane hangar. Karen Thompson hosted me, and she held a dinner with Conrad for a follow-up interview. The next day, Conrad, Karen, and I drove to the hatcheries and Point Davidson. Before my flight, Conrad took me to Ketchikan with his car on the ferry. We went to lunch, visited totem poles, and stopped by Ward Lake. Conrad brought me all the way to the Ketchikan airport, which was another ferry ride.
Fairbanks, *October 2017*	During the week of Elders and Youth at the AFN Conference, I flew to Fairbanks to re-interview Jorgy and Al.
Metlakatla, *August 2018*	I flew and took a ferry to Ketchikan with Emma Huntington since I was eight months pregnant. Max watched our toddler, Jada, in San Francisco. Karen Thompson drove us to historic World War II ruins and participated in an interview. Her granddaughter Ziesha showed us historic sites too.
Highland *Park, Illinois,* *January 2019*	I met Al Mecklenburger's daughter, Amy Thimmig, on a flight, and she helped me to arrange an interview with her father, who served in the Coast Guard in Alaska during World War II. My spouse, Max, watched our kids while I attended the American Historical Association conference in Chicago and when I spent an afternoon interviewing Al.
Vancouver, *Washington,* *April 2019*	I attended the Western Association of Women Historians conference in Portland and met with Larry and Pat Chercasen at their house in Vancouver. I brought sourdough bread from San Francisco, and Pat made beef stew. Max watched our kids while I traveled.

Fairbanks and Anchorage, August 2019	Follow-up interview with Louis Palmer at the Anchorage Pioneer Home coordinated with help by Bob Montague. Follow-up interview with Melva Withers at ASAC. Follow-up interview with Elizabeth Keating at the Anchorage ZJ Loussac Library. I flew to Fairbanks to spend a day with Jorgy. Nancy Martinez watched my son, Nash, while I spent the day in Fairbanks. My mom and Nancy watched Nash during the other interviews in Anchorage.
Juneau, July 2021	Visiting Scholar at the Sealaska Heritage Institute (SHI), coordinated with Marina LaSalle and Emily Pastore. Oral interview with Rosita Worl. Chuck Smythe coordinated a meeting with Juneau-Douglas City Museum staff Beth Weigel and Niko Sanguinetti. Meals and glacier visit with fellow SHI visiting scholar Ben Bridges. Group dinner with Crystal Worl.
Zoom, October 2021	Julie Abo and Kimiko from Tadaima Japanese American Memorial Pilgrimages coordinated a panel, "Unangax̂ WWII history," with Mike Livingston of APIA, Lauren Peters, Martin Stepetin Sr., Patricia Lekanoff-Gregory, alongside another panel, "Unangax̂ Pilgrimages & Oral Histories," with Mike Livingston, Uĝatinax̂, Rachel Mason of the National Park Service, and me. Contents on YouTube.
Zoom, November 2021	Journalist Caroline Lester put me in contact with Marie Matsuno after we worked on an audio project about Japanese incarceration and Unangax̂ relocation. Marie and I had a Zoom interview, and in spring 2022, she Zoomed into my undergraduate history class where my students interviewed her and she shared stories about internment and the Japanese American Citizens League.
Anchorage, April 2022	I interviewed Joseph Senungetuk. Martha Senungetuk and cousin Vicky Hykes helped with the interview. Anna Hoover filmed this interview that is now preserved with the Anchorage Museum with the help of Monica Shah. I met Marie Matsuno in person for an interview.

Fairbanks,
August 2022

I flew to Fairbanks for a day while my mom watched my daughter, Jada, in Anchorage. I spent the day with Al Wright for an interview. He took me to lunch at a diner that he and Jorgy used to go to weekly before Jorgy passed away.

Anchorage,
August 2022

Taylor Strelevitz arranged the Alaska Humanities Forum (AHF) conference room for an interview with Marie Matsuno. Taylor provided tea and scones and also intermittently watched my daughter, Jada, while offering snacks. 'Wáats'asdiyei Joe Yates filmed our interview with Marie Matsuno. In addition to the recording, my mom, Ella Anagick, daughter Jada, and I had afternoon tea with Marie Matsuno. I participated in a filming interview by 'Wáats'asdiyei Joe Yates for the multi-award-winning film *Indigenous Resistance: Now and Then* (2023), produced by the AHF. This A More Perfect Union project received $50,000 from the National Endowment for the Humanities. Prior to filming, I served as a historian and story developer steering a community advisory board. 'Wáats'asdiyei created this fantastic project intended to feature Native resistance history and to foster community dialogues.

Alaska Natives: The Indigenous peoples of Alaska spanning diverse tribal geographies and language families comprising 228 federally recognized tribes. Of note, many Alaska Natives not only identify with their specific tribe but also with the term *Alaska Native,* illustrating the impact of Indigenous solidarities that have existed since the early twentieth century with the Alaska Native Brotherhood and the Alaska Native Sisterhood as well as the Alaska Federation of Natives founded in 1966.

Aleut: The Russian colonial term for Unangax̂, Indigenous to the Aleutian Islands and Pribilof Islands. Of note, some elders used this colonial word in identifying their Native background.

Alutiit (sing. Alutiiq): A Russian colonial term for Sugpiat.

American Indian/Indigenous American/Native American: Terminology used interchangeably in this book to describe the first peoples of the Americas including Indigenous peoples from Alaska and the contiguous United States. Of note, *Indian* and *Aboriginal rights* are commonly found in the federal archives including papers related to Alaska, and *Indian* has been reappropriated to a degree.

Athabascan: Indigenous peoples of Interior Alaska who speak Athabaskan.

Atkan: Unangax̂ from the Aleutian Island of Atka.

Cupiit (sing. Cup'ik from Chevak/Cup'iq from Nunivak Island): Central Alaskan Yupiit from Chevak and Nunivak Island.

dAxunhyuu: Indigenous peoples of the Cordova region in South Central Alaska and northern Southeast Alaska.

Dene: The original term that interior Indigenous Alaskans call themselves, also known as the Athabascan spanning across Alaska and Canada.

Esk*mo: Colonial vocabulary to describe Iñuit. Considered offensive in Canada and

Greenland and by the younger generation of Iñuit Alaskans, who prefer the term *Iñuit*.

Iñuit: Indigenous peoples of northern and western Alaska spanning several national boundaries including Canada, Greenland, and Siberia. Alaskan Iñuit includes Iñupiat, Yupiit, and Cupiit.

Iñupiat (sing. Iñupiaq): Iñuit of northern Alaska, spanning from the southernmost village of Unalakleet up to Alaska's North Slope.

Issei: Japanese immigrants to the Americas.

J*p: A racial slur with dehumanizing connotations directed at Japanese people and Japanese Americans.

Nisei: Second-generation Japanese Americans, born in the Americas to Japanese immigrants (Issei).

Pribolobians: Unangax̂ from the Pribilof Islands of St. Paul and St. George.

Russians: People of Czarist Russia and sometimes used to describe people of the Soviet Union. As Alaska has a legacy of Russian colonization that predates and postdates the Soviet era, there is a slippage in how Alaska Natives and even US government officials identify people of this region as "Russians."

Squ*w: A racial slur directed at Native women.

Sugpiat (sing. Sugpiaq): The ancestral name for Indigenous peoples of Alaska's southern central coast including Kodiak; Russian colonial terminology includes "Alutiiq/Alutiit" and sometimes "Aleut." This includes Qikertarmiut or Qik'rtarmiut, Indigenous peoples of Qik'rtaq/Qikertaq (Kodiak Island).

Tlingit (sing. and pl.): Indigenous people of Southeast Alaska. There is a shift to spell this as Lingít.

Unangax̂ (sing. and pl.): Indigenous peoples of the Aleutian and Pribilof Islands. Depending on eastern or western regional dialects, Unangas or Unangan is plural, although both regions have agreed to use Unangax̂ for the plural form.

Yupiit (sing. Yup'ik): Southern Iñuit of western Alaska spanning across the Yukon-Kuskokwim Delta and coastal Alaska.

An Alaskan Introduction

1 Alice Petrivelli (Aleut), personal interview, November 6, 2014, and January 16, 2015.

2 Mortality rates are from Kohlhoff, *When the Wind*, 108–34.

3 In 1947, the Department of the Interior formally adopted the name Bureau of Indian Affairs (BIA), replacing Office of Indian Affairs. Since elders refer to this organization as the BIA, I will retain that name throughout this study. Mike Livingston, PhD, of the Aleutian Pribilof Islands Association, generously helped me obtain the full name of William "Bill" Dirks.

4 Dora Adams affidavit re: H. O. K. Bauer, January 3, 1943, Civilian Personnel Record for H. O. K. Bauer, National Archives and Records Administration (hereafter NARA), St. Louis, Missouri; and Guise, "Who Is Doctor Bauer?"

5 Bodnar, *"Good War,"* 1–9.

6 Samet, *Looking*, 7–23.

7 Enloe, *Bananas*.

8 Okihiro, *Encyclopedia*, 23–26.

9 Houston and Houston, *Farewell*.

10 For more on citizenry, see chapter 1.

11 On Latin American Japanese Americans incarcerated in the United States, see Chew, *Uprooting Community*.

12 On retained sovereignty despite wardship imposed on Native American nations, see Lomawaima, "Federalism."

13 On defining a racial hierarchy, see Omi and Winant, *Racial Formation*.

14 Jefferson, *Fighting for Hope*, 1–9.

15 "Hiroshima and Nagasaki Bombings," ICAN, accessed June 29, 2023, https://www.icanw.org/hiroshima_and_nagasaki_bombings.

16 Welcome page, JapanAirRaids.org, accessed November 30, 2023, https://www.japanairraids.org.

17 Takaki, *Hiroshima*, 23.

18 Brown, "Tewa Pueblos," 7–17.

19 Correspondence with Haliehana Stepetin, November 28, 2023; and Bergsland, *Aleut Dictionary*, 49.

20 McGreevy, "Venetian Glass Beads."

21 State of Alaska Department of Labor and Workforce Development Research and Analysis, 1940 Census Data for Alaska.

22 Haycox, "Mining," 203–9.

23 Naske and Rowinski, *Anchorage*, 127.

24 Nielson, *Armed Forces*, 106–7.

25 Gruening, *Many Battles*, 328–29.

26 Ernest Gruening to Harold Ickes, December 11, 1944, RG 126, box 331, NARA, College Park, Maryland (hereafter cited as NARA II).

27 Anthony Dimond to House of Representatives, December 15, 1944, Anthony Dimond, series 3, box 5, folder 44, Alaska and Polar Regions Collections and Archives at the University of Alaska Fairbanks (hereafter cited as UAF).

28 Ostler, *Surviving Genocide*.

29 Wyatt, "Alaska and Hawai'i," 565.

30 Jung, *Menace to Empire*, 9.

31 Haycox, *Alaska*.

32 Campbell, *Darkest Alaska*.

33 Cole, "Jim Crow," 429–49.

34 Hartman and Reamer, *Black Lives*.

35 On US imperialism after 1898 including Cuba, Guam, Hawai'i, the Philippines, and Puerto Rico, see Thompson, *Imperial Archipelago*; on Guam, see Camacho, *Sacred Men*; and on Hawai'i and the Philippines, see Gonzalez, *Securing Paradise*.

36 On US imperial extension through language of liberation in Guam, see Diaz, *Repositioning the Missionary*, 13–14. On language of liberation in the Philippines, see Salinas and Xu, *Philippines' Resistance*.

37 Dower, *Embracing Defeat*.

38 See, for example, JapanAirRaids.org; Yamazaki and Fleming, *Children*; and Allinson, *Japan's Postwar History*, 45–82.

39 Immerwahr, *How to Hide*, 3–20.

40   On Manchuria and the rise of Japan's imperialism, see Drea, *Japan's Imperial Army*; Duus, Myers, and Peattie, *Japanese Wartime Empire*; and Young, *Japan's Total Empire*. On Japan's colonial and imperial power in East Asia, see Mason and Lee, *Reading Colonial Japan*; and Yellen, *Greater East Asia*. On Japan's colonial agricultural control, see Fedman, *Seeds of Control*.

41   Young, *Japan's Total Empire*, 3–52.

42   Reid, *Sea Is My Country*.

43   Geiger, *Converging Empires*, 17–54.

44   Gruening, *Many Battles*, 361; and Marston, *Men of the Tundra*, 65 (refers to "Russian pilots" and "Russian soldiers" in 1942).

45   On "cacophony" by US colonialism and imperialism, see Byrd, *Transit of Empire*, xvii, 228–29.

46   Equilibrium as a concept gained popularity from mathematician John Forbes Nash Jr. The "equilibrium" I define does not represent or relate to theories about "Nash equilibrium." On Nash equilibrium, see Peterson, *Prisoner's Dilemma*, 1–9; and Fujiwara-Greve, *Non-cooperative Game Theory*, 48.

47   Hartman, *Scenes of Subjection*, 14.

48   Kelley, "Black Study," 14.

49   Silva, *Aloha Betrayed*, 1.

50   Estes, *Our History*, 21–24.

51   Simpson, *Mohawk Interruptus*, 11.

52   Thiong'o, *Decolonising the Mind*, 1–3.

53   Gilbert, *Education beyond the Mesas*.

54   Scott, *Domination*, xii–xiii.

55   Hoxie, *This Indian Country*, 4, 10.

56   Vizenor, *Manifest Manners*, vii; and Vizenor, *Survivance*, 1–23.

57   In Tuck et al., "Visiting."

58   For those interested in learning to conduct oral histories, see Ritchie, *Doing Oral History*.

59   Smith, *Decolonizing Methodologies*. I was also inspired by Wilson, *Remember This!*

60   Name cited with permission; Nataanii Hatathlie, email correspondence with the author, June 23, 2023.

61   Nicole Kuhn (Haida) reminded scholars at the Indigenous Borderlands symposium at the University of Washington not to apply a Western concept to Indigenous languages (April 2023).

62   Pegues, *Space-Time Colonialism*.

63 Moore, *Proud Raven*.

64 Demuth, *Floating Coast*.

65 Dunaway, *Defending the Arctic Refuge*.

66 Williams, *Alaska Native Reader*.

67 Million, *Therapeutic Nations*.

68 Dauenhauer and Dauenhauer, *Haa Kusteeyí*; and Dauenhauer and Dauenhauer, *Haa Shuká*.

69 Indigenous futures is a growing field in Native studies and literary studies; see Harjo, *Spiral to the Stars*; Simpson, *Lighting the Eighth Fire*; and Taylor, *Me Tomorrow*.

ONE Unangax̂ Relocation

1 Larry Chercasen, personal interview, May 6, 2015. Of note, Larry did not identify himself to me as Unangax̂, instead referring to himself as Aleut. As there has been a shift to use more correct original terminology and non-Russian colonial terminology, I have substituted *Unangax̂* for elders who identified as Aleut, except for Marie Matsuno whose mother might be Alutiiq, so it was simpler to write *Aleut* when unsure. *Unangax̂* is the more inclusive word that does not distinguish between eastern and western dialects, so this term is imperfect although a shift in direction from the blanket colonial term *Aleut*.

2 Ostler, *Surviving Genocide*.

3 On Warner Ranch removal, see Akins and Bauer, *We Are the Land*, 168, 184–89. On Rampart Dam, see Dunaway, *Defending the Arctic Refuge*, 38–40.

4 On wardship, see Lomawaima, *Prairie Light*; and Prucha, *Great Father*.

5 Madden, "Forgotten People," 55; and Kohlhoff, *When the Wind*, xiii. On potentiality of historic landmarks, see Mobley, *Aleut Relocation Camps*.

6 Edward Johnston to R. E. Barnes, July 7, 1942, NARA, Anchorage, Alaska. The exact location unknown as this site closed; I do have a photocopy of the document.

7 Dave Kiffer, "German POWs Helped Fismantle SE Alaska's 'White Elephant,'" *SitNews*, February 17, 2015, accessed November 29, 2023, http://www.sitnews.us/Kiffer/POWCamp/021715_prisoners_of_war.html.

8 On settler colonialism, mobility injustice, and Indigenous mobility in (not) choosing movements, see Carpio, Bard, and Barraclough, "Introduction."

9 Perras, *Stepping Stones*, 80–86.

10 Ford, *Short Cut to Tokyo*. Some newspapers spelled the surname Hodikoff as Hudakof.

11 Etta Jones statement, n.d., Etta Jones Collection, box 1, folder 8, Atwood Resource Center (hereafter cited as ARC).

12 Etta Jones statement, n.d., Etta Jones Collection, box 1, folder 8, ARC.

13 Drea, *Japan's Imperial Army*, 97–124.

14 Young, *Japan's Total Empire*, 55–114.

15 Alex Prossoff's testimony, in Ross Oliver, *Journal*, 242–48.

16 Henry Stewart report to APIA and Kirtland, "Preliminary Report Concerning the 1942 Japanese Invasion," World War II documentation legal preparation documents by Kirtland (hereafter cited as WWII Kirtland legal prep), folder, "Documents," APIA.

17 Masami Sugiyama, "On the Trail of the Picture: A Trip to the Aleutians," 1987, 102–12, APIA.

18 Golodoff, *Attu Boy*; and Stewart, "Aleuts in Japan."

19 "Ask a Historian: How Did Alaska Natives End Up Inside Japanese American Concentration Camps?," Densho, accessed January 21, 2023, https://densho.org/catalyst/alaska-natives-inside-japanese-american-concentration-camps/.

20 Michael Hagiwara to Ernest Gruening, October 20, 1942, RG 126 9-1-96 Foreign Relations World War, box 506, NARA II.

21 Alaska Defense Command proclamation, April 14, 1942, general correspondence of the Alaskan territorial governor (hereafter cited as Corresp. Alaska governor) 1909–1958, National Archives Microfilm Publication M939 (hereafter cited as M939), roll 338, NARA, Anchorage, Alaska.

22 Russell Maynard to E. L. Bartlett, April 22, 1942, Corresp. Alaska governor 1909–1958, M939, roll 338, NARA, Anchorage, Alaska.

23 Marie Matsuno, personal interview, August 10, 2022.

24 Ronald K. Inouye, "The World War II Evacuation of Japanese-Americans from the Territory of Alaska," report to NEH, Summer 1973, Elmer E. Rasmuson Library, University of Alaska Fairbanks.

25 Melva Wolcoff Withers, personal interview, August 26, 2019; and Hattie D'Orsay, "The Story a Little Esk*mo Girl Told Me," *The Magazine Alaska*, June 1941, Peter & Beulah Parisi Papers, box 4, folder 2, Archives and Special Collections, Consortium Library, University of Alaska Anchorage (hereafter cited as UAA).

26 "Death and Renewal," Charles Lucier Papers, box 9, folder 7, UAA.

27 Charles Foode to Ernest Gruening, November 24, Corresp. Alaska governor 1909–1958, M939, roll 338, NARA, Anchorage, Alaska.

28 Alice Stuart to Ernest Gruening, April 24, 1942, Corresp. Alaska governor 1909–1958, M939, roll 338, NARA, Anchorage, Alaska.

29 Leonard Allen to Indian Office in Juneau, April 8, 1942, Corresp. Alaska governor 1909–1958, M939, roll 338, NARA, Anchorage, Alaska.

30 Earl Ohmer to Bob Bartlett, April 18, 1942, Corresp. Alaska governor 1909–1958, M939, roll 338, NARA, Anchorage, Alaska.

31 Withers, interview, August 26, 2019.

32 Hays, *Alaska's Hidden Wars*, 7; Kashima, *Judgment without Trial*, 3–13; Okihiro, *Storied Lives*; Takaki, *Different Mirror*, 341–50; and Blum, *V Was for Victory*, 155–72.

33 Hinnershitz, *Japanese American Incarceration*.

34 On race formation and racial attitudes toward Asian Americans as "others," see Okihiro, *Margins*, 3–63.

35 Torrey, *Slaves of the Harvest*.

36 Haycox, *Alaska*, 53–87.

37 Specific language from primary documents about removal does not mention Soviet influence, and language by the US Navy claims to protect Unangax̂. This was confirmed with anthropologist Mike Livingston, email correspondence, November 15, 2023.

38 General Jake Lestenkof, personal interview, November 3, 2014. In keeping with referring to elders by their first name, I refer to him as "Jake."

39 Alfred Stepetin, testimony to the Commission on Wartime Relocation and Internment of Civilians for Public Hearings Testimonies, NARA II.

40 Williams, *Aleut Story*; and US Commander Jackson Tate, notice to residents, December 9, 1941, RG 181 Naval Districts and Shore Establishments, 17th Naval District Sitka, Naval Air Station General Files 1938–1946, box 21, NARA, Seattle, Washington.

41 General Buckner notice to residents, n.d., RG 181 Naval Districts and Shore Establishments, 17th Naval District Sitka, Naval Air Station General Files 1938–1946, box 21, NARA, Seattle, Washington.

42 Henry Stimson to Secretary, December 4, 1942, RG 126 "Foreign Relations," box 506, folder "WW Evacuation," NARA II.

43 Gruening to B. W. Thoron, June 24, 1944, RG 126 Foreign Relations World War, box 506, NARA II.

44 "John Collier," Densho, accessed April 24, 2023, https://encyclopedia.densho .org/John_Collier. On Indian reservations hosting incarcerated Japanese Americans organized by the Office of Indian Affairs, see D. E. Thomas to Ward Bower, July 21, 1942, RG 126 Foreign Relations World War, box 506, NARA II.

45 Maruyama, "On Common Ground."

46 Hobart Copeland to Commanding General, June 17, 1944, RG 75 Central Clas-

sified Files (hereafter CCF) on Alaska, box 50, NARA, Washington, DC (hereafter NARA I).

47   On blood quantum linked to land dispossession, see Kauanui, *Hawaiian Blood*, 1–35.

48   Mobley, *Aleut Relocation Camps*, 5–6.

49   Seiple, *Ghosts in the Fog*, 161.

50   Williams, *Aleut Story*.

51   On "American Plan," see Stern, *Trials*.

52   Petrivelli, personal interview.

53   Father Ishmael Gromoff, Commission on Wartime Relocation and Internment of Civilians for Public Hearings Testimonies, NARA II. Correct spelling of Gromoff's name confirmed by Mike Livingston.

54   *Alaska Weekly*, November 19, 1943, RG 126 Alaska Islands Leasing, box 304, NARA II.

55   J. A. Talbot to Ernest Gruening, May 27, 1943, RG 220 Records on the Commission of Wartime Relocation and Internment (hereafter cited as CWRI), box 51, NARA II.

56   Andronik Kashevarof, Elekonida Kashevarof, and Bonnie Mierzejek, personal interview, February 9, 2016.

57   Official log, August 31, 1943, RG 49, series 1, NARA, Anchorage, Alaska.

58   Ernest Gruening to Ira N. Gabrielson, September 22, 1943, Alaska's Digital Archives, https://vilda.alaska.edu/digital/collection/cdmg41/id/1134.

59   Berneta Block to Edward Johnston, October 14, 1943, RG PIM 1897–1974, box 22, folder "Misc. 1943," NARA, Seattle, Washington.

60   St. Paul Agent to Edward Johnston, May 22, 1941, RG PIM, box 21, folder "Misc. 1940–41," NARA, Seattle, Washington.

61   Edward Johnston to Ward Bower, May 7, 1944, NARA, Anchorage, Alaska.

62   Ruth Gruber to Harold Ickes, January 12, 1944, RG 126 "Alaska Islands, Leasing," box 304, NARA II.

63   Williams, *Aleut Story*.

64   Riley, *Fur Seal Industry*, 1.

65   Johnson, *Pribilof Islands*, 10–17.

66   For a few sources on ANCSA, see Huhndorf and Huhndorf, "Alaska Native Politics"; and Tuck, "ANCSA."

67   Torrey, *Slaves of the Harvest*. On sealing numbers and varied quantities by year, see Kohlhoff, *When the Wind*.

68   Edward Johnston, April 30, 1943, RG 220 CWRI, box 47, NARA II.

69   Seiple, *Ghosts in the Fog*, 170–71.

70 Log Book St. Paul, Alaska, May 24, 1944, RG 370 Pribilof Island Program (hereafter PIP) 1871–1984, box 36, NARA, Seattle, Washington.

71 Paul Thompson to Edward Johnston, April 6, 1943, RG 220 CWRI, box 47, NARA II.

72 Gromoff testimony.

73 L. C. McMillin to Edward Johnston, March 6, 1943, RG Pribilof Island Materials (hereafter PIM) 1897–1974, box 22, folder "Misc. 1943," NARA, Seattle, Washington.

74 Edward Johnston to Ward Bower, March 19, 1943, World War II Kirtland legal prep, folder "WWII Evacuation Military Correspondence," APIA.

75 Mary Jane Gaither to Anthony Dimond, April 7, 1943, World War II Kirtland legal prep, folder "WWII Evacuation Military Correspondence," APIA.

76 John Hanson et al. to government, April 26, 1943, RG 370 PIP, box 33, folder D, NARA, Seattle, Washington.

77 Torrey, *Slaves of the Harvest*, 131.

78 Official log, September 14–15, 1943, RG 49, series 1, vols. NOAA Pribilof Island, box 30, NARA, Anchorage, Alaska.

79 Morton report, August 14, 1943, RG 22 Reports on Fur Seal Drives (hereafter cited as RFSD), container 14, NARA II.

80 Department of Commerce Bureau of Fisheries report, RG 22 RFSD, container 16, NARA II.

81 Ward Bower memorandum, November 11, 1942, RG 22 RFSD, container 6, NARA II.

82 Morton report, August 14, 1943, RG 22 RFSD, container 14, NARA II.

83 Report killing fur seals St. George, July 31, 1944, RG 22 RFSD, container 6, NARA II; and Abstract of seals killed St. Paul 1944, October 17, 1944, RG 22 RFSD, container 14, NARA II. Pribolobian men harvested 51,560 pelts on St. Paul and 12,310 pelts on St. George, totaling 63,870 pelts in 1952. "Seal Killings St. George 1952," RG 22 RFSD, container 16, NARA II; and "Seal Killings St. Paul 1952," RG 22 RFSD, container 16, NARA II.

84 US Treasury calculations, 1943, RG 22 Fur Seal Service Ledgers, container 1, NARA II.

85 Harry May to Daniel Benson, September 2, 1943, RG 220 CWRI, box 47, vol. 5, NARA II. May states, "Due to War Department regulations, I will be unable to compensate the St. George Island [N]ative soldiers who blubbered 9,711 skins this season."

86 Haretina Kochutin et al. to US government, October 10, 1942, RG 370 PIP, box 33, folder D, NARA, Seattle, Washington.

87 Official log, November 1, 1943, RG 49, series 1, vols. NOAA Pribilof Island, box 13, NARA, Anchorage, Alaska.

88 John Misikin et al. to whom it may concern, February 17, 1944, RG PIP 1897–1974, Aleut Community St. Paul Association, box 5, folder "Church Affairs," NARA, Seattle, Washington.

89 Black, *Russians*, 223–30.

90 Sweetland Smith and Petrivelli, *Sure Foundation*.

91 Nicholai Lekanoff, personal interview with Patty Lekanoff-Gregory, February 6, 2016.

92 Chercasen, personal interview.

93 Lestenkof, personal interview.

94 Williams, *Aleut Story*.

95 I am grateful for Mike Livingston and Haliehana Stepetin who checked this Unangam Tunuu spelling. On Unangam Tunuu, translations, histories, and futures, see Stepetin, "Unangam Qaqamiiĝuu."

96 Chandonnet, "Recapture of Attu," 81–85.

97 Fred Geeslin letter, September 29, 1944, RG 181 Naval Districts and Shore Establishments 17th Naval District, Naval Op. Base Dutch Harbor, box 1, folder "Aleut Evacuees Atka & Akutan," NARA, Seattle, Washington.

98 Edward Johnston to Ward Bower, May 7, 1944, NARA, Anchorage, Alaska.

99 Alaska Indian Service to Commissioner of Indian Affairs, October 3, 1942, RG 370 NOAA PIP, box 33, folder D, NARA, Seattle, Washington.

100 Don Foster to John Collier, May 6, 1944, RG 75 Office File John Collier, box 24, NARA I.

101 St. Paul agent statement, March 19, 1945, RG PIP Materials Aleut Community St. Paul Association, box 5, NARA, Seattle, Washington.

102 St. Paul Island General Manager memorandum, June 25, 1944, RG 370 PIP Materials Aleut Community St. Paul Association, box 33, NARA, Seattle, Washington.

103 Al Wright, personal interview, January 28, 2016.

104 Williams, *Aleut Story*.

105 Alice Petrivelli PowerPoint, "Aleut Relocation and Restitution," APIA.

106 Rachel Napolitan and Tom Findtner, "Army Engineers Remove World War II-Era Explosives from National Historic Landmark on a Remote Alaskan Island," *US Army Corps of Engineers*, August 31, 2022, accessed June 29, 2023, https://www.poa.usace.army.mil/Media/News-Stories/Article/3146095/army-engineers-remove-world-war-ii-era-explosives-from-national-historic-landma/.

TWO Survivance Alliance

1   Petrivelli, personal interview.

2   Betty Samato, Klas Stope KINY radio interview, November 29, 2021.

3   On Japanese immigrants cultivating strawberries in the Pacific Northwest, see Neiwert, *Strawberry Days.*

4   Oleana Snigaroff, February 24, [no year], "Why I like Atka Better than Killisnoo," Ted Bank Collection, series 10, folder "Aleut Essays," UAA.

5   "Killisnoo—Atka Island Evacuees" report, 1942, NARA, Anchorage, Alaska. The exact location unknown as this site closed; I do have a photocopy of the document.

6   Henry Dirks testimony, RG 220 CWRI, box 67, 172-4, NARA II.

7   Seiple, *Ghosts in the Fog,* 167.

8   Seiple, *Ghosts in the Fog,* 167.

9   John Hall to Carl Hoverson, September 3, 1943, World War II Kirtland legal prep, folder "WWII Evacuation Military Correspondence," APIA.

10 Vizenor, *Survivance,* 11.

11 Dauenhauer and Dauenhauer, *Haa Shuká,* 448, 478. For more on the racial segregation in towns, see chapters 5 and 6.

12 On recognizing persistent Indigenous sovereignty, see Crandall, *These People*; Wilkins and Stark, *American Indian Politics,* 73–106; and Den Ouden and O'Brien, *Recognition,* 13–16.

13 On violence as a settler colonial construct enacted on Native lands, see, for example, Blackhawk, *Violence over the Land*; Jacoby, *Shadows at Dawn*; and Sleeper-Smith, Ostler, and Reid, *Violence and Indigenous Communities.*

14 Dauenhauer, Dauenhauer, and Black, *Anóoshi Lingít Aaní Ká.*

15 Torrey, *Slaves of the Harvest*; and Miller, *Kodiak Kreol.*

16 Dauenhauer, Dauenhauer, and Black, *Anóoshi Lingít Aaní Ká,* xxxviii.

17 Dauenhauer, Dauenhauer, and Black, *Anóoshi Lingít Aaní Ká,* xxxviii.

18 John Haile Cloe, "Military Development in Alaska 1867–2005 Draft Chronology," 3rd Wing History Office, Joint Base Elmendorf-Richardson, Anchorage, Alaska (hereafter cited as JBER), 5.

19 Kohlhoff, *When the Wind,* 170.

20 John Haile Cloe, "Military Development in Alaska 1867–2005 Draft Chronology," 3rd Wing History Office, JBER, 6.

21 Cook-Lynn, *Anti-Indianism.*

22 On savagery and the US imagination, see Pearce, *Savagism and Civilization.*

23 Witgen, *Infinity of Nations*.

24 Dauenhauer and Dauenhauer, *Haa Kusteeyí*, 291.

25 Dauenhauer and Dauenhauer, "Walter Soboleff," in *Haa Kusteeyí*, 567.

26 Dauenhauer and Dauenhauer, *Haa Kusteeyí*, 126, 290.

27 For more on boarding schools, see chapter 5.

28 Dauenhauer and Dauenhauer, *Haa Kusteeyí*, 567.

29 Gilbert, *Education*, xxx–xxxi. On boarding school histories, see also Lomawaima, *Prairie Light*; and Gram, *Education*.

30 Arnold, "Legacy," 38.

31 Arnold, "Legacy," 111.

32 Lauren Peters, email messages to the author, cited with permission, April 13, 2021, and June 16, 2023. Bob Sam relayed this to Peters, explaining that his uncle from Angoon, Mathew Fred, shared this history.

33 Arnold, "Legacy," 40.

34 Alaska Indian Service to Commissioner of Indian Affairs, October 3, 1942, RG 370 NOAA PIP, box 33, folder D, NARA, Seattle, Washington.

35 Edward Johnston to Donald Gibbins, November 2, 1942, folder "WWII Evacuation Military Correspondence," APIA.

36 Kohlhoff, *When the Wind*, 121.

37 Kohlhoff, *When the Wind*, 121.

38 Arnold, "Legacy," 40.

39 Larry Dirks Sr., Mr. Bergsl[a]nd, translator Michael Lekanoff Sr., "During the Time of War," 1970s, folder "WWII Evacuation Military Correspondence," APIA.

40 See chapters 5 and 6.

41 Roy Peratrovich to all ANB and ANS members, July 6, 1942, Walter Soboleff Papers (hereafter cited as Soboleff Papers), series 1, box 7, folder 21, Sealaska Heritage Institute, Juneau, Alaska (hereafter cited as SHI).

42 Tatiana Crevden, "Story of Mainland," n.d., Ted Bank Collection, series 10, folder "Aleut Essays," Archives and Special Collections, UAA. Name illegible, although identified by Mike Livingston using the 1940 census record.

43 Dirks, "During the Time of War."

44 Nadesta Golley, n.d., Ted Bank Collection, series 10, folder "Aleut Essays," Archives and Special Collections, UAA.

45 Oleana Snigaroff, February 24 [no year listed], "Why I like Atka Better than Killisnoo," Ted Bank Collection, series 10, folder "Aleut Essays," Archives and Special Collections, UAA.

46   Campbell, *In Darkest Alaska*.

47   Tatiana Crevden, "Story of Mainland," n.d., Ted Bank Collection, series 10, folder "Aleut Essays," Archives and Special Collections, UAA.

48   Kohlhoff, *When the Wind*, 141.

49   Kohlhoff, "'My Heart," 295.

50   Alice Petrivelli, personal interview by Carlene Arnold, September 7, 2010.

51   Johnson, *Pribilof Islands*, 21.

52   Don Foster to Fredericka Berenberg, November 18, 1947, RG 75 CCF "Alaska," series 734, box 185, NARA I. The archival document says "Alice Gromoff's father"; Mike Livingston helped me identify his name as Elary Gromoff, father to Alexandra "Alice" Gromoff. Foster initially had a typo, "Bromoff," then wrote "Gromoff."

53   Johnson, *Pribilof Islands*, 21.

54   John Collier to Senator Henrik Shipstead, March 2, 1944, Soboleff Papers, series 1, box 7, folder 21, SHI.

55   Fred Geeslin to Edward Johnston, March 20, 1943, RG 220 CWRI, box 47, NARA II.

56   Annual Medical Report of Pribilof Island Natives, March 31, 1944, PIM 1897–1974, box 21, folder "Medical 1946," NARA, Seattle, Washington; Edward Johnston to Ward Bower, October 10, 1942, location unknown, NARA, Anchorage, Alaska; and Carl Hoverson to George Barrett, November 6, 1943, PIM 1897–1974, box 21, folder "Funter Bay Alaska 1943," NARA, Seattle, Washington.

57   Tatiana Crevden, "Story of Mainland," n.d., Ted Bank Collection, series 10, folder "Aleut Essays," Archives and Special Collections, UAA.

58   Chercasen, personal interview.

59   Mary Jane Gaither to Anthony Dimond, April 7, 1943, World War II Kirtland legal prep, folder "WWII Evacuation Military Correspondence," APIA.

60   John Hall report, September 3–4, 1943, WWII Kirtland legal prep, folder "WWII Evacuation Military Correspondence," APIA.

61   Carl Hoverson to R. G. Morton, June 26, 1943, PIM 1897–1974 Aleut Community St. Paul Association, box 21, folder "Funter Bay 1943," NARA, Seattle, Washington.

62   Edward Johnston to Ward Bower, February 1944, PIM 1897–1974, box 21, folder "Native Affairs 1946," NARA, Seattle, Washington.

63   Bob Loescher, personal interview, May 14, 2013.

64   Hulan and Eigenbrod, *Aboriginal Original Traditions*, 7.

65   Nora Dauenhauer and Richard Dauenhauer, personal interview, May 15, 2013.

66   For more on gendered segregation of Native women by the military, see chapter 6.

67   Anonymous, personal interview, September 15, 2014.

68   Charlotte McConnell, personal interview, September 22, 2014.

69   Petrivelli, personal interview.

THREE War on Unangax̂ Soil

1   Ford, *Short Cut to Tokyo*, 125.

2   Yellen, *Greater East Asia*; Myers and Peattie, *Japanese Colonial Empire*; and Duus, Myers, and Peattie, *Japanese Wartime Empire*. On a history of Japan and Indigenous peoples of the Pacific including Ainu, Okinawans, Micronesians, and Taiwan, see Ziomek, *Lost Histories*.

3   Hays, *Alaska's Hidden Wars*, xi, 9–11; Garfield, *Thousand-Mile War*, 31–55, 59; Hammett and Colodny, *Battle*, 4–5, 24; and War Department, *Capture of Attu*, 5–9.

4   Garfield, *Thousand-Mile War*, 101. On Buckner and bases, see Hays, *Alaska's Hidden Wars*, xv.

5   Etta Jones round robin, August 31, 1941, Etta Jones Collection, box 1, folder 3, ARC.

6   Salinas and Xu, *Philippines' Resistance*; and Diaz, *Repositioning the Missionary*.

7   On sexual enslavement of women by Japan's military in colonized territories, see Kimura, *"Comfort Women" Debates*; Tanaka, *Japan's Comfort Women*; and Yoshiaki, *Comfort Women*.

8   Hall, *Beneath the Backbone*, 5.

9   Garfield, *Thousand-Mile War*, 274–75.

10   Townsend, *World War II*, 134.

11   Garfield, *Thousand-Mile War*.

12   National Park Service, "Battle of Attu: 60 Years Later," accessed June 29, 2023, https://www.nps.gov/articles/000/battle-of-attu-60-years.htm.

13   Perras, *Stepping Stones*, 133.

14   Lesser, "Report"; Associated Press, "Attu Cold and Fighting Described by Veterans: 200 at San Francisco Hospital Suffer from Frostbite and Are Unable to Walk," *The Sun*, June 8, 1943, 260; Hess, "Alaska Native Veterans," 9; and Harding, "What We Learned."

15   Hays, *Alaska's Hidden Wars*, 23; Harding, "What We Learned"; and Hess, "Alaska Native Veterans," 9. Harding identified that twenty-nine Japanese POWs remained.

16   Harding, "What We Learned"; Hays, *Alaska's Hidden Wars*, 22–23; and Dower, *War without Mercy*, 11–12.

17 War Department, *Capture of Attu*, 33–34.

18 Perras, *Stepping Stones*, 152–54.

19 Perras, *Stepping Stones*, 155–56.

20 Anonymous, personal interview, 2015. This elder consented to have their story included in publications on Alaska history and to be recorded by audio, although they did not sign a written consent form, only giving verbal consent. As such, I censored their name.

21 *Patriotism of the Unangax̂*, wall text, Aleutian World War II National Historic Area Visitor Center, Unalaska, Alaska; and Hudson, "Aleuts in Defense," 161–64.

22 "Simeon Peter Pletnikoff," *Anchorage Daily News*, February 27, 1997.

23 Hudson, "Aleuts in Defense," 163.

24 Wheeler, *Pacific Is My Beat*, 365.

25 Simon Bolivar Buckner to H. H. Arnold, December 8, 1941, RG 547 Records US Army Forces Alaska, box 1 290-39-12-2, NARA II.

26 General Buckner KFAR message delivered by Colonel L. E. Schick, 1943, RG 547 Official Correspondence Buckner, box 1 290-39-12-2, NARA II.

27 Hess, "Alaska Native Veterans," 6.

28 Rosier, *Serving Their Country*, 9.

29 Townsend, *World War II*.

30 Jefferson, *Fighting for Hope*, 6.

31 Kantrowitz, *More than Freedom*, 3–9.

32 Moyd, *Violent Intermediaries*, 35.

33 Sergeant George Meyers, "Alaska Scouts: Rugged Outdoor Band Landed from Subs to Chart Aleutian Invasions," *Washington Post*, March 12, 1944, RG 220 CWRI, box 51, NARA II.

34 On Tlingit code talkers, see Clara Miller, "Talking in Code: How the Tlingit, Navajo Tribes Helped End WWII," *Juneau Empire*, November 25, 2016. On Navajo code talkers, see Townsend, *World War II*, 143–50.

35 Meyers, "Alaska Scouts."

36 Corey Ford and Alastair MacBain, "Castner's Cutthroats," n.d., Walter Bradshaw Scrapbook, UAA.

37 Hess, "Alaska Native Veterans," 6.

38 See "No-no boys," Densho, accessed December 1, 2023, https://encyclopedia.densho.org/No-no_boys/.

39 Hudson, "Aleuts in Defense," 162–63. On the life of Henry Swanson, see Swanson, *Unknown Islands*, 151–89.

40 Hudson, "Aleuts in Defense," 163.

41 "Pagano Gives the National Guard His Best," *Tundra Times* (Fairbanks), December 28, 1983.

42 Hudson, "Aleuts in Defense," 163.

43 *Patriotism of the Unangax̂.*

44 "Official Log, St. Paul Island, Alaska 1944," May 24, 1944, RG 49, NOAA Pribilof Island, box 13, NARA, Anchorage, Alaska.

45 "Appendix L: Location of Alaska Territorial Guard Units," July 1, 1944, 673d Air Base Wing History Office (hereafter cited as ABWHO), JBER.

46 "Evacuation and Internment, 1942–1945," National Park Service, last updated February 4, 2018; and *Patriotism of the Unangax̂.*

47 "Soldier's Medals, Air Medals, Awards for Valor, and Awards" and "Wounded in Action," RG 75 "Records Related to Indians in World War," NARA I.

48 Ethel Ross Oliver, "Simeon Oliver (Nutchuk)," n.d., Billy Blackjack Johnson Papers, box 2, folder 2/26, UAA.

49 "Editorial: Gordon Gould and Simeon Oliver," *Tundra Times* (Fairbanks), May 14, 1980.

50 "Editorial: Gordon Gould and Simeon Oliver."

51 Lillian C. Harle, "Readers Inquire Whereabouts of Famous Author Simeon Oliver," *Tundra Times* (Fairbanks), January 27, 1967.

52 "Editorial: Gordon Gould and Simeon Oliver"; Simeon Oliver, unidentified interviewer and Al Bramstedt, 1940s, Oral History 75–16, Oral History Program, Elmer E. Rasmuson Library, University of Alaska Fairbanks.

53 Patrick Pletnikoff to Paul Carrigan, May 17, 1979, folder "WWII Evacuation Military Correspondence," APIA.

54 Townsend, *World War II*, 62, 64.

55 Townsend, *World War II*, 2, 31–60, 81; and Holm, "White Man's War," 69–83.

56 Loew, "Back of the Homefront," 82–103.

57 Townsend, *World War II*, 150; RG 75 Division of Information Records Relating to Indians in WWI and WWII, NARA I. Exact numbers on Native servicemen/officers are difficult to access since Indians received the classification of "white" when inducted into the military. As no statistics are available, these numbers occlude Native officers.

58 Loew, "Back of the Homefront," 98.

59 Echohawk, *Drawing Fire*, 1–3.

60 "Soldier's Medals, Air Medals, Awards for Valor, and Awards," RG 75 Records Related to Indians in World War, NARA I.

61 "American Indians of Every Tribe Take War Path against the Axis," n.d., Walter Bradshaw Scrapbook, UAA.

62 Holm, "Fighting," 73.

63 This rate is from 1945 adjusted for inflation in 2023. Townsend, *World War II*, 186.

64 Gruening, *Many Battles*, 311.

65 Shoemaker, "Powers of Persuasion," 38; and Al Sahlin, personal interview, August 25, 2015.

66 Arnold Booth, personal interview, July 24, 2008, September 20, 2014.

67 On applied stereotypes of "Indianness," see Gouveia, "'We Also Serve,'" 153–82.

68 On "noble savagery," see Deloria, *Playing Indian*, 20–21; and Dower, *War without Mercy*, 150.

69 Jefferson, *Fighting for Hope*; and Takaki, *Different Mirror*, 350–59. On segregated African American units in Alaska, see Morgan, "Race Relations"; and Hendricks, "Challenge to the Status Quo?" On segregation in the military and African American attitudes toward the military, see Cox, *Segregated Soldiers*, 1–9.

70 Conrad Ryan, personal interview, September 20, 2014, February 27, 2016, and October 13, 2017.

71 S.A.S.S.Y., *Learning to Live Together*, 19. Another elder, Nelson Frank (Native from Hydaburg), described witnessing segregation while in the military when he saw "all the African Americans were in the kitchen."

72 Oscar Drake to Superintendent Office of Indian Affairs, January 13, 1943, RG 126, box 202, NARA II.

73 For more on Elizabeth Peratrovich, see chapter 5.

74 Earl Wineck, personal interview, January 19, 2017.

75 Alfred Wright, personal interview, March 12, 2015, January 28, 2016, April 6, 2017, August 3, 2022.

76 Jorgensen and Lester, *Jorgy*, 72–77. For more on Alberta Schenck, see chapter 5.

77 Holger "Jorgy" Jorgensen, phone interview, October 20, 2015. A photo of Jorgy and other Alaska Scouts is featured in Lenz and Barker, *Bethel*, 106.

78 Coen, "'Shoot It Down,'" 1–19.

79 F. W. Laskowski to all posts, camps, and stations, Alaskan Department, October 5, 1945, RG 547 AK Department Adjutant General Section, box 415, NARA II.

80 Supported by AFN, journalist Bill Hess wrote, "Alaska Native Veterans."

81 C. L. Smith, *Aleut Service Members of the Aleutians East*, website, Aleut Corporation, 2017, https://aleut.info.

FOUR The Alaska Territorial Guard

1   Hess, "Alaska Native Veterans." On the great blackout, see William Schneider and Wendy Arundale, Greta Akpik Interview, Quliaqtuat Iñupiat Nunafiññiñ — The Report of the Chipp-Ikpikpuk River and Upper Meade River Oral History Project, 1987, Tape 037, Iñupiat Heritage Center.

2   On the significance of Iñupiat whaling ventures, music, and culture, see Sakakibara, *Whale Snow*, 150–86.

3   Salinas, *Pinay Guerrilleras*.

4   Conversation with Melissa Bokovoy, September 1, 2022, Albuquerque, NM.

5   Marston, *Men of the Tundra*; Martz, *Uncle Sam's Men*; and Wooley and Martz, "Tundra Army," 155–60.

6   World War II was the first time that Alaska experienced a significant influx of military equipment and servicemen. From 1867 to 1877 the US Army had forts at Wrangell, St. Paul Canal, Kodiak Island, and Kenai. Even during the gold rush, when the Royal Canadian Mounted Police occupied the Yukon Territory, the US Army refrained from sending the army to Alaska. US Army, "USARAK History," September 9, 2016, https://www.army.mil/article/163011/usarak_history.

7   Woodman, *Duty Station Northwest*, 19.

8   Alex DeMarban, "23 Territorial Guardsmen Honored for WWII Service," *Arctic Sounder* (Anchorage), October 21, 2004.

9   Adjutant General, Department of the Army, "Chapter 18: Local Defense Forces Alaska National Guard Official History of the Alaskan Department," Record Series World War II Histories 1940–45, series 1, box 1, folder 3, 673d ABWHO, JBER.

10 Barbara Cane, "Territorial Guard Honored," *Tundra Times* (Fairbanks), July 24, 1989.

11 The following Native news sources cite Marston investing in Native leadership for the ATG: "Muktuk Marston Will Be the No. 1 Musher," *Tundra Times* (Fairbanks), November 16, 1987; and Steve Pilkington, "New Armory Memorializes Gen. Marston," *Tundra Times* (Fairbanks), July 13, 1987.

12 Adjutant General, Department of the Army, "Chapter 18," 1. On Japanese bomb balloons, see Sheila Turner, "'Muktuk' of ATG Fame Farms near Unalakleet," *Tundra Times* (Fairbanks), June 2, 1967; and Coen, "If One."

13 Adjutant General, Department of the Army, "Chapter 18," 1.

14 Turner, "'Muktuk' of ATG"; and Marston, *Men of the Tundra*, 141–42.

15 Gruening, *Many Battles*, 310.

16 Morgan, "Race Relations," 274.

17 *Eskimo Guardsmen*, 1940–1950, film strip with audio, 45 minutes, Alaska Film Archives, UAF.

18 "Margaret Panigeo Gray Passes in Barrow," *Tundra Times* (Fairbanks), September 27, 1995.

19 *Eskimo Guardsmen*.

20 Turner, "'Muktuk' of ATG."

21 Marston, *Men of the Tundra*, 76.

22 Thomas A. Snapp, "Esk*mo Grandmother Wins Irish Sweepstakes Prize," *Fairbanks Daily News-Miner*, March 29, 1961.

23 Marston, *Men of the Tundra*, 231–32. This percentage is based on identifying twenty-nine feminine names from the ATG roster. The percentage might be higher since I only counted names that appear feminine; other names might also be feminine.

24 Marston, *Men of the Tundra*, 231–32.

25 "Indian Women Work for Victory," n.d., RG 75, box 1, "Records Related to Indians in World War II," NARA I.

26 "Eskimos Help Win War," n.d., Walter Bradshaw scrapbook, UAA.

27 This rate is from 1945 adjusted to inflation in 2023.

28 Townsend, *World War II*, 19.

29 Townsend, *World War II*, 191.

30 Holger Jorgensen, phone interview, October 20, 2015.

31 Hess, "Alaska Native Veterans," 10; Richard Frank, Bernice Joseph, and Bill Schneider, Fairbanks Native Association Project Jukebox Interview, October 2, 1991; and Mary Beth Smetzer, "Respected Athabascan Elder Richard Frank Dies," *Fairbanks Daily News-Miner*, September 20, 2012.

32 Marston, *Men of the Tundra*, 120–21.

33 La Verne Kopp to Marston, February 6, 1945, Otto Geist Collection, series 16, box 1, folder 10, UAF.

34 Alex Okitkun to Otto Geist, April 20, 1946, Otto Geist Collection, series 16, box 1, folder 10, UAF.

35 Alex Okitkun to ATG headquarters in Nome, June 8, 1946, Otto Geist Collection, series 16, box 1, folder 10, UAF.

36 Robert Mayokok to Ernest Gruening, December 11, 1946, RG 101, series 79-35, box 461, folder 461-2, Alaska State Archives (hereafter cited as ASA).

37 Perea, *Sound Relations*, 6.

38 Tone-Pah-Hote, *Crafting*, 5.

39 Wooley and Martz, "Tundra Army," 159. Racialization of Natives was inextricably tied to racialization of African Americans.

40 Gruening, *Many Battles*, 309.

41 Marston, *Men of the Tundra*, 196.

42 Marston, *Men of the Tundra*, 194.

43 Marston, *Men of the Tundra*, 109.

44 Wooley and Martz, "Tundra Army," 159.

45 Wooley and Martz, "Tundra Army," 159–60; and Turner, "'Muktuk' of ATG."

46 Marston, *Men of the Tundra*, 195.

47 Wooley and Martz, "Tundra Army," 160; Turner, "'Muktuk' of ATG"; and Gruening, *Many Battles*, 311.

48 "Army National Guard Scout Battalion in Tactical Tests: Massive Air Transport Assembles ATG Men," *Tundra Times* (Fairbanks), February 13, 1970.

49 Carl Gidlund, "Guard Celebrates 350th Anniversary," *Tundra Times* (Fairbanks), December 8, 1986.

50 Marston, *Men of the Tundra*, 152 (see chapter 13, "Jade Mountain"). While Marston encouraged ATG captain Joe Sun of Shungnak to stake claims, and Native artists carved jade, it does call into question how much Native people of the region profited from massive resource extraction extending to global geographies, including Germany and China.

51 Joseph Upicksoun, "ASNA Asks Special Consideration," *Tundra Times* (Fairbanks), May 13, 1970.

52 Wesley Ugiaqtaq Aiken, personal interview, May 26, 2017, May 27, 2017.

53 Mercedes Angerman, "90-Year-Old WWII Veteran Receives Training to Help Fellow Veterans," *Alaska Native News*, November 18, 2016.

54 Angerman, "90-Year-Old WWII Veteran."

55 On the Iñupiat duck-in protest of 1961, see Edwardson, *History of the Iñupiat*.

56 David Ungrudruk Leavitt Sr., personal interview, May 30, 2017.

57 Kashevarof family, personal interview.

58 Lekanoff, personal interview.

59 Nicholai Lekanoff et al., National Park Service Interview with Nicholai S. Lekanoff, June 8, 2004; and Hudson and Mason, *Lost Villages*, 265–71.

60 Lestenkof, personal interview.

61 Dana Petersen, "Retired Major General Jake Lestenkof," *Tribal College Journal of American Indian Higher Education*, February 15, 2012, accessed December 2, 2023, https://tribalcollegejournal.org/reaching-hearts-hands/jake-lestenkof/.

62 Sahlin, personal interview.

63 "Know Your Leaders—AFN Sergeant at Arms Frank Degnan Leads a Varied Life," *Tundra Times* (Fairbanks), January 9, 1970.

64 Wooley and Martz, "Tundra Army," 160.

65 June Degnan, personal interview, May 14, 2013.

66 Irwin Bahr, personal interview, June 1, 2013.

67 Wilfred Eakon, personal interview, June 3, 2013.

68 Carrighar, *Moonlight*, 170.

69 According to sec 8147 of the Department of Defense Appropriations Act, 2000 (P.L. 106-259, 38 U.S.C. 106); and Adjutant General, Department of the Army, "Chapter 18."

70 Sprott, Craig, and Lehman, *Aanas and Taatas*.

71 Aiken, personal interview.

72 Alaska Native Veterans Association, "Alaska Territorial Guard Statue Project," grant proposal, accessed November 21, 2023, https://omb.alaska.gov/ombfiles /09_budget/CapBackup/proj49233.pdf.

73 "Louis Reich Jr. Obituary," *Alaska Dispatch News* (Anchorage), January 22, 2017. Louis Reich Jr.'s obituary mentioned both his parents, Norma Reich and Louis P. Reich, as members of the ATG.

FIVE **Racing and Erasing Natives**

1   Gruening, *Many Battles*, 319.

2   ANB Resolution, March 29, 1940, RG 101, series 79-35, box 460, folder 460-2, ASA.

3   Glenda Gilmore, conversation during a graduate seminar, in which she quickly termed *frozen Jim Crow* after I described Alaskan segregation directed at Native people, spring 2013, New Haven, CT.

4   Smith, "Exceeding Beringia."

5   Woodward, *Strange*, 1–10.

6   Camarillo, "Navigating Segregated Life," 645–62.

7   Lowery, *Lumbee*.

8   Takaki, *Iron Cages*. This conceptualization builds from Takaki's analysis that power transmits through culture, politics, and the economy and from conversations I had with Matthew Jacobson when I was a graduate student in 2011 to 2014.

9   On defining racial hierarchy, see Omi and Winant, *Racial Formation*, 8.

10 Carpio, *Collisions*, 1–21.

11 On Indigenous refusal that maintains sovereignty, see Simpson, *Mohawk Interruptus*, 1–12.

12 Eakon, personal interview.

13 Anonymous, personal interview, July 30, 2008.

14 Theresa Nanouk, personal interview, July 30, 2008.

15 Mary Ann Haugen, personal interview, July 30, 2008.

16 Frances Charles, personal interview, June 3, 2013.

17 S.A.S.S.Y., *Learning to Live Together*, 10.

18 S.A.S.S.Y., *Learning to Live Together*, 11.

19 S.A.S.S.Y., *Learning to Live Together*, 25.

20 Booth, personal interview; and S.A.S.S.Y., *Learning to Live Together*, 14. Another elder, Argyll Dennard of Sitka, spoke of "No Natives Allowed" signs when interviewed.

21 Gruening, *Many Battles*, 318.

22 On the Metlakatla Indian reservation settled in 1887 as an outlier of Alaska history regarding Indian reservations and Father Duncan, see Geiger, *Converging Empires*, 66–68.

23 Holloway, *Jim Crow Wisdom*, 9.

24 Alberta Schenck, "To Whom It May Concern," *Nome Nugget*, March 3, 1944.

25 Marston, *Men of the Tundra*, 133. Of note, Alberta mentioned to Marston, "I have been thinking so much about the Negro slaves down there and what Lincoln did for them!"

26 Otto Geist to Muktuk Marston, January 17, 1945, Otto Geist Collection, series 16, box 15, UAF.

27 For a longer source, see Guise, "Elizabeth Peratrovich."

28 "Superior Race Theory Hit in Hearing: Native Sisterhood President Hits at Rights Bill Opposition," *Daily Alaska Empire* (Juneau), February 6, 1945.

29 Vern Metcalfe, "Roy Peratrovich Sets Columnist Straight," *Tundra Times* (Fairbanks), September 14, 1987.

30 Elizabeth Peratrovich to ANB/ANS Executives, February 11, 1946, Soboleff Papers, series 1, box 6, folder 1, SHI.

31 Marcelo Quinto Jr., personal interview, May 15, 2013.

32 Elizabeth Peratrovich to Miss Fohn-Hansen, October 5, 1944, Soboleff Papers, series 1, box 6, folder 1, SHI.

33 Elizabeth and Roy Peratrovich to National Council of American Indians, October 20, 1945, Soboleff Papers, series 1, box 1, folder 10, SHI.

34 William L. Paul Jr. to 2nd division voters, May 1, 1945, Soboleff Papers, series 1, box 1, folder 10, SHI.

35 Haycox, "William Paul, Sr."

36 Frank Price proclamation, March 30, 1925, Soboleff Papers, series 1, box, 1, folder 1, SHI.

37 Harmon, *Rich Indians*, 227.

38 Arnett, "Unsettled Rights."

39 Metcalfe, *Dangerous Idea*. For sources on Alaskan fishing rights, see Groat, "Changing Tides"; Paul, *Then Fight for It*, 34–40; Alaska Federation of Natives, "Subsistence Chronology: A Short History of Subsistence Policy in Alaska since Statehood," AFN, 1998; and Steve Colt, "Salmon Fish Traps in Alaska: An Economic History Perspective," ISER Working Paper, February 15, 2000. Of note, in speaking with elders on wartime Alaska, fishing rights did not emerge as a topic by the elders whom I interviewed. While some elders spoke about fishing and subsistence generally, they did not speak about litigation.

40 Alfred Widmark to all ANB and ANS camps, June 11, 1946, Soboleff Papers, series 1, box 6, folder 11, SHI.

41 William Paul Jr. to Frank Marshall, October 27, 1943, Soboleff Papers, series 1, box 7, folder 21, SHI.

42 Andrew Hope to all land suit communities, February 20, 1945, Soboleff Papers, series 1, box 6, folder 4, SHI.

43 William Paul Jr. to Ralph Rivers, November 10, 1945, Soboleff Papers, series 1, box 7, folder 21, SHI.

44 Grosfoguel, *Colonial Subjects*. As a shortcoming of my analysis, I will not be analyzing sexuality, and I focus on race and gender.

45 Byrd, *Transit of Empire*, 221; and Estes, *Our History*.

46 Harmon, *Indians in the Making*.

47 Shoemaker, *Strange Likeness*, 142.

48 Harmon, *Indians in the Making*, 160.

49 Ostler, *Surviving Genocide*.

50 War Department Publication, *What Has Alaska to Offer Postwar Pioneers?*, 1944, Atwood Frances and William Ray Collection, box 1, folder 4, ARC.

51 John Adams, "This Is Matanuska!," in the *Alaska Sportsman*, May 1938, Felix S. Cohen Papers, box 18, folder 318, Beinecke Rare Book and Manuscript Library, Yale University (hereafter cited as Beinecke Library).

52 Department of the Interior report, "The Problem of Alaskan Development," April 1940, Felix S. Cohen Papers, box 18, folder 317, Beinecke Library.

53 Nielson, *Armed Forces*, 106–7.

54 Nielson, *Armed Forces*, 106–7; and Gruening, *Many Battles*, 270–71.

55 Wilkins and Stark, *American Indian*, 62.

56 Ernest Gruening to Harold Ickes, December 11, 1944, RG 126, box 331, NARA II.

57 Theodore Haas to Felix Cohen, June 21, 1946, Felix S. Cohen Papers, box 23, folder 379, Beinecke Library (source discusses Frank Johnson of Kake, who said "subtle propaganda" circulated and "instilled fears and misunderstandings of the effect of reserves"); Thodore Haas to D'Arcy McNickle, July 22, 1946, Felix S. Cohen Papers, box 23, folder 379, Beinecke Library (source says Natives from Kake feared losing citizenship and their franchise and feared restrictions on their movements from a reservation); and Don Foster to William Zimmerman, April 26, 1944, RG 75 John Collier, box 24 P1-163 entry 178, NARA I. Of note, Iñupiat in Shishmaref voted 13 to 47 not in favor of establishing an Indian reservation. This might be attributed to "Mr. Goshaw," a white trapper who intimidated locals and "threatened and bulldozed the people."

58 Earenfight, *Kiowa's Odyssey*, 4.

59 "The Nelson Act," Alaskool, accessed November 29, 2023, http://www.alaskool .org/native_ed/law/nelson.html.

60 Raibmon, *Authentic Indians*, 195.

61 Commissioner of Education to Don Foster, August 23, 1945, RG 101, box 460, series 79-35, folder 460-3, ASA.

62 Alaska Territorial Board of Education (estimated date 1947), RG 101, series 79-35, box 460, folder 460-3, ASA.

63 Fort Yukon residents to Ernest Gruening, June 28, 1939, RG 101, series 79-35, box 460, folder 460-2, ASA.

64 W. J. Dowd to John Troy, June 12, 1939, RG 101, series 79-35, box 460, folder 460-2, ASA.

65 Don Foster to Ernest Gruening, January 11, 1946, RG 101, series 79-35, box 460, folder 460-3, ASA.

66 Petersburg Chamber of Commerce education committee to Claude Hirst, November 3, 1938, RG 101, series 79-35, box 460, folder 460-2, ASA.

67 William Warne to Secretary Krug, October 8, 1949, RG 101, series 79-35, box 460, folder 460-3, ASA.

68 John W. Fletcher to Governor John Weir Troy, May 25, 1939, RG 101, series 79–35, box 460, folder 460-2, ASA.

69 Report on Palmer community meeting, October 5, 1949, RG 101, series 79-35, box 460, folder 460-3, ASA.

70 For more on the vernacular of *Squ*w*, see chapter 6.

71 Alaska Territorial Board of Education (estimated date 1947), RG 101, series 79-35, box 460, folder 460-3, ASA.

72 Nick Alokli, personal interview with author and Peter Boskofsky, August 9, 2008.

73 Weinberg, *Keep Talking*.

74 Nora Dauenhauer and Richard Dauenhauer, personal interview, May 15, 2013.

75 Carol Brady, personal interview, September 18, 2014; and Brady, *Through the Storm*. For more about Carol and her experience with gendered segregation during World War II, see chapter 6.

76 Helen Sarabia, personal interview, May 14, 2013.

77 Selina Everson, personal interview, May 15, 2013.

78 Rosa Miller, personal interview, September 19, 2014.

79 M. W. Johnson speech, n.d., M. Walter Johnson Papers (hereafter cited as Johnson Papers), folder 18, UAA.

80 Richard L. Neuberger, "Scourge of the North," *Survey Graphic*, December 1947, Johnson Papers, folder 35, UAA.

81 Harry Barnett et al., "Medical Conditions in Alaska: A Report by a Group Sent by the American Medical Association," October 25, 1947, Johnson Papers, folder 35, UAA.

82 Alaska Historical Society talk by Walter Johnson, "The 200-Year Tuberculosis Epidemic among Alaska Natives," November 7, 1970, Johnson Papers, folder 37, UAA.

83 Wallace Philoon to Don Foster, May 31, 1945, RG 101, series 79-35, box 461, folder 461-2, ASA.

84 Ceniza Choy, *Empire of Care*; and Imada, "Promiscuous Signification."

85 Pauline Burkher, "Chapter 11: The Fight for Tuberculosis Hospitals in Alaska," n.d., Johnson Papers, folder 31, UAA.

86 M. W. Johnson, "Brief History of Tuberculosis in Alaska," Johnson Papers, folder 8, UAA.

87 Walter Johnson, "'Who Knows What Sickness They May Bring Us?' The Historical Review of Tuberculosis as an Agent of Change for the Alaska Native," n.d., Johnson Papers, folder 33, UAA.

88 Nulato petition to Ernest Gruening, June 26, 1942, RG 101, series 79-35, box 461, folder 461-2, ASA.

89 Esmailka and Tribal Council to Office of Indian Affairs, December 1936, RG 101, box 461, series 79–35, folder 461-2, ASA.

90 Donald Tyer to Governor John W. Troy, March 29, 1939, RG 101, series 79-35, box 461, folder 461-2, ASA.

91 Hugh Fulton to Roy Peratrovich, March 7, 1944, Soboleff Papers, series 1, box 7, folder 5, SHI.

92 William L. Paul Jr. proposed executive committee resolution by the ANB, October 8, 1945, Soboleff Papers, series 1, box 1, folder 10, SHI.

93 William Paul Jr. to C. C. Carter, January 27, 1944, Soboleff Papers, series 1, box 7, folder 21, SHI.

94 Paul and Paul, *Home Care of the Tuberculosis in Alaska*, RG 75, Records of the BIA Juneau Area Office, box 1, folder 2, NARA, Seattle, Washington.

95 Gruening, *Many Battles*, 319.

SIX War and Sexual Violence

1 Brady, *Through the Storm*.

2 Brady, personal interview.

3 Huhndorf, *Going Native*, 3; and Stoler, *Carnal Knowledge*, 41–111.

4 Byrd, *Transit of Empire*, xv–xxxix.

5 For a foundational source in the field of sexual violence, see Block, *Rape and Sexual Power*, 1–15. For a key source on sexual violence and defining rape, see Freedman, *Redefining Rape*, 1–11. On violence against Black women and white patriarchy, see hooks, *Ain't I a Woman*, 15–49. On sexual violence in Native America, see Deer, *Beginning and End*.

6 Stephen and Speed, *Indigenous Women*, 22.

7 Million, *Therapeutic Nations*, 7.

8 Enloe, *Bananas*, 125–73.

9 Barman, "Taming Aboriginal Sexuality," 237–66.

10 On the colonial gaze that infused power by sexualizing Esk*mo women as conquest, see Huhndorf, *Going Native*, 107–28.

11 Stanley Pogozelski correspondence, box 1, folder 1, Beinecke Library. Stationery also found in the Earl J. Lucier Collection, World War II photo album, UAA.

12 Holloway, *Jim Crow Wisdom*, 42–43.

13 Pearce, *Savagism and Civilization*; Said, *Orientalism*, 1–28; and Rasmussen, *Queequeg's Coffin*, 1–16.

14 Deloria, *Playing Indian*, 28–32.

15 Huhndorf, *Going Native*, 111.

16 Huhndorf, *Going Native*, 6, 18.

17 On colonial markets generating power from propaganda on Indigenous history, see Cothran, *Remembering the Modoc War*, 20–21.

18 On "commodity racism," see McClintock, *Imperial Leather*, 207–8.

19 Tijuana Bibles Collection, Beinecke Library.

20 Wexler, *Tender Violence*.

21 Jacobson, *Barbarian Virtues*, 139–72 (photographic insert "Madonnas of Many Lands").

22 Navy Seabee photograph album, UAA.

23 Library of Congress Prints and Photographs Online Catalog, "Mickaninies Kow-Kow," by Frank H. Nowell, accessed February 7, 2018, https://www.loc .gov/item/91794617/.

24 On consumerism that manifests power through the commercialization of ethnic bodies, see Thompson, *Eye for the Tropics*.

25 This is from checking eBay.com, accessed June 5, 2023.

26 Deloria, *Indians in Unexpected Places*, 8.

27 Adakian collection, folder 1:16–20, Beinecke Library.

28 Adakian collection, folder 1:16–20, Beinecke Library.

29 O'Brien, *Firsting*, xxi–xxvi.

30 Fanon, *Black Skin*, 89–92.

31 Piatote, *Domestic Subjects*, ix.

32 Geiger, *Converging Empires*, 79.

33 Driscoll, *War Discovers Alaska*, 11.

34 On race formation, white supremacy, and humor, see Pérez, *Souls of White Jokes*, 5.

35 "Weather Stations Rogers" report, April 6, 1945, series World War II Histories 1940–1945, box 1, folder 4, 673d ABWHO, JBER.

36 Beulah Marrs Parisi to family, March 2, 1945, Peter and Beulah Parisi Papers, box 1, folder 5, UAA (underlines replicate Parisi's).

37 Rosita Worl, personal interview, July 16, 2021.

38 On "playing Indian," see Deloria, *Playing Indian*, 1–8.

39 Jack Hunt photograph, Vern Brickley Collection, box 29, Anchorage Museum.

40 Theobald, *Reproduction*, 1–14.

41 Phillips, *Staging Indigeneity*, 1–13.

42 Reesly Heurkie to Ernest Gruening, September 26, 1944, RG 101, series 79–35, box 462, folder 462-2, ASA.

43 Pascoe, *What Comes Naturally*.

44 Hodes, *White Women*.

45 I use the terms *prostitution* and *prostitute* in this discussion as these are the terms used in the primary documents.

46 Bailey and Farber, *First Strange Place*, 95–132; and Padoongpatt, *Flavors of Empire*, 32–37.

47 Mrs. John Birkeland to Ernest Gruening, June 22, 1942, M939, roll 338, NARA, Anchorage, Alaska.

48 Lieutenant Corporal of Engineers T. J. Haines to Daniel Berry Mayor of Haines, September 4, 1943, M939, roll 338, NARA, Anchorage, Alaska.

49 Harry McCain to C. M. Archbold Care of US Forest Service, June 9, 1942, M939, roll 338, NARA, Anchorage, Alaska.

50 Langdon White to Wayne Ramsey, May 22, 1942, M939, roll 338, NARA, Anchorage, Alaska.

51 Barman, "Taming Aboriginal Sexuality," 243.

52 "Esk*mos Help Win War: Women Make Army Parkas and Men Work on Docks," Walter Bradshaw Scrapbook, UAA.

53 Barman, "Taming Aboriginal Sexuality," 240.

54 Don Foster to Wallace Philoon, June 8, 1945, RG 101, box 461, folder 461-2, ASA.

55 Enloe, *Bananas*, 17.

56 Enloe, *Bananas*, 22, 137–38.

57 Roy Peratrovich to USO Board of Directors, February 16, 1943, [Rare Book] *A Recollection of Civil Rights Leader Elizabeth Peratrovich, 1911–1958* (hereafter cited as *A Recollection*), UAA.

58 Claude Hirst to Ernest Gruening, May 20, 1943, RG 101, series 79-35, box 461, folder 461-6, ASA.

59 Metcalfe, *Dangerous Idea*, 72; and Gruening, *Many Battles*, 328-37.

60 Alaska Native Brotherhood minutes, January 19, 1942, Soboleff Papers, series 2, box 19, folder 2, SHI.

61 Ernest Gruening to Simon Bolivar Buckner, May 20, 1943, [Rare Book] *A Recollection*, UAA.

62 Ernest Gruening, "Message to the 31st Annual Convention of the ANB at Kake," November 1944, William Lewis Paul Papers, box 3, folder 67, University of Washington Libraries Special Collections.

63 Simon Bolivar Buckner to Ernest Gruening, June 7, 1943, RG 101, series 79-35, box 461, folder 461-6, ASA.

64 Arnold Brower plus fifty-seven residents to Ernest Gruening, April 8, 1946, RG 126, box 201, NARA II.

65 Walter Soboleff to Simon Bolivar Buckner, June 24, 1943, [Rare Book] *A Recollection*.

66 Anthony Dimond to Frank Knox, June 28, 1943, RG 126, box 201, NARA, II.

67 Claude Hirst to Roy Peratrovich, July 9, 1943, [Rare Book] *A Recollection*.

68 Anthony Dimond to Frank Knox, November 13, 1943, RG 126, box 201, NARA II.

69 Harold Ickes to Frank Knox, December 8, 1943, RG 126, box 201, NARA II.

70 Robert Patterson to Harold Ickes, July 27, 1943, RG 126, box 201, NARA II.

71 Ruth Gruber to John Collier, January 26, 1944, RG 75, Alaska 1940–57, box 195, NARA I.

72 Irwin Silverman to B. W. Thoron, February 18, 1944, RG 126, box 202, NARA II.

73 Enloe, *Bananas*, 17, 22, 148–49.

74 Homer Stockdale to Evelyn Butler, February 5, 1942, RG 126, box 202, NARA II.

75 Stockdale names the girl, but I will not print it here as she was a child and never consented for this story to be told.

76 Karl Brunstad to "Sir," December 16, 1943, RG 126, box 202, NARA II.

77 Deer, *Beginning and End*, xx.

78 Block, *Rape and Sexual Power*, 12.

79 Freedman, *Redefining Rape*, 3.

80 Freedman, *Redefining Rape*, 11.

81 Fred Dimler to Fred Geeslin, January 7, 1943, RG 101, box 502, folder 502-6, ASA.

82 Harold Ickes to President Franklin Delano Roosevelt, May 13, 1944, RG 126, box 202, NARA II.

83 FDR to Harold Ickes, May 22, 1944, RG 126, box 202, NARA II.

84 Miller, personal interview.

85 Departmental Order No. 82-1943, December 22, 1943, RG 181 Naval District and Shore Establishment, 17th Naval District Kodiak, Alaska, Alaska Sea Frontier Central Subject Files 1945 entry 132, box 19, folder "Domestic Relations," NARA, Seattle, Washington.

86 McRoberts, *North Country*, 95–96.

87 McRoberts, *North Country*, 97, 111.

88 McRoberts, *North Country*, 94.

89 McRoberts, *North Country*, 98.

90 Martha Benzel, personal interview, September 16, 2014.

91 Ralph Boaz memorandum to headquarters US troops in Juneau, May 9, 1944, RG 101, box 462, folder 462-2, ASA.

92 G. W. MacLane to Ernest Gruening, June 3, 1944, RG 101, box 462, folder 462-2, ASA.

93 Shah, *Contagious Divides*, 11–16.

94 Edgar Norris to Ernest Gruening, June 13, 1944, RG 101, box 462, folder 462-2, ASA.

95 Orvel Holum to Ernest Gruening, April 10, 1944, RG 126, box 202 (likely although exact box unrecorded—I retain photocopies of this document made onsite), NARA II.

96 G. W. MacLane to his units, July 31, 1944, RG 101, box 462, folder 462-2, ASA.

97 Restricted areas map, July 31, 1944, RG 101, box 462, folder 462-2, ASA.

98 Ernest Gruening to Ruth Hampton, August 17, 1944, RG 126, box 202, NARA II.

99 Jorgensen, personal interview.

100 Poor, *Artist Sees Alaska*, 95.

101 Pascoe, *What Comes Naturally*, 6.

102 P. W. Danielson to Fred Daiker, November 4, 1948, RG 75, CCF "Alaska," series 741, box 186, NARA I.

103 Fred Daiker to Darcy McNickle, November 9, 1948, RG 75, CCF "Alaska," series 741, box 186, NARA I.

Epilogue

1 Napoleon, *Yuuyaraq*.

2 DeLucia, *Memory Lands*, 328.

3 O'Neill, *Firecracker Boys*.

4 Alaska v. Native Village of Venetie Tribal Government, 522 U.S. 520 (1998).

5 Takaki, *Hiroshima*, 46.

6 Takaki, *Hiroshima*, 47.

7 Immerwahr, *How to Hide*, 18–19, 400.

SELECTED BIBLIOGRAPHY

This is organized by prioritizing oral history interviews I conducted followed by archives and published sources consulted.

Oral History Interviews: Indigenous Alaskan Interviews

Adams, Bertrand Kadashan, Sr. (Tlingit), Anchorage, July 11, 2008

Ahwinona, Jacob (Iñupiaq), Nome, July 18, 2008

Aiken, Wesley Ugiaqtaq (Iñupiaq), Utqiaġvik, May 26, 2017; May 27, 2017

Alokli, Nick (Alutiiq), Kodiak, August 9, 2008

Anonymous (Iñupiaq), Anchorage, January 14, 2015

Anonymous (Iñupiaq), Unalakleet, June 3, 2013

Anonymous (Iñupiaq), Unalakleet, June 3, 2013; August 30, 2015

Anonymous (Iñupiaq), Unalakleet, September 24, 2015

Anonymous (Tlingit), Juneau, September 15, 2014

Anonymous (Tlingit), Juneau, September 16, 2014

Bahr, Irwin (Iñupiaq), Unalakleet, June 1, 2013

Benzel, Martha (Tlingit), Juneau, September 16, 2014

Booth, Arnold (Tsimshian), Metlakatla, July 24, 2008; September 20, 2014; February 27, 2016

Brady, Carol Feller (Tlingit), Juneau, September 18, 2014

Callahan, Alice (Native; did not specify tribe), Anchorage, August 4, 2008

Charles, Frances (Iñupiaq), Unalakleet, June 3, 2013

Chercasen, Lawrence "Larry" (Aleut), Anchorage and Dutch Harbor, May 6, 2015; June 2, 2017

Dauenhauer, Nora (Tlingit), Juneau, May 15, 2013

Degnan, June (Yup'ik), Juneau, May 14, 2013

Didrickson, Kristian (Tsimshian), Metlakatla, July 24, 2008

Doyle, Marilyn (Tlingit), Juneau, May 13, 2013

Eakon, Wilfred "Mallak" (Iñupiaq), Unalakleet, June 3, 2013

Everson, Selina (Tlingit), Juneau, May 15, 2013

Fawcett, Barbara (Tsimshian), Metlakatla, July 24, 2008

Hammond, Bella Gardner (Yup'ik), phone interview, May 24, 2013

Haugen, Mary Ann (Iñupiaq), July 30, 2008, June 3, 2013

John, Adam (Athabascan), Fairbanks, January 27, 2016

Johnson, William (Athabascan), Fairbanks, April 10, 2017

Johnson, William "Bill" (Tlingit), Anchorage, July 15, 2008

Jorgensen, Holger "Jorgy" (Iñupiaq), Fairbanks, March 11, 2015; March 12, 2015; January 27, 2016; April 9, 2017; October 20, 2017

Karmun, Dan (Iñupiaq), Nome, July 17, 2008

Kashevarof, Andronik P. (Aleut), Anchorage, February 9, 2016

Kashevarof, Elekonida "Ella" (Aleut), Anchorage, February 9, 2016

Keating, Elizabeth (Athabascan), Anchorage, February 29, 2016

Kendall, Shirley (Tlingit), Anchorage, July 26, 2008; May 4, 2015

Kinegak, Ella (Yup'ik), Bethel, May 2, 2015

Knagin, Dennis (Alutiiq), Kodiak, August 9, 2008

Knagin, Julie (Alutiiq), Kodiak, August 9, 2008

Kookesh, Jackie D'Cafango (Tlingit), Juneau, May 13, 2013

Leavitt, David Ungrudruk, Sr. (Iñupiaq), Utqiaġvik, May 30, 2017

Lekanoff, Nicholai S. (Aleut), Dutch Harbor, February 6, 2016

Lekanoff-Gregory, Patty (Aleut), Dutch Harbor, February 6, 2016

Lestenkof, Jake (Aleut), Anchorage, November 3, 2014, February 8, 2016

Loescher, Bob (Tlingit), Juneau, May 14, 2013

Matsuno, Marie (Aleut/Japanese American), Anchorage, November 27, 2021; April 4, 2022; August 10, 2022

McClean, Mary (Athabascan), Fairbanks, January 28, 2016

McConnell, Charlotte (Tlingit), Juneau, September 22, 2014

Mierzejek, Bonnie (Aleut), Anchorage, February 9, 2016

Miller, Rosa (Tlingit), Juneau, July 22, 2008; September 19, 2014

Morris, Madeline (Tlingit/Athabascan), Juneau, September 23, 2014

Nanouk, Theresa (Iñupiaq), Unalakleet, July 30, 2008

O'Brien, William P. (Aleut), Anchorage, May 24, 2013

Oman, Lela Kiana (Iñupiaq), Nome, July 17, 2008

Omiak, James (Iñupiaq), Nome, August 25, 2015

Owens, Dorothy (Tlingit/Filipino, "Indipino"), Juneau, September 17, 2014

Peters, Helen Joseph (Athabascan), Fairbanks, March 11, 2015

Petrivelli, Alice (Aleut), Anchorage, November 6, 2014; January 16, 2015; April 29, 2015; August 19, 2015

Pikonganna, Vince (Iñupiaq), Anchorage, July 15, 2008

Quinto, Marcelo, Jr. (Tlingit/Filipino, "Indipino"), Juneau, May 15, 2013

Riley, Grover "Butch" (Athabascan), Anchorage, July 28, 2008

Ryan, Conrad F., Sr. (Tsimshian), Metlakatla, September 20, 2014; February 27, 2016; October 12, 2017; October 13, 2017

Sahlin, Alfred "Al" (Iñupiaq), Nome, August 25, 2015

Sarabia, Helen (Tlingit), Juneau, May 14, 2013

Senungetuk, Joseph (Iñupiaq), Anchorage, April 5, 2022

Senungetuk, Ron (Iñupiaq), Fairbanks, March 6, 2015

Smith, Margaret Wolcoff (Aleut), Anchorage, May 24, 2013

Soboleff, Walter (Tlingit), Juneau, July 22, 2008

Soxie, Francis (Iñupiaq), Unalakleet, June 1, 2013

Stephan, Alberta (Athabascan), Anchorage, July 12, 2008; January 25, 2016

Stephan, Lee (Athabascan), Anchorage, July 12, 2008; January 25, 2016

Thomas, Edward (Tlingit), Juneau, May 15, 2013

Thompson, Karen Blandov (Tsimshian/Yup'ik), Metlakatla, September 21, 2014

Titus, Lawrence "Larry" (Athabascan), Fairbanks, March 7, 2015

Trigg, Lincoln (Iñupiaq), Nome, July 18, 2008, August 26, 2015

Trigg, Lucy (Iñupiaq), Nome, July 18, 2008

Withers, Melva Wolcoff (Aleut), Anchorage, May 28, 2013; August 26, 2019

Wolcoff, Mary (Aleut), Anchorage, May 24, 2013

Worl, Rosita (Tlingit), Juneau, July 16, 2021

Wright, Alfred "Al" (Athabascan), Fairbanks, March 12, 2015; January 28, 2016; April 6, 2017; October 20, 2017; August 3, 2022

Oral History Interviews: Alaskan Non-Native Interviews and World War II Veterans

Beltz, Arne, Anchorage, August 5, 2008

Berman, Elaine, Menlo Park, CA, March 22, 2015

Berman, Herb, Menlo Park, CA, March 22, 2015

Bowen, Dorothy, Juneau, May 16, 2013

Dauenhauer, Richard "Dick," Juneau, May 15, 2013

Fiala, Glenn L., Anchorage, May 22, 2013

Green, Alice S., Anchorage, June 6, 2013; January 18, 2017

Hoogendorn, William "Bill," Nome, August 27, 2015

Hurley, Katie, Wasilla, May 29, 2013

Lute/Washington, Nicola, Anchorage, May 22, 2013

Mecklenburger, Alvin "Al," Highland Park, IL, January 3, 2019

Palmer, Louis, Anchorage, June 6, 2013; January 18, 2017; August 26, 2019

Reader, Caroline, Nome, July 18, 2008

Uhr, Jonathan, San Francisco, CA, November 8, 2014

von der Heydt, James A., Anchorage, August 15, 2008

von der Heydt, Verna, Anchorage, August 15, 2008

Weimer, Robert "Pete," Anchorage, May 30, 2013

Whitehead, Lucy, Anchorage, January 18, 2017

Wilson, Juliana "Jan," Anchorage, January 11, 2015

Wineck, Earl, Anchorage, January 19, 2017

Oral History Interviews by Others

Akpik, Greta (Iñupiaq), 1987, Iñupiat Heritage Center

Brady, Isabella (Tlingit), 1996, Seniors and Sitka Sound Youth (S.A.S.S.Y.)

Buckingham, Althea, 1996, S.A.S.S.Y.

Chikigak, Thomas (Yup'ik), January 2, 2011, Alaska Veterans Museum

Dennard, Argyll, 1996, S.A.S.S.Y.

Frank, Nelson (Native from Hydaburg), 1996, S.A.S.S.Y.

Herman, Sam, Sr. (Cup'ik), October 18, 2011, Alaska Veterans Museum

Jorgensen, Holger "Jorgy" (Iñupiaq), 1999, Oral History Program, University of
    Alaska Fairbanks

Karras, Bertha (Tlingit), 1996, S.A.S.S.Y.

Lekanoff, Nicholai S. (Aleut), June 8, 2004, National Park Service

Petrivelli, Alice (Aleut), September 7, 2010, Carlene Arnold

Wineck, Earl, Alaska Veterans Museum

Archives

Alaska State Archives, Juneau, Alaska

Aleutian Pribilof Islands Association Heritage Library, Anchorage, Alaska
    World War II Legal Preparation Documents by John C. Kirtland

Anchorage Museum, Anchorage, Alaska
  Hilscher Collection
  Vern Brickley Collection
Hoover Institution Library and Archives, Stanford, California
Joint Base Elmendorf-Richardson, 673d Air Base Wing History Office,
  Anchorage, Alaska
  World War II Histories 1940–45, Series 1
National Archives and Records Administration, Anchorage, Alaska (before closure)
National Archives and Records Administration, College Park, Maryland
  Records of the Commission on Wartime Relocation and Internment
    of Civilians
National Archives and Records Administration, St. Louis, Missouri
National Archives and Records Administration, Seattle, Washington
  National Oceanic and Atmospheric Administration Pribilof Island Program
    Log Books 1871–1984
National Archives and Records Administration, Washington, DC
  Division of Information Records Relating to Indians in World War I and
    World War II
  Records Related to Indians in World War
  Sealaska Heritage Institute, William L. Paul Sr. Archives, Juneau, Alaska
  Walter Soboleff Papers
  Tuzzy Consortium Library, Iḷisaġvik College, Utqiaġvik, Alaska
UAA/APU Consortium Library, Archives and Special Collections, University of
  Alaska, Anchorage, Alaska
  Benjamin B. Talley Papers
  Ted Bank Papers
University of Alaska Fairbanks
  Alaska Film Archives, Alaska and Polar Regions Collections & Archives
    (APRCA)
  Anthony J. Dimond Papers
  Otto W. Geist Papers
University of Washington Libraries Special Collections, Seattle, Washington
  William Lackey Paul Papers
  William Lewis Paul Papers
Yale University, Beinecke Rare Books and Manuscript Library, New Haven, Con-
  necticut
  Adakian Collection
  Felix S. Cohen Papers

Published Sources

Akins, Damon B., and William J. Bauer Jr. *We Are the Land: A History of Native California*. Oakland: University of California Press, 2021.

Aleut Evacuation: The Untold War Story. Anchorage: Aleutian Pribilof Islands Association, 1992. DVD.

Allinson, Gary D. *Japan's Postwar History*. Ithaca, NY: Cornell University Press, 1997.

Arnett, Jessica Leslie. "Unsettled Rights in Territorial Alaska: Native Land, Sovereignty, and Citizenship from the Indian Reorganization Act to Termination." *Western Historical Quarterly* 48, no. 3 (Autumn 2017): 233–54.

Arnold, Carlene. "The Legacy of Unjust and Illegal Treatment of Unangan during World War II and Its Place in Unangan History." MA thesis, University of Kansas, 2011.

Asaka, Megan. *Seattle from the Margins: Exclusion, Erasure, and the Making of a Pacific Coast City*. Seattle: University of Washington Press, 2022.

Bailey, Beth, and David Farber. *The First Strange Place: Race and Sex in World War II Hawaii*. Baltimore: Johns Hopkins University Press, 1992.

Barman, Jean. "Taming Aboriginal Sexuality: Gender, Power, and Race in British Columbia, 1850–1900." *BC Studies*, no. 115–16 (1997): 237–66.

Bennett, Pamela. "Sometimes Freedom Wears a Woman's Face: American Indian Women Veterans of World War II." PhD diss., University of Arizona, 2012. ProQuest (3505019).

Bergsland, Knut. *Aleut Dictionary: Unangam Tunudgusii*. Fairbanks: Alaska Native Language Center, 1994.

Black, Lydia T. *Russians in Alaska, 1732–1867*. Fairbanks: University of Alaska Press, 2004.

Blackhawk, Ned. *Violence over the Land: Indians and Empires in the Early American West*. Cambridge, MA: Harvard University Press, 2006.

Block, Sharon. *Rape and Sexual Power in Early America*. Chapel Hill: University of North Carolina Press, 2006.

Blum, John Morton. *V Was for Victory: Politics and American Culture during World War II*. San Diego: Harcourt Brace, 1976.

Bodnar, John. *The "Good War" in American Memory*. Baltimore: Johns Hopkins University Press, 2010.

Brady, Carol Feller. *Through the Storm towards the Sun*. Bloomington, IN: AuthorHouse, 2006.

Brown, Dmitri Joseph. "Tewa Pueblos at the Dawn of Atomic Modernity." PhD diss., University of California, Davis, 2022.

Byrd, Jodi A. *The Transit of Empire: Indigenous Critiques of Colonialism*. Minneapolis: University of Minnesota Press, 2011.

Camacho, Keith L. *Sacred Men: Law, Torture, and Retribution in Guam*. Durham, NC: Duke University Press, 2019.

Camarillo, Albert M. "Navigating Segregated Life in America's Racial Borderhoods, 1910s–1950s." *Journal of American History* 100, no. 3 (December 2013): 645–62.

Campbell, Robert. *In Darkest Alaska: Travel and Empire along the Inside Passage*. Philadelphia: University of Pennsylvania Press, 2007.

Carpio, Genevieve. *Collisions at the Crossroads: How Place and Mobility Make Race*. Oakland: University of California Press, 2019.

Carpio, Genevieve, Natchee Blu Barnd, and Laura Barraclough. "Introduction to the Special Issue: Mobilizing Indigeneity and Race within and against Settler Colonialism." *Mobilities* 17, no. 2 (2022): 179–95.

Carrighar, Sally. *Moonlight at Midday*. New York: Knopf, 1958.

Ceniza Choy, Catherine. *Empire of Care: Nursing and Migration in Filipino American History*. Durham, NC: Duke University Press, 2003.

Chandonnet, Fern, ed. *Alaska at War, 1941–1945: The Forgotten War Remembered*. Fairbanks: University of Alaska Press, 2008.

———. "The Recapture of Attu." In *Alaska at War, 1941–1945: The Forgotten War Remembered*, edited by Fern Chandonnet, 81–85. Fairbanks: University of Alaska Press, 2008.

Chew, Selfa A. *Uprooting Community: Japanese Mexicans, World War II, and the U.S.-Mexico Borderlands*. Tucson: University of Arizona Press, 2015.

Chiang, Connie Y. *Nature behind Barbed Wire: An Environmental History of the Japanese American Incarceration*. New York: Oxford University Press, 2018.

Child, Brenda J. *Boarding School Seasons: American Indian Families, 1900–1940*. Lincoln: University of Nebraska Press, 1998.

Coates, K. S., and W. R. Morrison. *The Alaska Highway in World War II: The U.S. Army of Occupation in Canada's Northwest*. Norman: University of Oklahoma Press, 1992.

Coen, Ross. "'If One Should Come Your Way, Shoot It Down': The Alaska Territorial Guard and the Japanese Balloon Bomb Attack of World War II." *Alaska History* 25, no. 2 (Fall 2010).

Cole, Terrence M. "Jim Crow in Alaska: The Passage of the Alaska Equal Rights Act of 1945." *Western Historical Quarterly* 23, no. 4 (1992): 429–49.

Cook-Lynn, Elizabeth. *Anti-Indianism in Modern America: A Voice from Tatekeya's Earth*. Urbana: University of Illinois Press, 2001.

Cothran, Boyd. *Remembering the Modoc War: Redemptive Violence and the Making of American Innocence*. Chapel Hill: University of North Carolina Press, 2014.

Cox, Marcus S. *Segregated Soldiers: Military Training at Historically Black Colleges in the Jim Crow South*. Baton Rouge: Louisiana State University Press, 2013.

Crandall, Maurice. *These People Have Always Been a Republic: Indigenous Electorates in the U.S.-Mexico Borderlands, 1598–1912*. Chapel Hill: University of North Carolina Press, 2019.

Dauenhauer, Nora Marks, and Richard Dauenhauer. *Haa Kusteeyí, Our Culture: Tlingit Life Stories*. Seattle: University of Washington Press, 1994.

———. *Haa Shuká, Our Ancestors: Tlingit Oral Narratives*. Seattle: University of Washington Press, 1987.

Dauenhauer, Nora Marks, Richard Dauenhauer, and Lydia T. Black. *Anóoshi Lingít Aaní Ká: Russians in Tlingit America: The Battles of Sitka, 1802 and 1804*. Seattle: University of Washington Press, 2008.

Deer, Sarah. *The Beginning and End of Rape: Confronting Sexual Violence in Native America*. Minneapolis: University of Minnesota Press, 2015.

Deloria, Philip J. *Indians in Unexpected Places*. Lawrence: University Press of Kansas, 2004.

———. *Playing Indian*. New Haven, CT: Yale University Press, 1998.

DeLucia, Christine M. *Memory Lands: King Philip's War and the Place of Violence in the Northeast*. New Haven, CT: Yale University Press, 2018.

Demuth, Bathsheba. *Floating Coast: An Environmental History of the Bering Strait*. W. W. Norton, 2019.

Den Ouden, Amy E., and Jean M. O'Brien. *Recognition, Sovereignty Struggles, and Indigenous Rights in the United States: A Sourcebook*. Chapel Hill: University of North Carolina Press, 2013.

Diaz, Vicente M. *Repositioning the Missionary: Rewriting the Histories of Colonialism, Native Catholicism, and Indigeneity in Guam*. Honolulu: University of Hawaiʻi Press, 2010.

Dower, John W. *Embracing Defeat: Japan in the Wake of World War II*. New York: W. W. Norton, 1999.

———. *War without Mercy: Race and Power in the Pacific War*. New York: Pantheon Books, 1986.

Drea, Edward J. *Japan's Imperial Army: Its Rise and Fall, 1853–1945*. Lawrence: University Press of Kansas, 2009.

Driscoll, Joseph. *War Discovers Alaska*. Philadelphia: J. B. Lippincott, 1943.

Dunaway, Finis. *Defending the Arctic Refuge: A Photographer, an Indigenous Nation, and a Fight for Environmental Justice*. Chapel Hill: University of North Carolina Press, 2021.

Duus, Peter, Ramon H. Myers, and Mark R. Peattie. *The Japanese Wartime Empire, 1931–1945*. 1996; repr., Princeton, NJ: Princeton University Press, 2010.

Earenfight, Phillip. *A Kiowa's Odyssey: A Sketchbook from Fort Marion*. Seattle: University of Washington Press, 2007.

Echohawk, Brummett, with Mark R. Ellenbarger. *Drawing Fire: A Pawnee, Artist, and Thunderbird in World War II*. Edited by Trent Riley. Lawrence: University Press of Kansas, 2018.

Edwardson, Rachel Naninaaq, dir. *History of the Iñupiat: 1961, The Duck-In*. Utqiaġvik, AK: North Slope Borough School District, 2005. Film screening, March 24, 2022, by Sovereign Iñupiat for a Living Arctic.

Enloe, Cynthia. *Bananas, Beaches and Bases: Making Feminist Sense of International Politics*. 2nd ed. Berkeley: University of California Press, 2014.

Estes, Nick. *Our History Is the Future*. London: Verso, 2019.

Fanon, Frantz. *Black Skin, White Masks*. New York: Grove Press, 1952.

———. *The Wretched of the Earth*. New York: Grove Press, 1963.

Fedman, David. *Seeds of Control: Japan's Empire of Forestry in Colonial Korea*. Seattle: University of Washington Press, 2020.

Fienup-Riordan, Ann. *Freeze Frame: Alaska Esk*mos in the Movies*. Seattle: University of Washington Press, 1995.

Ford, Corey. *Short Cut to Tokyo: The Battle for the Aleutians*. New York: Charles Scribner's Sons, 1943.

Fredrickson, George M. *Racism: A Short History*. Princeton, NJ: Princeton University Press, 2002.

Freedman, Estelle B. *Redefining Rape: Sexual Violence in the Era of Suffrage and Segregation*. Cambridge, MA: Harvard University Press, 2013.

Fujiwara-Greve, Takako. *Non-cooperative Game Theory*. Tokyo: Springer, 2015.

Garfield, Brian. *The Thousand-Mile War: World War II in Alaska and the Aleutians*. Fairbanks: University of Alaska Press, 1969.

Geiger, Andrea. *Converging Empires: Citizens and Subjects in the North Pacific Borderlands, 1867–1945*. Chapel Hill: University of North Carolina Press, 2022.

Gilbert, Matthew Sakiestewa. *Education beyond the Mesas: Hopi Students at Sherman Institute, 1902–1929*. Lincoln: University of Nebraska Press, 2010.

Gilman, William. *Our Hidden Front: The Complete Report on Alaska and the Aleutians.* New York: Reynal and Hitchcock, 1944.

Golodoff, Nick. *Attu Boy: A Young Alaskan's WWII Memoir.* Edited by Rachel Mason. Anchorage: National Park Service, 2012.

Gonzalez, Vernadette Vicuña. *Securing Paradise: Tourism and Militarism in Hawai'i and the Philippines.* Durham, NC: Duke University Press, 2013.

Gordon, Linda, and Gary Y. Okihiro. *Impounded: Dorothea Lange and the Censored Images of Japanese American Internment.* New York: W. W. Norton, 2006.

Gouveia, Grace Mary. "'We Also Serve': American Indian Women's Role in World War II." *Michigan Historical Review* 20, no. 2 (Fall 1994): 153–82.

Gram, John R. *Education at the Edge of Empire: Negotiating Pueblo Identity in New Mexico's Indian Boarding Schools.* Seattle: University of Washington Press, 2015.

Groat, Bridget. "The Changing Tides of Bristol Bay: Salmon, Sovereignty, and Alaska Natives." PhD diss., Arizona State University, 2019.

Grosfoguel, Ramón. *Colonial Subjects: Puerto Ricans in a Global Perspective.* Berkeley: University of California Press, 2003.

Gruening, Ernest. *Many Battles: The Autobiography of Ernest Gruening.* New York: Liveright, 1973.

Grummett, Karleen. *Quiet Defiance: Alaska's Empty Chair Story.* Juneau: Empty Chair Project, 2016.

Guise, Holly Miowak. "Alaskan Segregation and the Paradox of Exclusion, Separation, and Integration." In *Transforming the University: Alaska Native Studies in the 21st Century,* edited by Beth Ginondidoy Leonard et al., 274–304. Minneapolis: Two Harbors Press, 2014.

———. "Elizabeth Peratrovich, the Alaska Native Sisterhood, and Indigenous Women's Activism, 1943–1947." In *Suffrage at 100: Women in American Politics since 1920,* edited by Stacie Taranto and Leandra Zarnow, 147–62. Baltimore: Johns Hopkins University Press, 2020.

———. "Who Is Doctor Bauer? Rematriating a Censored Story on Internment, Wardship, and Sexual Violence in Wartime Alaska, 1941–1944." *Western Historical Quarterly* 53, no. 2 (Summer 2022): 145–65.

Hall, Ryan. *Beneath the Backbone of the World: Blackfoot People and the North American Borderlands, 1720–1877.* Chapel Hill: University of North Carolina Press, 2020.

Hammett, Dashiell, and Robert Colodny. *The Battle of the Aleutians: A Graphic History, 1942–1943.* Adak, AK: Intelligence Section, Field Force Headquarters, 1943.

Handleman, Howard. *Bridge to Victory: The Story of the Reconquest of the Aleutians.* New York: Random House, 1943.

Harding, Stephen. "What We Learned . . . from the Battle of Attu." *Military History* 25, no. 6 (February/March 2009): 17.

Harjo, Laura. *Spiral to the Stars: Mvskoke Tools of Futurity*. Tucson: University of Arizona Press, 2019.

Harmon, Alexandra. *Indians in the Making: Ethnic Relations and Indian Identities around Puget Sound*. Berkeley: University of California Press, 1998.

———. *Rich Indians: Native People and the Problem of Wealth in American History*. Chapel Hill: University of North Carolina Press, 2010.

Hartman, Ian C., and David Reamer. *Black Lives in Alaska: A History of African Americans in the Far Northwest*. Seattle: University of Washington Press, 2022.

Hartman, Saidiya V. *Scenes of Subjection: Terror, Slavery, and Self-Making in Nineteenth Century America*. New York: Oxford University Press, 1997.

Haycox, Stephen W. *Alaska: An American Colony*. Seattle: University of Washington Press, 2002.

———. "Mining the Federal Government: The War and the All-America City." In *Alaska at War, 1941–1945: The Forgotten War Remembered*, edited by Fern Chandonnet, 203–9. Fairbanks: University of Alaska Press, 2008.

———. "William Paul, Sr., and the Alaska Voters' Literacy Act of 1925." *Alaska History* 2, no. 1 (Winter 1986/87): 17–38.

Hays, Otis, Jr. *Alaska's Hidden Wars: Secret Campaigns on the North Pacific Rim*. Fairbanks: University of Alaska Press, 2004.

Hendricks, Charles. "A Challenge to the Status Quo?" In *Alaska at War, 1941–1945: The Forgotten War Remembered*, edited by Fern Chandonnet, 277–83. Fairbanks: University of Alaska Press, 2008.

Hess, Bill. "Alaska Native Veterans." *Alaska's Village Voices* 5, no. 5 (Winter 2001/2002): 6.

Hinnershitz, Stephanie. *Japanese American Incarceration: The Camps and Coerced Labor during World War II*. Philadelphia: University of Pennsylvania Press, 2021.

Hodes, Martha. *White Women, Black Men: Illicit Sex in the Nineteenth-Century South*. New Haven, CT: Yale University Press, 1997.

Holloway, Jonathan Scott. *Jim Crow Wisdom: Memory and Identity in Black America since 1940*. Chapel Hill: University of North Carolina Press, 2013.

Holm, Tom. "Fighting a White Man's War: The Extent and Legacy of American Indian Participation in World War II." *Journal of Ethnic Studies* 9, no. 2 (Summer 1981): 69–83.

hooks, bell. *Ain't I a Woman: Black Women and Feminism*. Boston: South End Press, 1981.

Houston, Jeanne Wakatsuki, and James D. Houston. *Farewell to Manzanar: A True*

Story of Japanese American Experience during and after the World War II Internment. 1973; repr., Boston: Houghton Mifflin Harcourt, 2002.

Hoxie, Frederick. *This Indian Country: American Indian Activists and the Place They Made.* New York: Penguin Books, 2012.

Hudson, Ray. "Aleuts in Defense of Their Homeland." In *Alaska at War, 1941–1945: The Forgotten War Remembered*, edited by Fern Chandonnet, 161–64. Fairbanks: University of Alaska Press, 2008.

Hudson, Ray, and Rachel Mason. *Lost Villages of the Eastern Aleutians: Biorka, Kashega, Makushin.* Washington, DC: National Park Service, 2014.

Huhndorf, Roy M., and Shari M. Huhndorf. "Alaska Native Politics since the Alaska Native Claims Settlement Act." *South Atlantic Quarterly* 110, no. 2 (Spring 2011): 385–401.

Huhndorf, Shari M. *Going Native: Indians in the American Cultural Imagination.* Ithaca, NY: Cornell University Press, 2001.

Hulan, Renée, and Renate Eigenbrod, eds. *Aboriginal Oral Traditions: Theory, Practice, Ethics.* Halifax: Fernwood Publishing, 2008.

Imada, Adria L. *Aloha America: Hula Circuits through the U.S. Empire.* Durham, NC: Duke University Press, 2012.

———. "Promiscuous Signification: Leprosy Suspects in a Photographic Archive of Skin," *Representations* 138, no. 1 (Spring 2017): 1–36.

Immerwahr, Daniel. *How to Hide an Empire: A History of the Greater United States.* New York: Picador, 2019.

Jacobson, Matthew Frye. *Barbarian Virtues: The United States Encounters Foreign Peoples at Home and Abroad, 1876–1917.* New York: Hill and Wang, 2000.

Jacoby, Karl. *Shadows at Dawn: A Borderlands Massacre and the Violence of History.* New York: Penguin Books, 2008.

Jagodinsky, Katrina. *Legal Codes and Talking Trees: Indigenous Women's Sovereignty in the Sonoran and Puget Sound Borderlands, 1854–1946.* New Haven, CT: Yale University Press, 2016.

Jefferson, Robert F. *Fighting for Hope: African American Troops of the 93rd Infantry Division in World War II and Postwar America.* Baltimore: Johns Hopkins University Press, 2008.

Johnson, Susan Hackley. *The Pribilof Islands: A Guide to St. Paul, Alaska.* St. Paul, AK: TDX Corporation, 1978.

Jorgensen, Holger "Jorgy," and Jean Lester. *Jorgy: The Life of Native Alaskan Bush Pilot and Airline Captain Holger "Jorgy" Jorgensen.* Ester, AK: Ester Republic Press, 2007.

Jung, Moon-Ho. *Menace to Empire: Anticolonial Solidarities and the Transpacific Origins of the US Security State.* Oakland: University of California Press, 2022.

Kantrowitz, Stephen. *More than Freedom: Fighting for Black Citizenship in a White Republic, 1829–1889.* New York: Penguin, 2012.

Kashima, Tetsuden. *Judgment without Trial: Japanese American Imprisonment during World War II.* Seattle: University of Washington Press, 2003.

Kauanui, J. Kehaulani. *Hawaiian Blood: Colonialism and the Politics of Sovereignty and Indigeneity.* Durham, NC: Duke University Press, 2008.

Kelley, Robin D. G. "Black Study, Black Struggle." *Boston Review*, March 1, 2016.

Kimura, Maki. *Unfolding the "Comfort Women" Debates: Modernity, Violence, Women's Voices.* New York: Palgrave Macmillan, 2016.

Kohlhoff, Dean. "A Matter Very Close to the Aleut Heart: The Politics of Restitution." In *Alaska at War, 1941–1945: The Forgotten War Remembered*, edited by Fern Chandonnet, 297–99. Fairbanks: University of Alaska Press, 2008.

———. "'It Only Makes My Heart Want to Cry': How Aleuts Faced the Pain of Evacuation." In *Alaska at War, 1941–1945: The Forgotten War Remembered*, edited by Fern Chandonnet, 291–95. Fairbanks: University of Alaska Press, 2008.

———. *When the Wind Was a River: Aleut Evacuation in World War II.* Seattle: University of Washington Press, 1995.

Lekanof, Flore, Sr. "Aleut Evacuation: Effects on the People." In *Alaska at War, 1941–1945: The Forgotten War Remembered*, edited by Fern Chandonnet, 307–8. Fairbanks: University of Alaska Press, 2008.

Lenz, Mary, and James H. Barker. *Bethel: The First 100 Years.* Bethel, AK: City of Bethel Centennial History Project, 1985.

Lesser, Albert. "Report of Immersion Foot Casualties from the Battle of Attu." *Annals of Surgery* 121, no. 3 (March 1945): 257–71.

Loew, Patty. "The Back of the Homefront: Black and American Indian Women in Wisconsin during World War II." *Wisconsin Magazine of History* 82, no. 2 (Winter 1998–1999): 82–103.

Lomawaima, K. Tsianina. "Federalism: Native Federal, and State Sovereignty." In *Why You Can't Teach United States History without American Indians*, edited by Susan Sleeper-Smith et al., 273–86. Chapel Hill: University of North Carolina Press, 2015.

———. *They Called It Prairie Light: The Story of Chilocco Indian School.* Lincoln: University of Nebraska Press, 1994.

Lowery, Malinda Maynor. *Lumbee Indians in the Jim Crow South: Race, Identity, and the Making of a Nation.* Chapel Hill: University of North Carolina Press, 2010.

Madden, Ryan. "The Forgotten People: The Relocation and Internment of Aleuts during World War II." *American Indian Culture and Research Journal* 16, no. 4 (1992): 55–76.

Marston, Muktuk. *Men of the Tundra: Alaska Esk*mos at War*. 2nd ed. New York: October House, 1972.

Martz, Mike, dir. *Uncle Sam's Men*. Bethel, AK: Bethel Broadcasting, 1995. DVD.

Maruyama, Hana C. "On Common Ground: Concentration Camps in the 'Home of the Free' at the Southwest Border and in History." *Radical History Review*, September 10, 2019.

Mason, Michele M., and Helen J. S. Lee, eds. *Reading Colonial Japan: Text, Context, and Critique*. Stanford, CA: Stanford University Press, 2012.

McClintock, Anne. *Imperial Leather: Race, Gender and Sexuality in the Colonial Contest*. New York: Routledge, 1995.

McGreevy, Nora. "Venetian Glass Beads May Be Oldest European Artifacts Found in North America." *Smithsonian Magazine*, February 10, 2021.

McRoberts, Ted, and Gene Medaris. *North Country Marshal*. Anchorage: Great Northwest Publishing and Distributing, 1986.

Metcalfe, Peter. *A Dangerous Idea: The Alaska Native Brotherhood and the Struggle for Indigenous Rights*. Fairbanks: University of Alaska Press, 2014.

Miller, Gwenn A. *Kodiak Kreol: Communities of Empire in Early Russian America*. Ithaca, NY: Cornell University Press, 2010.

Million, Dian. *Therapeutic Nations: Healing in an Age of Indigenous Human Rights*. Tucson: University of Arizona Press, 2013.

Mobley, Charles M. *World War II Aleut Relocation Camps in Southeast Alaska*. Anchorage: National Park Service, 2015.

Moore, Emily L. *Proud Raven, Panting Wolf: Carving Alaska's New Deal Totem Parks*. Seattle: University of Washington Press, 2018.

Morgan, Lael. "Minority Troops and the Alaskan Advantage during World War II." In *Alaska at War, 1941–1945: The Forgotten War Remembered*, edited by Fern Chandonnet, 271–75. Fairbanks: University of Alaska Press, 2008.

Moyd, Michelle R. *Violent Intermediaries: African Soldiers, Conquest, and Everyday Colonialism in German East Africa*. Athens: Ohio University Press, 2014.

Myers, Ramon H., and Mark R. Peattie. *The Japanese Colonial Empire, 1895–1945*. Princeton, NJ: Princeton University Press, 1984.

Napoleon, Harold. *Yuuyaraq: The Way of the Human Being*. Edited by Eric Madsen. Fairbanks: Alaska Native Knowledge Network, 1996.

Naske, Claus-M., and Ludwig J. Rowinski. *Anchorage: A Pictorial History*. Virginia Beach, VA: Donning Company, 1981.

Naske, Claus-M., and Herman E. Slotnick. *Alaska: A History*. Norman: University of Oklahoma Press, 1979.

Neiwert, David A. *Strawberry Days: How Internment Destroyed a Japanese American Community*. New York: St. Martin's Press, 2005.

Nielson, Jonathan M. *Armed Forces on a Northern Frontier: The Military in Alaska's History, 1867–1987.* New York: Praeger, 1988.

Nutchuk. *Back to the Smoky Sea*. New York: Julian Messner, 1946.

———. *Son of the Smoky Sea*. New York: Julian Messner, 1941.

O'Brien, Jean M. *Firsting and Lasting: Writing Indians Out of Existence in New England*. Minneapolis: University of Minnesota Press, 2010.

Okihiro, Gary Y., ed. *Encyclopedia of Japanese American Internment*. Westport, CT: Greenwood, 2013.

———. *Margins and Mainstreams: Asians in American History and Culture*. Seattle: University of Washington Press, 1994.

———. *Storied Lives: Japanese American Students and World War II*. Seattle: University of Washington Press, 1999.

Omi, Michael, and Howard Winant. *Racial Formation in the United States*. 3rd ed. New York: Routledge, 2015.

O'Neill, Dan. *The Firecracker Boys: H-Bombs, Inupiat Eskimos, and the Roots of the Environmental Movement*. 1994; repr., New York: Basic Books, 2007.

Ostler, Jeffrey. *Surviving Genocide: Native Nations and the United States from the American Revolution to Bleeding Kansas*. New Haven, CT: Yale University Press, 2020.

Padoongpatt, Mark. *Flavors of Empire: Food and the Making of Thai America*. Oakland: University of California Press, 2017.

Pascoe, Peggy. *What Comes Naturally: Miscegenation Law and the Making of Race in America*. New York: Oxford University Press, 2009.

Paul, Fred. *Then Fight for It! The Largest Peaceful Redistribution of Wealth in the History of Mankind and the Creation of the North Slope Borough*. Victoria, BC: Trafford Publishing, 2003.

Pearce, Roy Harvey. *Savagism and Civilization: A Study of the Indian and the American Mind*. Rev. ed. Berkeley: University of California Press, 1988.

Pegues, Juliana Hu. *Space-Time Colonialism: Alaska's Indigenous and Asian Entanglements*. Chapel Hill: University of North Carolina Press, 2021.

Perea, Jessica Bissett. *Sound Relations: Native Ways of Doing Music History in Alaska*. New York: Oxford University Press, 2021.

Pérez, Raúl. *The Souls of White Jokes: How Racist Humor Fuels White Supremacy*. Stanford: Stanford University Press, 2022.

Perras, Galen Roger. *Stepping Stones to Nowhere: The Aleutian Islands, Alaska, and American Military Strategy, 1867–1945*. Annapolis, MD: Naval Institute Press, 2003.

Personal Justice Denied: Report of the Commission on Wartime Relocation and Internment of Civilians. 1982; repr., Seattle: University of Washington Press, 1997.

Peterson, Martin, ed. *The Prisoner's Dilemma*. Cambridge: Cambridge University Press, 2015.

Phillips, Katrina M. *Staging Indigeneity: Salvage Tourism and the Performance of Native American History*. Chapel Hill: University of North Carolina Press, 2021.

Piatote, Beth H. *Domestic Subjects: Gender, Citizenship, and Law in Native American Literature*. New Haven, CT: Yale University Press, 2013.

Poor, Henry Varnum. *An Artist Sees Alaska*. New York: Viking Press, 1945.

Potter, Jean. *Alaska under Arms*. New York: Macmillan Company, 1942.

Prucha, Francis Paul. *The Great Father: The United States Government and the American Indians*. Lincoln: University of Nebraska Press, 1984.

Raibmon, Paige. *Authentic Indians: Episodes of Encounter from the Late-Nineteenth-Century Northwest Coast*. Durham, NC: Duke University Press, 2005.

Rasmussen, Birgit Brander. *Queequeg's Coffin: Indigenous Literacies and Early American Literature*. Durham, NC: Duke University Press, 2012.

Reid, Joshua L. *The Sea Is My Country: The Maritime World of the Makahs*. New Haven, CT: Yale University Press, 2015.

Riley, Francis. *Fur Seal Industry of the Pribilof Islands, 1786–1965*. Washington, DC: United States Department of the Interior, 1967.

Ringsmuth, Katherine Johnson. *Alaska's Skyboys: Cowboy Pilots and the Myth of the Last Frontier*. Seattle: University of Washington Press, 2015.

Ritchie, Donald A. *Doing Oral History: A Practical Guide*. 2nd ed. New York: Oxford University Press, 2003.

Rosier, Paul C. *Serving Their Country: American Indian Politics and Patriotism in the Twentieth Century*. Cambridge, MA: Harvard University Press, 2009.

Ross Oliver, Ethel. *Journal of an Aleutian Year*. Seattle: University of Washington Press, 1988.

Said, Edward W. *Orientalism*. New York: Vintage Books, 1978.

Sakakibara, Chie. *Whale Snow: Iñupiat, Climate Change, and Multispecies Resilience in Arctic Alaska*. Tucson: University of Arizona Press, 2020.

Salinas, Stacey Anne Baterina, and Klytie Xu. *Philippines' Resistance: The Last Allied Stronghold in the Pacific*. San Francisco: Pacific Atrocities Education, 2017.

———. *Pinay Guerrilleras: The Unsung Heroics of Filipina Resistance Fighters during the Pacific War*. San Francisco: Pacific Atrocities Education, 2019.

Samet, Elizabeth D. *Looking for the Good War: American Amnesia and the Violent Pursuit of Happiness.* New York: Picador, 2021.

Schneider, William. *So They Understand: Cultural Issues in Oral History.* Logan: Utah State University Press, 2022.

———. *The Tanana Chiefs: Native Rights and Western Law.* Fairbanks: University of Alaska Press, 2018.

Scott, James C. *Domination and the Arts of Resistance.* New Haven, CT: Yale University Press, 1990.

Seiple, Samantha. *Ghosts in the Fog: The Untold Story of Alaska's WWII Invasion.* New York: Scholastic Press, 2011.

Seniors and Sitka Sound Youth (S.A.S.S.Y.). *Learning to Live Together: Conversations with Sitka Elders.* Sitka, AK: S.A.S.S.Y., 1996.

Shah, Nayan. *Contagious Divides: Epidemics and Race in San Francisco's Chinatown.* Berkeley: University of California Press, 2001.

Sherman, Dean F. *Alaska Cavalcade.* Seattle: Alaska Life Publishing Company, 1943.

Shoemaker, Lou-Ann. "The Powers of Persuasion: Poster Art of World War I and II." *Antiques and Collecting Magazine* 112, no. 5 (July 2007).

Shoemaker, Nancy, ed. *Negotiators of Change: Historical Perspectives on Native American Women.* New York: Routledge, 1995.

———. *A Strange Likeness: Becoming Red and White in Eighteenth-Century North America.* New York: Oxford University Press, 2004.

Silva, Noenoe K. *Aloha Betrayed: Native Hawaiian Resistance to American Colonialism.* Durham, NC: Duke University Press, 2004.

Silverman, Jeffry, dir. *For the Rights of All: Ending Jim Crow in Alaska.* Lincoln, NE: Vision Maker Media, 2009. DVD.

Simpson, Audra. *Mohawk Interruptus: Political Life across the Borders of Settler States.* Durham, NC: Duke University Press, 2014.

Simpson, Leanne. *Lighting the Eighth Fire: The Liberation, Resurgence, and Protection of Indigenous Nations.* Winnipeg, MB: Arbeiter Ring Publishing, 2008.

Sleeper-Smith, Susan, Jeffrey Ostler, and Joshua L. Reid. *Violence and Indigenous Communities: Confronting the Past and Engaging the Present.* Evanston, IL: Northwestern University Press, 2021.

Smith, E. Valerie. "The Black Corps of Engineers and the Construction of the Alaska (ALCAN) Highway." *Negro History Bulletin* 51/57, no. 1/12 (December 1993): 22–37.

Smith, Jen Rose. "'Exceeding Beringia': Upending Universal Human Events and Wayward Transits in Arctic Spaces." *Environment and Planning D: Society and Space* 39, no. 1 (2021): 158–75.

Smith, Linda Tuhiwai. *Decolonizing Methodologies: Research and Indigenous Peoples.* London: Zed Books, 1999.

Sprott, Julie, Rachel Craig, and Judy Lehman. *Aanas and Taatas: Noorvik Elders Share Their Life Stories.* Vol. 2, *Iñupiaq Childrearing Study.* N.p.: n.p., 1998.

Stepetin, Haliehana. "Unangam Qaqamiiĝuu [Unangax̂ Subsistence] Cosmologies: Protocols of Sustainability, or Ways of Being Unangax̂." PhD diss., University of California, Davis, 2023.

Stephen, Lynn, and Shannon Speed, eds. *Indigenous Women and Violence: Feminist Activist Research in Heightened States of Injustice.* Tucson: University of Arizona Press, 2021.

Stern, Scott Wasserman. *The Trials of Nina McCall: Sex, Surveillance, and the Decades-Long Government Plan to Imprison "Promiscuous" Women.* Boston: Beacon Press, 2018.

Stewart, Henry. "Aleuts in Japan, 1942–1945." In *Alaska at War, 1941–1945: The Forgotten War Remembered,* edited by Fern Chandonnet, 301–4. Fairbanks: University of Alaska Press, 2008.

Stoler, Ann Laura. *Carnal Knowledge and Imperial Power: Race and the Intimate in Colonial Rule.* Berkeley: University of California Press, 2002.

Suzack, Cheryl, Shari M. Huhndorf, Jeanne Perreault, and Jean Barman. *Indigenous Women and Feminism: Politics, Activism, Culture.* Vancouver: UBC Press, 2010.

Swanson, Henry. *The Unknown Islands: Life and Tales of Henry Swanson.* Unalaska, AK: Cuttlefish–Unalaska City School District, 1982.

Sweetland Smith, Barbara, and Patricia J. Petrivelli. *A Sure Foundation: Aleut Churches in World War II.* Anchorage: Aleutian Pribilof Islands Association, 1994.

Swensen, Thomas Michael. "The Relationship between Indigenous Rights, Citizenship, and Land in Territorial Alaska: How the Past Opened the Door to the Future." *Alaska Native Studies Journal* 2 (2015): 44–58.

Takaki, Ronald. *A Different Mirror: A History of Multicultural America.* New York: Back Bay Books, 1993.

———. *Double Victory: A Multicultural History of America in World War II.* Boston: Little, Brown, 2000.

———. *Hiroshima: Why America Dropped the Atomic Bomb.* Boston: Little, Brown, 1995.

———. *Iron Cages: Race and Culture in 19th-Century America.* Rev. ed. New York: Oxford University Press, 2000.

Takei, George, Justin Eisinger, Steven Scott, and art by Harmony Becker. *They Called Us Enemy.* Marietta, GA: Top Shelf Productions, 2019.

Tanaka, Yuki. *Japan's Comfort Women: Sexual Slavery and Prostitution during World War II and the US Occupation*. London: Routledge, 2002.

Taylor, Drew Hayden. *Me Tomorrow: Indigenous Views on the Future*. Madeira Park, BC: Douglas and McIntyre, 2021.

Teves, Stephanie Nohelani. *Defiant Indigeneity: The Politics of Hawaiian Performance*. Chapel Hill: University of North Carolina Press, 2018.

Theobald, Brianna. *Reproduction on the Reservation: Pregnancy, Childbirth, and Colonialism in the Long Twentieth Century*. Chapel Hill: University of North Carolina Press, 2019.

Thiong'o, Ngũgĩ wa. *Decolonising the Mind: The Politics of Language in African Literature*. Nairobi: East African Educational Publishers, 1986.

Thompson, Krista A. *An Eye for the Tropics: Tourism, Photography, and Framing the Caribbean Picturesque*. Durham, NC: Duke University Press, 2006.

Thompson, Lanny. *Imperial Archipelago: Representation and Rule in the Insular Territories under U.S. Dominion after 1898*. Honolulu: University of Hawaiʻi Press, 2010.

Tone-Pah-Hote, Jenny. *Crafting an Indigenous Nation: Kiowa Expressive Culture in the Progressive Era*. Chapel Hill: University of North Carolina Press, 2019.

Torrey, Barbara Boyle. *Slaves of the Harvest*. St. Paul, AK: TDX Corporation, 1978.

Townsend, Kenneth William. *World War II and the American Indian*. Albuquerque: University of New Mexico Press, 2000.

Tuck, Eve. "ANCSA as X-Mark." In *Transforming the University: Alaska Native Studies in the 21st Century*, edited by Beth Ginondidoy Leonard, Jeane Táaw xíwaa Breinig, Lenora Acʼaralek Carpluk, Sharon Chilux Lind, and Maria Shaa Tláa Williams, 240–72. Minneapolis: Two Harbors Press, 2014.

Tuck, Eve, Haliehana Stepetin, Rebecca Beaulne-Stuebing, and Jo Billows. "Visiting as an Indigenous Feminist Practice." *Gender and Education* 35, no. 2 (2023): 144–55. https:doi.org/10.1080/09540253.2022.2078796.

Vizenor, Gerald. *Manifest Manners: Postindian Warriors of Survivance*. Hanover, NH: Wesleyan University Press, 1994.

———, ed. *Survivance: Narratives of Native Presence*. Lincoln: University of Nebraska Press, 2008.

War Department. *The Capture of Attu: As Told by the Men Who Fought There*. Washington, DC: The Infantry Journal, 1944.

Weinberg, Karen Lynn, dir. *Keep Talking*. Chicago: Ten Trees Productions, 2018. YouTube, 1:19:30, https://www.youtube.com/watch?v=L9_7LzIZRcQ.

Wexler, Laura. *Tender Violence: Domestic Visions in an Age of US Imperialism*. Chapel Hill: University of North Carolina Press, 2000.

Wheeler, Keith. *The Pacific Is My Beat*. New York: E. P. Dutton, 1943.

Wilkins, David E., and Heidi Kiiwetinepinesiik Stark. *American Indian Politics and the American Political System*. 4th ed. Lanham, MD: Rowman and Littlefield, 2017.

Williams, Maria Shaa Tláa, ed. *The Alaska Native Reader: History, Culture, Politics*. Durham, NC: Duke University Press, 2009.

Williams, Marla, dir. *Aleut Story*. Lincoln, NE: Vision Maker Video, 2005. DVD.

Wilson, Waziyatawin Angela. *Remember This! Dakota Decolonization and the* Eli Taylor Narratives. Lincoln: University of Nebraska Press, 2005.

Witgen, Michael. *An Infinity of Nations: How the Native New World Shaped Early North America*. Philadelphia: University of Pennsylvania Press, 2012.

———. *Seeing Red: Indigenous Land, American Expansion, and the Political Economy of Plunder in North America*. Chapel Hill: University of North Carolina Press, 2022.

Woodman, Lyman L. *Duty Station Northwest: The U.S. Army in Alaska and Western Canada, 1867–1987*. Anchorage: Alaska Historical Society, 1996.

Woodward, C. Vann. *The Strange Career of Jim Crow*. Commemorative ed. New York: Oxford University Press, 2001.

Wooley, Chris, and Mike Martz. "The Tundra Army: Patriots of Arctic Alaska." In *Alaska at War, 1941–1945: The Forgotten War Remembered*, edited by Fern Chandonnet, 155–60. Fairbanks: University of Alaska Press, 2008.

Wyatt, Victoria. "Alaska and Hawai'i." In *The Oxford History of the American West*, edited by Clyde A. Milner II, Carol A. O'Connor, and Martha A. Sandweiss, 565–601. New York: Oxford University Press, 1994.

Yamazaki, James N., with Louis B. Fleming. *Children of the Atomic Bomb: An American Physician's Memoir of Nagasaki, Hiroshima, and the Marshall Islands*. Durham, NC: Duke University Press, 1995.

Yaw Davis, Nancy. "Childhood Memories of the War: Sitka." In *Alaska at War, 1941–1945: The Forgotten War Remembered*, edited by Fern Chandonnet, 265–67. Fairbanks: University of Alaska Press, 2008.

Yellen, Jeremy A. *The Greater East Asia Co-prosperity Sphere: When Total Empire Met Total War*. Ithaca, NY: Cornell University Press, 2019.

Yoshiaki, Yoshimi. *Comfort Women: Sexual Slavery in the Japanese Military during World War II*. Translated by Suzanne O'Brien. New York: Columbia University Press, 2000.

Young, Louise. *Japan's Total Empire: Manchuria and the Culture of Wartime Imperialism*. Berkeley: University of California Press, 1998.

Ziomek, Kirsten L. *Lost Histories: Recovering the Lives of Japan's Colonial Peoples*. Cambridge, MA: Harvard University Asia Center, 2019.

INDEX

Italicized page numbers refer to a figure.

with, 172–73; vernacular violence, 167–71; violence directed at, 25, 179, 181–82, 188

Alaskan Combat Intelligence Platoon. *See* Alaska Scouts

Alaskan Fisheries Division, 38

Alaskan Indians, ancestral lands of, 7

Alaskan settler colony, demographics, 7–9

Alaska Office of Veterans Affairs, ATG Task Force, 125

Alaska "purchase" (1867), 12, 195

Alaska Scouts: about, 82; Jorgensen in, 96–97, *97*; members of, 83–84; role in recapture of Attu, 77, 78

Alaska-Siberia Lend-Lease program (1941–45), 11, 194

Alaska State Defense Force, 125

Alaska Statehood Act (1958), 140

Alaska Steamship Company, 184

Alaska Territorial Board of Education, on assimilation/segregation, 146–47

Alaska Territorial Guard: about, 100–103; Alaska Natives in, 84; dancing, *114*, 115; disbanding of, 116–17; drill practice, *124*; financial support gained through, 112; as fitting around subsistence lifestyle, 111–12; former members of, 118–27; harpoon carving, 105–6, *106*; Indigenizing, 104–15; leadership, 103; map, *xviii*; membership of, *105*, 105–6; oral histories, 118–27; racial bias, 115–18; racism impact on, 115–16; social events, 112; statue in Utqiaġvik, *126*; tasks of, 103; transitioning out, 118; Unangax̂ involvement in, 120;

women scouts, 108, 228n23; women's role in, 106–7

Alaska Veterans Museum, 92, 125

Alaska Voters' Literacy Act (1925), 139

ALCAN (Alaska-Canada) Highway, xv, 7–8, 194

Aleut: Sugpiat, 6; Unangax̂, 6; Unangax̂ vs., 214n1

Aleutian campaign (1942–43), 10

Aleutian Islands: bureaucratic fight over return fare, 48; Indigenous removal from, 49, 75; Japanese invasion of, 6, 23, 25–26, 75, 88, 102; map, *xviii*; military pollution of, 50; span of archipelago, 6; as Unangax̂ homeland, 6; Unangax̂ return to, 94. *See also specific islands*

Aleutian Pribilof Islands Association (APIA) Heritage Library, 18

Aleutian Pribilof Islands Restitution Trust, 51

Aleut Story (film), 50

Allen, Robert M., 146

Alokli, Nick, 147–48

Amchitka, detonations at, 192

American Federation of Labor, 140

American Indians: Alaska Natives compared with, 195; battle casualties, 86; as dual citizens, 15; in military service, 84, 225n57; war bond purchases, 87; in World War II, 85–86

Anagick, Betty, 189, 192, 199

Anagick, Lowell, 153, *193*

Anagick family photo, *193*

ANB. *See* Alaska Native Brotherhood

ANCSA (Alaska Native Claims Settlement Act; 1971), 37–38, 73, 195

Freedman, Estelle, 179
Freeman, C. S., 172
Funter Bay cannery, 23
Funter Bay mine, 23
Funter Bay Relocation Camp: absence
of clean water, 56; depictions of, 73;
deplorable conditions in, 47–48;
disease at, 56; disembarkation at, 34;
map, *xviii*; photo of, *43*; pilgrimages
to, 52; sewage problems, 56; transportation to, *33*
FWS. *See* Fish and Wildlife Service

Galanin, Ferman, 38–39
Galanin, Laurence, 38–39
Galanin, Moses, 38–39
Geiger, Andrea, 11, 168
Geist, Otto, 111, 135–36
German POWS, 24
Gibbins, Donald, 63
Gilbert, Matthew Sakiestewa, 14–15, 61
Gilmore, Glenda, 128–29
Glover, Eva, 108
Golley, Sergeus, 67
Golodoff, Nick (Attuan), 27
Gordaoff, George, 62
Grant, James, 125
Green, Kate, 108
Gregg, Laura, 108
Gromoff, Alexandra (Alice), 222n52
Gromoff, Elary, 68, 222n52
Gromoff, Ishmael, Father, 34–35, 39
Grosfoguel, Ramón, 141
Gruber, Ruth, 36, 38, 177–78
Gruening, Ernest: Alaska Equal Rights
Act signing, 137, *138*; anti-Semitic
views, 143; Bartlett's alliance with,
68; on Buckner, 115; camp conditions

inaction, 35; career and views of,
8; correspondence, 27, 28–29, 176,
177–78, 183; denying land rights, 156;
on discrimination, 132–33; on healthcare legislation, 155; opposition to
Alaskan Indian reservations, 143; on
segregation, 174–75; visit to St. Lawrence Island, 87; on white veterans as
settlers, 143
Guard Retirement Act (1972), 124
Gundersen, Paul, 83–84
Gunnison, Judge, 144

Hagiwara, Michael, 27
Haida: alliance with US military, 7;
labor negotiations, 68; map, *5*
Hall, John, 56
Hall, Ryan, 76
Hallingstad, Amy, 145
Hampton, Ruth, 184
Hanson, John, 44
Harmon, Alexandra, 141, 142
Harper, Francis S., 86
harpoon carving, 105–6, *106*
Hartman, Annie M., 108
Hartman, Ian, 9
Hartman, Saidiya V., 13
Hatathlie, Nataanii, 19
Haugen, Maryann, 131
Hawai'i, Indigenous resistance in, 14
Haycox, Stephen, 9, 139
Hayward, John, 150, *151*, 153
Hayward, Joseph, *152*
healthcare: activism, 68–69, 154–55;
advocacy, 69, 155; Alaska VA System,
119; banishing nurse Lambert, 154;
banishing physician Bauer, 2, 3, 13,
34, 154; degrading, 34; discrimination

in, 147, 154–55; invasive, 34; at Ket-
chikan hospital, 35; segregation in,
153; shortcomings, 2–3; Tlingit, 64
Hensley, Priscilla G., 108
Hess, Dora, 108
Heurkie, Reesly, 170–71
Hiroshima, bombing of, 4–5, 194,
196–97
Hirst, Claude, 56, 177–78
Hodes, Martha, 172
Hodikoff, George, 26–27
Hodikoff, Mike, 25, 26–27, 74
Hokkaido POW camp, Attuans taken
to, 75
Holloway, Jonathan, 134, 160–61
Holum, Orvel, 183–84
Hoopes, Robert, 139
Hope, Andrew, 140–41
Hope, Harriet, 34
Hope, Henry, 29
Hope, William B., 84
Hopson, Eddie, 116, 120
Houston, James, 4
Houston, Jeanne Wakatsuki, 4
Howarth, Pauline, 108
Hoxie, Frederick, 15
Huhndorf, Shari, 158, 162
Hunnicutt, Susie, 108

Ickes, Harold, 87, 177–78, 180
Ilisagvik Tribal College, 118
Immerwahr, Daniel, 10, 197
Indian Citizenship Act (1924), 139
Indian Reorganization Act, 109
Indian reservations: Alaska Natives' oppo-
sition to, 143, 233n57; Gruening on, 8
Indians, genocide, 9, 22
Indian Wars (19th century), 22

Indigenous people: and blood quantum,
33; and land rights, 140; partnerships
with environmentalists, 19; patriotism of, 66, 81; resistance of, 1–2,
14; sovereignty of, 15, 20, 31, 57; and
talking circles, 189–90
"Indigenous sexuality," exploitation of,
160
infrastructure construction, 7–8
Inman, Irene, 184
integration: of Alaskan towns, 96; of
American Indian and Alaska Native
servicemen, 89; of Nome Dream
Theater, 134–36
intergenerational, 52, 147, 198–99
internment camps. See Japanese Americans
intertribal warfare, 58–59
Iñuit: from Big Diomede, as Soviet residents, 86; blanket toss, 113; geography and linguistics, 6; Scouts, 102
Iñupiat, 6
Itta, Irene, 100, 108
Itta, Miles, 104
Ituk, Gertrude, 108
ivory carving, 95
Iwo Jima, Battle of Attu compared with, 77

Jackson, Peter N., 84
Jacobson, Matthew, 163–64
jade mining, 117, 229n50
Japan: alliances to defend against, 74,
75; bomb balloons from, 98; invasion of Aleutian Islands, 6, 23, 88;
invasion of Manchuria and Kuril
Islands (1931), 10, 26; map, xviii; mass
suicides, 77; POW mortality rate, 26;
Unangax̂ alliance choices, 74, 99

JapanAirRaids.org, 4–5
Japanese, Alaska Natives resemblance
   to, 80
Japanese Alaskans, 27–28
Japanese Americans: apology and res-
   titution, 51; Executive Order 9066,
   xv, 27, 32; incarceration of, 3–4, 50;
   "No-no boys," 83; villainized as "out-
   side" white America, 30; as wartime
   enemies, 4
"Japanese hunting licenses," 80, 81
Japanese Latin Americans, incarceration
   of, 4
Japanese soldiers' bodies, bone frag-
   ments from, 77
Jefferson, Robert, 4, 83
Jesse Lee Home, Dutch Harbor, AK, 85
Jewish refugees, 8, 143
Jim Crow, in the far north, 129. *See also*
   discrimination
Johnson, Susan Hackley, 37
Johnston, Edward C., 39–40, 63
Jones, Charles: alert of Japanese inva-
   sion, 25; Attu burial, 26; interroga-
   tion of, 74–75
Jones, Etta, 26, 74–75
Jorgensen, Holger (Jorgy): author's in-
   teractions with, 199; camping in the
   snow, 97; integrating Nome Dream
   Theater, 134–35; on interracial dating,
   185; on Iñuit clothing for the mili-
   tary, 109; in military service, 95–98;
   military service certificate, 96; photo
   of, 198
Jorgensen, Noel, 199
Jorgensen, Roberta, 199
Jumping Eagle, Irving, 84
Jung, Moon-Ho, 9

Kake, AK, US Navy attack on, 59
Kamani, Mr. (Japanese soldier), 27
Kantrowitz, Stephen, 82
Karras, Bertha, 132
Kashevarof, Andronik: ATG involve-
   ment, 120–21; measles treatment, 35;
   on return trip to Funter Bay, 52; on
   Tlingit in Juneau, 64–65
Kashevarof, Bonnie. *See* Mierzejek,
   Bonnie Kashevarof
Kashevarof, Elekonida (Ella), 35, 44, 46,
   64–65
Kashevarof family, 44, 46
Katchatag, Fred, 116
Keep Talking (documentary, 2018), 148
Kelley, Robin D. G., 13
Kelly, Patay, 172
Kendall, Shirley, 189
Kendall-Miller, Heather, 195
Ketchikan, AK: discrimination in, 133;
   Restricted Areas, 184, 185
Ketchikan Industrial Union Council,
   183–84
Ketchikan Spruce Mill, 47
Killisnoo (Southeast Alaska) (Woosh-
   deidatetl' Seét): about, 60; absence of
   clean water, 55; BIA physician expul-
   sion from, 2, 3, 13; cannery as relo-
   cation site, 55; fishing at, 49; Golley's
   store in, 67; map, xviii; measles and
   TB at, 51–52; mortality rate, 55; pil-
   grimages to, 73; relocation to, 1, 54–55
Killisnoo herring reduction plant, 23
Kiska Island, AK: Japanese invasion
   of, xviii, 6, 25, 74, 102; US military
   ill-prepared for, 78
Knox, Frank, 177–78
Kochutin, Haretina, 44

Russian-American Company, 37, 58–59
Russian Orthodox religion: church in
    Juneau, 64–65, 65; clergy, 61
Russo-Japanese War (1904–1905), 26
Ryan, Conrad F., Sr., 91, 189, 190, 191

Sahlin, Al, 87, 87, 122–23
Salinas, Stacey Anne Baterina, 101
Samato, Annie, 54–55, 56, 73
Samato, Betty, 54, 73
Samato, Harry, 54, 55
Samet, Elizabeth D., 3
Sarabia, Helen, 149
S.A.S.S.Y. (Seniors and Sitka Sound
    Youth), 132
Savok, Lydia G., 108
Schaeffer, John, 103
Schenck, Alberta: integration of Nome
    Dream Theater, 96, 134–35; letter to
    Nome Nugget, 135; on US slavery,
    231n25
Schenck, "Whitey," 135
Schick, L. E., 80
Scott, Annie Curtis, 108
Scott, James C., 15
Scott, Tolbert, 139
Sealaska Heritage Institute (SHI), 18, 70,
    73, 177
seal pelts: forced labor, 23–24, 30–31,
    36–42, 37; prices/profits, 39, 48;
    record harvests, 41, 41, 218n83; as
    reflecting unpaid or underpaid labor,
    39, 40, 42, 63, 67–68, 218n83
segregation: of African Americans, 89,
    91; of Alaska Natives, 92; of Alaska
    Native women, 171–72, 177–78; an-
    ti-Black, 91, 115; anti-Indian, 88–89;

anti-Indigenous, 91; anti-Native, 102,
    115; in the armed forces, 4, 30, 82, 91;
    and assimilation, 147–50; Black pla-
    toons, xv, 7–8, 115; in education, xvi,
    144–47; in employment and public
    accommodations, xvi, 4; ending,
    187; gendered, 157–58; Gruening on,
    174–75; in Killisnoo, 60; military or-
    dinances role in, 171–87; racial,
    91. See also discrimination; racial
    bias
Seniors and Sitka Sound Youth
    (S.A.S.S.Y.), 132
settler colonialism: capitalism and, 141;
    components of, 129; Indigenous
    order vs., 14; Indigenous peoples
    displacement by, 129; Indigenous re-
    sistance to, 3, 12; labor extraction, 31;
    Native sovereignty and, 155–56; racial
    hierarchies in, 130; reappropriating
    structures left by, 190; resistance
    during World War II, 56–57; role in
    resettlement, 49; selective adoption
    of elements of, 14–15; sequential,
    26; US troops in vacated Native
    houses, 32; Western sexualization of
    Indigenous women, 158–59. See also
    colonization
settler institutions, 15
Shaaxeidi Tlaa (Anna Hunter Soboleff),
    61
Shah, Nayan, 183
Shaishnikoff, Sergie, 40
Sharai, Harvey, 29
Shattuck, Allen, 139
Shattuck, Curtis, 139
Sheldon, Genevieve Nancy, 108

US government (*cont.*)
Fur Company partnering with, 30–31; intimidation by, 40, 41; labor exploitation, 42, 67–68; material from Nevada test site relocated to Alaska, 194; propaganda, 40, 142; white supremacy exhibited by, 4

US military: Alaska Natives relationship with, 19; Alaska Native women vs., 187; Alaska VA Healthcare System, 119; battlefields and bases, *xviii*; church vandalism, 51; cold weather gear (Iñuit), 101, 108–9; combat intelligence, 76, 78, 82–83, 85, 102; damage to Native houses, 52; demographic changes of Alaska, 7; environmental damage, 50, 51, 192; gender violence adjacent to bases, 180; incarcerated families of service personnel, 83; Indigenous identity as hazard, 78, 80; Indigenous racial identity in, 82–83; Indigenous role in the Arctic, 117; Natives in life-threatening situations, 89; policing of interracial sex and marriage, 158; prostitution in conjunction with, 172; releases for sealing, 38–39; segregation by exclusion ordinances, 159; sex as a perk, 167; social activities regulated by, 50; social equality with uniforms, 88–89; troops in vacated Native houses, 32; women in, 100–101; WWII influx of equipment and personnel, 227n6

US Navy: claims of protecting Unangax̂, 216n37; lethal attacks by, 59

USO functions, Alaska Native women barred from, 174, 177, 183

US profit from Indigenous sources, 38, 41. *See also* forced labor; seal pelts

US War Department, 42, 158, 187; *What Has Alaska to Offer Postwar Pioneers?*, 142

Utqiaġvik: defense of, 100; Town Hall, 126

venereal disease, 172–73, 178, 183

Venetie case, 195

Venevedez, Jose P., 84

veterans: elders, 88–99; totem pole honoring, 98

violence: in language, 167–71; in material culture, 160–67

Vizenor, Gerald, 15, 56–57

Wacker City, AK: illustrations, *161*, 161–63; promotional literature, 161; stationery, 160, *161*, 164–65

Walsh, M. J., 139

Walton, Rudolph, 144

War Discovers Alaska (Driscoll), 168

Ward Lake Civilian Conservation Corps (CCC) camp, *xviii*, 23, *33*, 51

Washington, Laura O., 108

Weber, Evelyn, 108

Weinberg, Karen Lynn: *Keep Talking* (documentary, 2018), 148

Wells, Alfred Qaaġraq, 124

Wexler, Laura, 163

Whaley, Frank, 139

What Has Alaska to Offer Postwar Pioneers? (US War Department), 142

White, Langdon, 172–73

white supremacy: in language, 168; in US government, 4; in Western settlement, 129

Indigenous
Confluences

CHARLOTTE COTÉ AND COLL THRUSH *Series Editors*

Indigenous Confluences publishes innovative works that use decolonizing perspectives and transnational approaches to explore the experiences of Indigenous peoples across North America, with a special emphasis on the Pacific Coast.